GRENDEL GRENDEL GRENDEL

ANIMATION: KEY FILMS/FILMMAKERS

Series Editor: Chris Pallant

Titles in the Series:
Toy Story: How Pixar Reinvented the Animated Feature edited by Susan Smith, Noel Brown and Sam Summers
Princess Mononoke: Understanding Studio Ghibli's Monster Princess edited by Rayna Denison
Norman McLaren: Between the Frames by Nichola Dobson
Hayao Miyazaki: Exploring the Early Work of Japan's Greatest Animator by Raz Greenberg
Allegro non troppo: Bruno Bozetto's Animated Music by Marco Bellano
Snow White and the Seven Dwarfs: New Perspectives on Production, Reception, Legacy edited by Chris Pallant and Christopher Holliday

GRENDEL GRENDEL GRENDEL

Animating *Beowulf*

Dan Torre and Lienors Torre

BLOOMSBURY ACADEMIC
NEW YORK · LONDON · OXFORD · NEW DELHI · SYDNEY

BLOOMSBURY ACADEMIC
Bloomsbury Publishing Inc
1385 Broadway, New York, NY 10018, USA
50 Bedford Square, London, WC1B 3DP, UK
29 Earlsfort Terrace, Dublin 2, Ireland

BLOOMSBURY, BLOOMSBURY ACADEMIC and the Diana logo
are trademarks of Bloomsbury Publishing Plc

First published in the United States of America 2021
This paperback edition published 2023

Copyright © Dan Torre and Lienors Torre, 2021

For legal purposes the Acknowledgements on p. xii constitute
an extension of this copyright page.

Cover design: Louise Dugdale
Cover image © Estate of Alexander Stitt, used with permission

This work is published open access subject to a Creative Commons Attribution-NonCommercial-NoDerivatives 3.0 licence (CC BY-NC-ND 3.0, https://creativecommons.org/licenses/by-nc-nd/3.0/). You may re-use, distribute, and reproduce this work in any medium for non-commercial purposes, provided you give attribution to the copyright holder and the publisher and provide a link to the Creative Commons licence.

Bloomsbury Publishing Inc does not have any control over, or responsibility for, any third-party websites referred to or in this book. All internet addresses given in this book were correct at the time of going to press. The author and publisher regret any inconvenience caused if addresses have changed or sites have ceased to exist, but can accept no responsibility for any such changes.

Library of Congress Cataloging-in-Publication Data
Names: Torre, Dan, author. | Gardner, John,
1933-1982. Grendel. | Torre, Lienors, author.
Title: Grendel, Grendel, Grendel : animating Beowulf
Dan Torre and Lienors Torre.
Description: New York : Bloomsbury Academic, 2021. |
Series: Animation: key films/filmmakers; book 6 |
Includes bibliographical references and index.
Identifiers: LCCN 2021006771 (print) |
LCCN 2021006772 (ebook) | ISBN 9781501337826 (hardback) |
ISBN 9781501337819 (ebook) | ISBN 9781501337802 (pdf)
Subjects: LCSH: Grendel, Grendel, Grendel (Motion picture)
Classification: LCC NC1766.A83 G737 2021 (print) |
LCC NC1766.A83 (ebook) | DDC 791.43/72–dc23
LC record available at https://lccn.loc.gov/2021006771
LC ebook record available at https://lccn.loc.gov/2021006772

ISBN:	HB:	978-1-5013-3782-6
	PB:	978-1-5013-8111-9
	ePDF:	978-1-5013-3780-2
	eBook:	978-1-5013-3781-9

Series: Animation: Key Films/Filmmakers

Typeset by Integra Software Services Pvt. Ltd.

To find out more about our authors and books visit www.bloomsbury.com
and sign up for our newsletters.

CONTENTS

List of Illustrations — vi
Acknowledgements — xii

Introducing Grendel — 1

Chapter 1
THE GENEALOGY OF GRENDEL — 9

Chapter 2
SCENES OF *GRENDEL GRENDEL GRENDEL* — 31

Chapter 3
THEMES OF *GRENDEL GRENDEL GRENDEL* — 99

Chapter 4
MAKING *GRENDEL GRENDEL GRENDEL* — 121

Chapter 5
AESTHETICS OF *GRENDEL GRENDEL GRENDEL* — 157

Chapter 6
GRENDEL'LL GET YOU — 171

Concluding Grendel — 183

A Guide to Further Research — 186
Bibliography — 191
Filmography — 194
Index — 196

LIST OF ILLUSTRATIONS

Introducing Grendel

0.1   Director Alexander Stitt, Melbourne, 2007 (photo by Lienors Torre)   3

Chapter 1: The Genealogy of Grendel

1.1   The first page of the oldest surviving manuscript of the original *Beowulf* poem (this surviving copy was transcribed in *c.* AD 1000)   11
1.2   The character of Grendel as conceived by earlier visual artists: (a) an illustration by J.R. Skelton in *Beowulf, Told to the Children* by Henrietta E. Marshall (1908); (b) an illustration by J. H. F. Bacon in *Myths and Legends – The British Race* by Maud Isabel Ebbutt (1910)   12
1.3   Image of Grendel, the (almost) loveable monster, from *Grendel Grendel Grendel* (Alexander Stitt, 1981)   20
1.4   Characters from the 3D animated film, *Beowulf* (Robert Zemeckis, 2007) which incorporate both the vocal talents and the movement and likeness of well-known Hollywood actors. From left to right: Ray Winstone as Beowulf; Anthony Hopkins as King Hrothgar; Robin Wright Penn as Queen Wealtheow. Although relatively photo-realistic in their depiction, these animated characters often appear somewhat zombie-like in their movement (thus bordering on the monstrous)   26

Chapter 2: Scenes of Grendel Grendel Grendel

2.1   King Hrothgar with his loyal subjects, Wiglaf and Dung, watch as One-eyed Arthur and Basil run away after discovering Grendel's giant footprint (*Grendel Grendel Grendel*, Alexander Stitt, 1981)   35
2.2   Grendel makes a surprise appearance (*Grendel Grendel Grendel*, Alexander Stitt, 1981)   35
2.3   Title sequence (*Grendel Grendel Grendel*, Alexander Stitt, 1981)   36

List of Illustrations   vii

2.4   Grendel takes a melancholic stroll through the countryside and inadvertently frightens the wildlife (*Grendel Grendel Grendel*, Alexander Stitt, 1981)   38

2.5   (a) Grendel enters into his mother's cave; (b) Grendel carefully washes his hands as he speaks to his off-screen mother (*Grendel Grendel Grendel*, Alexander Stitt, 1981)   40

2.6   (a) King Hrothgar, Wiglaf and Dung ponder Grendel's form, which is stuck in a tree (b); Grendel's Mum (her character name in Stitt's film), depicted as a black silhouette, carefully rescues Grendel (*Grendel Grendel Grendel*, Alexander Stitt, 1981)   43

2.7   Unferth, after capturing Wiglaf and Dung, reluctantly rescues the King from a bear trap in the forest (*Grendel Grendel Grendel*, Alexander Stitt, 1981)   44

2.8   King Hrothgar's nose is accidently bumped by Unferth; a minor event that later will be greatly exaggerated and heralded as a great act of bravery (*Grendel Grendel Grendel*, Alexander Stitt, 1981)   47

2.9   (a) The Shaper gently touches his own nose in a display of empathy for the King's injured nose; (b) the Shaper and the Shaper's Boy sing of the King's bravery (*Grendel Grendel Grendel*, Alexander Stitt, 1981)   52

2.10   King Hrothgar meeting his new wife, Queen Wealtheow, as Unferth and the Foreign King look on (*Grendel Grendel Grendel*, Alexander Stitt, 1981)   55

2.11   The Shaper sings 'God halved his image into man and wife'. These words, along with the Shaper's strategic positioning, suggest the burgeoning rift in the relationship between the King and Queen (*Grendel Grendel Grendel*, Alexander Stitt, 1981)   57

2.12   (a) Grendel meets the Dragon, who (b) momentarily morphs into a red block (*Grendel Grendel Grendel*, Alexander Stitt, 1981)   60

2.13   The Priests offer a sacrifice to the Great Dragon God (*Grendel Grendel Grendel*, Alexander Stitt, 1981)   64

2.14   Grendel refuses to fight Unferth, and instead humiliates him with apples (*Grendel Grendel Grendel*, Alexander Stitt, 1981)   68

2.15   Grendel again refuses to do battle with Unferth, and instead carefully returns him to the meadhall (*Grendel Grendel Grendel*, Alexander Stitt, 1981)   70

2.16   Grendel, standing near the Sculptor's rock carvings, sings his 'Soliloquy' (*Grendel Grendel Grendel*, Alexander Stitt, 1981)   72

2.17   Grendel interacts with the oysters while singing his 'Soliloquy' (*Grendel Grendel Grendel*, Alexander Stitt, 1981)   73

2.18   The Shaper and Shaper's Boy perform 'We Know a Lovely Monster' (*Grendel Grendel Grendel*, Alexander Stitt, 1981)   79

2.19 Queen Wealtheow in the nude (a) as she appears at her window and (b) in her chambers (*Grendel Grendel Grendel*, Alexander Stitt, 1981) — 80

2.20 The Dragon impersonates Humphrey Bogart as he speaks with Grendel (*Grendel Grendel Grendel*, Alexander Stitt, 1981) — 82

2.21 King Hrothgar poisons the Shaper (*Grendel Grendel Grendel*, Alexander Stitt, 1981) — 83

2.22 An arrogant Beowulf arrives at Hrothgar's meadhall (*Grendel Grendel Grendel*, Alexander Stitt, 1981) — 85

2.23 Beowulf, with Troll, dines at the meadhall (*Grendel Grendel Grendel*, Alexander Stitt, 1981) — 86

2.24 The pious priests are deeply insulted by Beowulf's 'heresy'; note the strategic placement of Beowulf's sword in the foreground, mockingly suggesting the Christian cross (*Grendel Grendel Grendel*, Alexander Stitt, 1981) — 87

2.25 (a) Grendel discovers the body of Unferth, who has just been murdered by Beowulf at the behest of the King; (b) he then contemplates the bloody stain left on his hands (*Grendel Grendel Grendel*, Alexander Stitt, 1981) — 92

2.26 Beowulf rips off Grendel's arm (*Grendel Grendel Grendel*, Alexander Stitt, 1981) — 93

2.27 The King stares at an apple that has just fallen from Grendel's dismembered arm (being held aloft by Beowulf on left) – implying that Grendel had merely intended to pelt the King with apples (*Grendel Grendel Grendel*, Alexander Stitt, 1981) — 94

2.28 Grendel dies alone under the stars (*Grendel Grendel Grendel*, Alexander Stitt, 1981) — 95

2.29 Frame grabs from the closing credits sequence (*Grendel Grendel Grendel*, Alexander Stitt, 1981) — 96

Chapter 3: Themes of Grendel Grendel Grendel

3.1 The Dragon multiplying himself in order to add emphasis to his lyrical performance (*Grendel Grendel Grendel*, Alexander Stitt, 1981) — 109

3.2 (a) Dancing and singing oysters engage with Grendel (*Grendel Grendel Grendel*, Alexander Stitt, 1981); a sequence that is reminiscent of (b) John Tenniel's illustration in Lewis Carroll's *Through the Looking Glass* (1872) — 113

3.3 The Sculptor at work (*Grendel Grendel Grendel*, Alexander Stitt, 1981) — 115

3.4 Grendel speaks to the Dragon through a human-made effigy of the Dragon God (*Grendel Grendel Grendel*, Alexander Stitt, 1981) — 116

3.5 Grendel attempts to mimic the Sculptor's engravings; also note the use of 'mock-runes' (*Grendel Grendel Grendel*, Alexander Stitt, 1981) — 117

3.6 (a) As Grendel sings out the letters G-R-E-N-D-E-L and N-E-M-E-S-I-S, they appear as 'concretized speech' above his dancing form; (b) examples of 'concretized speech' from Grendel's Mum during the opening title song; (c) the Dragon, after conjuring into existence the word 'GAMES', adjusts the backwards facing letter 'E' (*Grendel Grendel Grendel*, Alexander Stitt, 1981) — 119

Chapter 4: Making of Grendel Grendel Grendel

4.1 A page from the first version of the storyboard for *Grendel Grendel Grendel* (copyright Estate of Alexander Stitt, used with permission; courtesy Bruce Smeaton/National Library of Australia) — 127

4.2 A page from the second version of the storyboard for *Grendel Grendel Grendel* (copyright Estate of Alexander Stitt, used with permission; courtesy RMIT Design Archives) — 128

4.3 (left to right) Alexander Stitt, Peter Ustinov and Phillip Adams at the first recording session in Sydney, 1978 (photo by Mary Smeaton, used with permission) — 133

4.4 (left to right) Peter Ustinov, Bruce Smeaton and Arthur Dignam rehearse before recording session (Albert's Studio, Sydney, September 1978) (photo by Mary Smeaton, used with permission) — 136

4.5 Character model sheet from *Grendel Grendel Grendel* (copyright Estate of Alexander Stitt, used with permission; courtesy RMIT Design Archives) — 140

4.6 Al et al studio where *Grendel Grendel Grendel* was produced, Melbourne, Australia (photo by Mary Smeaton, used with permission) — 142

4.7 (left) Animation director Frank Hellard and (right) animator David Atkinson at work on *Grendel Grendel Grendel* (photo by Mary Smeaton, used with permission) — 143

4.8 Layout drawing for *Grendel Grendel Grendel* describing composition and indicating paint colours and placement of cel overlay (so that background characters can appear to emerge from forest); notation states, 'Yobbos out from behind here' (copyright Estate of Alexander Stitt, used with permission; courtesy RMIT Design Archives) 144

4.9 Early test cels showing the original design style of the film (with inked, black outlines on both the characters and the background elements) (copyright Estate of Alexander Stitt, used with permission; courtesy RMIT Design Archives) 146

4.10 A production cel set up (used in a camera pan sequence) displays the finalized, line-free, look of the film (copyright Estate of Alexander Stitt, used with permission; courtesy RMIT Design Archives) 147

4.11 A page from the third (and final) version of the storyboard for *Grendel Grendel Grendel* (copyright Estate of Alexander Stitt, used with permission; courtesy RMIT Design Archives) 148

4.12 Production cel depicting a silhouetted Grendel, carrying dead bodies past a towering pedestal, which proudly displays a sculpture of King Hrothgar's head from *Grendel Grendel Grendel* (copyright Estate of Alexander Stitt, used with permission; courtesy RMIT Design Archives) 153

Chapter 5: Aesthetics of Grendel Grendel Grendel

5.1 These two images show the difference in character detail between (a) production drawing (copyright Estate of Alexander Stitt, used with permission; courtesy RMIT Design Archives) and (b) corresponding frame grab from the film (*Grendel Grendel Grendel*, Alexander Stitt, 1981) 158

5.2 Unusual rock formations, reminiscent of Viking helmets, populate the film's landscape (*Grendel Grendel Grendel*, Alexander Stitt, 1981) 160

5.3 Personified plants in Grendel's cave; note that Grendel is also sitting on a spotted rock which seems to mimic his general form and patterned design (*Grendel Grendel Grendel*, Alexander Stitt, 1981) 161

5.4 Periodic use of dramatic lighting, which both underscores mood and provides dimensionality to the otherwise flatly rendered forms (*Grendel Grendel Grendel*, Alexander Stitt, 1981) 162

5.5	Unconventional shifting from (a) black silhouetted forms to (b) coloured forms – in order to emphasize the dark shift in mood; in this case when the Shaper and Unferth plot to overthrow the King (*Grendel Grendel Grendel*, Alexander Stitt, 1981)	162
5.6	Frequent and unconventional use of black-screen space; (a) King Hrothgar trapped in Unferth's bear pit (b) a frightened King, seen through an open window, during Grendel's night-time attack on the meadhall (*Grendel Grendel Grendel*, Alexander Stitt, 1981)	164
5.7	A black matte (actually the reverse side of a scroll) effectively cutting a visual hole into the Dragon (*Grendel Grendel Grendel*, Alexander Stitt, 1981)	165
5.8	Three sequences (read from left to right) which utilize animated black-screen elements: (a) the film's live-action introductory sequence featuring Phillip Adams entering a darkened soundstage (b) King Hrothgar's men attack neighbouring villages and burst into a darkened home and (c) Beowulf and his men arrive at the meadhall (*Grendel Grendel Grendel*, Alexander Stitt, 1981)	166

Chapter 6: Grendel'll Get You

6.1	Promotional bumper sticker featuring the catchphrase, 'Grendel'll get you!' (copyright Estate of Alexander Stitt, used with permission; courtesy Paddy Stitt)	172
6.2	Promotional newspaper advertisements for *Grendel Grendel Grendel* (copyright Estate of Alexander Stitt, used with permission; courtesy RMIT Design Archives)	172
6.3	Promotional, animated film tie-in, tissue box for *Grendel Grendel Grendel* (courtesy Bruce Smeaton)	173
6.4	Promotional poster for *Grendel Grendel Grendel* (copyright Estate of Alexander Stitt, used with permission; courtesy RMIT Design Archives)	175
6.5	Promotional badge featuring the catchphrase, 'Grendel'll get you!' (copyright Estate of Alexander Stitt, used with permission; courtesy RMIT Design Archives)	179

ACKNOWLEDGEMENTS

The authors would like to thank:
Phillip Adams, Richard Allen, David Atkinson, Maggie Geddes, Frank Hellard, Neil Robinson, Simone Rule, Bruce Smeaton, Mary Smeaton, Dennis Tupicoff, Malcolm Turner, The National Film and Sound Archives, The National Library of Australia, RMIT Design Archives.

Very special thanks to Paddy Stitt.
All film stills, production artwork, film script excerpts and song lyrics pertaining to *Grendel Grendel Grendel*, copyright Estate of Alexander Stitt, used with permission.

INTRODUCING GRENDEL

This book examines the animated feature film, *Grendel Grendel Grendel* (1981),[1] which was written, designed and directed by the Australian animator and graphic designer, Alexander Stitt (1937–2016). The film showcases a very unique design aesthetic; most notably, it is devoid of outlines and utilizes bold flat planes of colour and mostly limited animation. It features the vocal talents of Peter Ustinov, Keith Michell, Arthur Dignam and Julie McKenna, and the music of Bruce Smeaton. It was produced on a shoe-string budget in a small independent design studio in Melbourne, Australia. Although it was not a commercial success, this uniquely designed film has enjoyed critical praise and occupies a unique place in Australian and international animation history. It also occupies a unique place in literary history as it is based on, and distinctively extends upon renowned American author, John Gardner's seminal novel, *Grendel* – which is arguably one of the most original retellings of the Anglo-Saxon poem, *Beowulf*.

It is believed that the *Beowulf* poem was first written in around the eighth century by a talented (but anonymous) poet; however, the oldest surviving manuscript copy of this poem dates from around AD 1000. *Beowulf* was written in what we now regard as Old English, and is therefore mostly unreadable, except in its modern translated form. The original *Beowulf* poem takes place in Scandinavia and recounts the heroic exploits and the political development of a warrior named Beowulf. His first adventure involves a confrontation with the monster, Grendel, a giant troll-like creature that had been terrorizing the Kingdom of Hrothgar. Next, he battles Grendel's mother, who seeks to avenge her son's death. Finally, some fifty years later as an aged king, Beowulf battles a great dragon. Although he succeeds in killing the dragon, it inflicts a mortal wound, eventually killing him as well.

In 1971, American author, John Gardner published his novel, *Grendel*, which represented an innovative retelling of the *Beowulf* poem. Gardner's unconventional narrative covers just the first third of the poem and, importantly, is told from the monster, Grendel's, perspective. Gardner's novel received very high praise and also brought the author, scholar and professor, some renown. In recent years, *Grendel* has continued to grow in stature, particularly in North America, where it has become an important text in high school and university literature courses. As a result of this continued academic study, a vast number of scholarly articles, texts and PhD thesis have been devoted to Gardner's novel.

Alexander Stitt's animated film, *Grendel Grendel Grendel*, in turn, marks a rather innovative retelling of Gardner's novel. Stitt explains this approach in the introduction to his 1981 publication, *Grendel Grendel Grendel – The Book of the Animated Feature Film*:

> Grendel is a monster and a very elderly one. He features in a long and ancient Anglo-Saxon epic poem called Beowulf. In the original telling of the story we don't find out much about him other than that he lives beneath a lake with his Mum and eats people.
>
> In 1971, the American writer, John Gardner, devoted an entire novel to Grendel himself, plausibly and entertainingly filling in the blanks. It is this novel that was used as the basis for the animated feature film, *Grendel Grendel Grendel*, and in turn, this record of the film.
>
> For the sake of Mr Gardner's readers and reputation, I hasten to add that it's a very free adaptation. Many of the complexities and subtleties of his *Grendel* defy reworking into ninety minutes of animation. *Grendel Grendel Grendel* must be regarded as a separate entity that I, as the designer and director, Bruce Smeaton as the composer, Phillip Adams as the producer and dozens of animators, painters, actors, musicians and technicians found satisfying to fashion alongside Mr Gardner's inspirational work.[2]

John Gardner's novel is a complex and multilayered piece of contemporary literature, and Stitt took a bold step in choosing to adapt *Grendel* into his first feature animated film. Gardner's unconventional narrative jumps back and forth in time, is told exclusively from the point of view of a schizophrenic monster, and exudes equal amounts of philosophy and acerbic social criticisms. Director, Alexander Stitt, was an artist and a graphic designer with a very distinct aesthetic and a relentlessly creative world view. He had developed a deep intellectual understanding of Gardner's novel (and of the original *Beowulf* epic) – and his animated feature is deceptively simple, being far more complex in terms of both design and literary content than it might initially appear.

The year 2021 marks the fortieth anniversary of the release of the film *Grendel Grendel Grendel* (1981) and the fiftieth anniversary of John Gardner's novel, *Grendel* (1971), on which the film is based. Gardner's novel, along with the original *Beowulf* poem, has enjoyed widespread critical discourse. The publication of this book represents an opportune time for a dedicated study of the film, *Grendel Grendel Grendel*.

An Australian animated feature

Grendel Grendel Grendel is a film that is international in its inspiration, but distinctively Australian in its subtext. The feature was made entirely in Melbourne, Australia, at a small design and animation studio called, 'Al et al'. The studio director, Alexander Stitt, also wrote, designed and directed the feature. It was clearly the vision of one filmmaker/designer, but also an adaptation of a very American novel; at the same time, it was a unique adaptation of one of the oldest and most significant literary works in the English language. Although it is an Australian animated film, it does not necessarily look or sound like one. The voice actors, although mostly Australian, primarily adopted British-sounding accents (although you might hear hints of an Australian accent in some character performances). However, as some have suggested that the original poem may, in fact, have been written in northern England, Stitt's choice of accents does follow a certain degree of logic.

Many Australian cartoonists and animators have struggled as to how to go about expressing Australian culture in their illustrations and films. Some have resorted to the featuring of native animals (koalas, kangaroos, wombats) as a means of projecting their Australian-ness. Many have, in fact, found it very difficult to represent Australia or Australian culture in cartoon form without resorting to bush animals. The Australian animator Harry Julius, in addressing this issue in 1938 noted that 'this problem has always rankled with Australian

FIGURE 0.1 Director Alexander Stitt, Melbourne, 2007 (photo by Lienors Torre).

cartoonists. It has never been solved. [...] When you are dealing in animals it is easy. The dressed-up kangaroo is recognizable at once – and he is exclusive.'³ An Australian accent and vernacular can also provide an easily identifiable sense of national origin; some have used this – although until more recently, it has been a dialect that has tended not to 'play well' in America. Some Australian studios such as Air Programs International (API) opted to use a 'mid-Atlantic' voice (one that sits somewhere between an American and a British accent), or else utilize a very exaggerated character voice – one devoid of any recognizable dialect.

Grendel Grendel Grendel was produced by Phillip Adams – a film producer, advertising executive and writer, who had played a huge role in reviving Australia's feature film industry. He had also played a significant part in securing Government support for the Australian film industry, having had prepared a report for the then prime minister, John Gordon, strongly advocating that 'it is time to see our own landscapes, hear our own voices and dream our own dreams'. Nearly all of the films with which Adams was involved sought to 'define or defend whatever was left of something called the Australian character'. Stitt's film, however, was an anomaly – 'it had absolutely no overt connection with Australia at all'. However, it was one strongly supported by Adams, primarily because of his extremely high regard for Stitt's work, and his strong belief that animation could be used to tell very complex ideas (see Chapter 4). Adams did note that there are certainly glimpses of Australian humour and ethos in *Grendel Grendel Grendel*. For example, one common theme in many Australian films is an 'obsession with loss, with defeat'. Gardner's novel expressed this idea perfectly. The main character's final words, 'Poor Grendel has had an accident', are mournfully uttered as he is left dying beneath the stars.⁴ Nevertheless, Stitt was not particularly interested in making a quintessentially 'Australian' film, but an animated feature film based on the literary novel, *Grendel*, which he held in very high regard.

At the time that *Grendel Grendel Grendel* was released, there had been only a handful of animated features produced in Australia, and in some ways, the animation industry was still finding its feet. On the other hand, Australia had already had a surprisingly rich and lengthy history of animation production.⁵

Animation production in Australia commenced at the turn of the twentieth century. A few filmmakers and cartoonists began experimenting with the medium between 1905 and 1914. In 1915, cartoonist and advertising artist, Harry Julius, began producing what can be regarded as the first Australian animation series, *Cartoons of the Moment*, which screened weekly in cinemas before the scheduled feature film. After a brief working holiday in America (where Julius was briefly employed at Roald Barre's animation studio in New York) he returned to Sydney and founded the nation's first significant animation studio, Cartoon Filmads. As the name suggests, the studio primarily focused on producing animated advertisements for cinemas (as well as animated instructional and training films for industry). What was most remarkable about the studio was that it quickly blossomed into an international empire, with offices throughout Asia, the Middle East and parts of Europe. The Cartoon Filmads studio cornered the market for animated advertising in Australia and in other parts of the world until about 1930, at which time the studio began to decline. A few other Australian animation studios also emerged in the 1930s and 1940s, but it was not until the comparatively late arrival of television in Australia in 1956 that domestic animation production finally began to flourish.

Although a significant portion of animation production in Australia continued to be dedicated to the lucrative advertising markets, a number of animated series also emerged in the early days of television, including *Freddo the Frog* (1962); the animated documentary series, *The Challenge of Flight & the Challenge of the Sea* (1962), as well as *Popular Misconceptions* (1963); the Indigenous-themed, stop-motion series *Wambidgee* (1962); the educational series *Eddie's Alphabet* (1967); and the internationally popular comedy *Arthur! And the Square Knights of the Round Table* (1966). Additionally, dozens of long form animated television specials were also produced at this time. The most prominent of these were API's series of animated adaptations of literary classics, including *A Christmas Carol, The Prince and the Pauper, Moby-Dick, The Swiss Family Robinson, Around the World in 80 Days, Journey to the Centre of the Earth* and *Rip Van Winkle*. These animated feature-length television specials were broadcast both in Australia and in many international markets, including North America. During this period, Australia had also become an important centre for productions of overseas animation studios, producing animated series for King Features and Hanna-Barbera. By the late 1970s Hanna-Barbera had set up their own major animation studio in Sydney and began producing hundreds of hours' worth of animated television series, specials and advertisements, which were screened both in Australia and around the world.

Although *Grendel Grendel Grendel* was not the first animated feature produced in Australia, only a handful of other theatrically released features had been made. In 1972, Eric Porter Studios completed Australia's first animated feature to be released in cinemas, *Marco Polo Jnr vs. the Red Dragon* (Eric Porter 1972). It was, in fact, a co-production between Porter and the American comic book artist, Sheldon Moldoff. Later, in 1977, Yoram Gross Studios began producing a series of cinema released animated features based on traditional Australian stories. These were not entirely animated, as the animated characters were composited primarily on to live-action backgrounds. The first three of these features were *Dot and the Kangaroo* (Yoram Gross 1977), *The Little Convict* (Yoram Gross 1979) and *Around the World with Dot* (Yoram Gross 1981).

Despite the fact that there were a number of studios in operation across Australia and a substantial amount of animation being produced, most domestically financed productions were, in fact, very small and made with very limited resources. In 1977, when Alexander Stitt began developing *Grendel Grendel Grendel*, the idea of making a fully animated feature film was still regarded as a highly risky venture in Australia.

Overview of this book

This text examines the animated feature, *Grendel Grendel Grendel*, from a variety of perspectives, and is divided into six chapters, each covering a different facet.

In Chapter 1, 'The Genealogy of Grendel', the history and development of the *Beowulf* story are considered, with particular emphasis on the history of the monster Grendel. It describes the evolution and genealogy of Grendel and how he has been depicted in a variety of *Beowulf* inspired narratives, spanning a wide range of media and eras. It begins with a discussion of the original *Beowulf* epic, then follows its development in popular literature. It further considers how the *Beowulf* story and the character of Grendel have evolved through their cinematic iterations, as well as their appearances in other forms of popular culture such as comics, video games, novels and a major opera production.

Chapter 2, 'Scenes of *Grendel Grendel Grendel*', simultaneously provides a detailed scene-by-scene synopsis with a brief critical analysis of the film *Grendel, Grendel, Grendel*. Each of the film's seventy-odd scenes (sixty-eight plus the introduction and end credit sequence) is discussed. Where appropriate, comparisons are made with Gardner's book, and with the original *Beowulf* epic.

Chapter 3, 'Themes of *Grendel Grendel Grendel*', builds upon the previous chapter by further investigating several themes that pervade the animated film. These include the importance and fundamental role of monsters, the curse of Cain, the character of the Dragon (and the Dragon God), the recurring allusions to Lewis Carroll's *Alice in Wonderland*, and the complimentary roles of the Shaper and of the Sculptor. Some of these subjects are exemplified both in Gardner's novel and in the film, while others (such as the Sculptor, the Dragon God and references to *Alice in Wonderland*) are uniquely represented in Stitt's animated feature.

Chapter 4, 'Making of *Grendel Grendel Grendel*', describes the production of *Grendel Grendel Grendel*, from its initial concept through to the completed animated film. It commences with a pre-history of the film's production in which the origins of the Al et al studio, the backgrounds of the director and of several of the key animators, and the composer of the film score are highlighted. It also describes the vocal recording sessions and the animation process for the film.

Chapter 5, 'Aesthetics of *Grendel Grendel Grendel*', addresses the aesthetics and design of the film. Most fundamental to the film's design was the decision to do away with any outlines around the characters or background elements. But there were also many other unique design choices that make the film distinctive. Particular emphasis is placed on how these aesthetics and approaches to animation are used to extend the film's tone and narrative.

Chapter 6, 'Grendel'll Get You', focuses on the marketing and reception of the film. Once the production of *Grendel Grendel Grendel* was complete, the producers faced the equally difficult task of promotion, and of convincing audiences actually to go and see the animated feature. 'Grendel'll get you!' became the celebrated marketing catchphrase for the film. This chapter further contextualizes the film among other animated films from the era.

Finally, there is a short conclusion chapter, 'Concluding Grendel', which is followed by a 'Guide to Further Research' section that provides an annotated listing of suggested texts and media for those who are interested in further sources of study of these themes.

John Gardner had a great love of animation and described Grendel as being one of his 'short-legged, overweight, twitching cartoon creations'.[6] Viewing his novel in this light it could be said that Gardner played a significant role in helping to *animate* the original *Beowulf* narrative. Stitt, working in the medium of animation, quite literally set out to animate both *Grendel* and a number of themes from the original *Beowulf* epic. This text, *Grendel Grendel Grendel – Animating Beowulf*, provides not only a substantial analysis of the animated feature, but it also illustrates how Stitt's film helps to further *animate* our understanding and appreciation of both John Gardner's novel and the greater Beowulf legacy.

Notes

1. Although *Grendel Grendel Grendel* was completed and copyrighted in November of 1980, it was not released for screening until June 1981.
2. Alexander Stitt, *Grendel Grendel Grendel – the Book of the Animated Feature Film* (Melbourne: Penguin Australia, 1981), p. 4.
3. Harry Julius, *The Sydney Morning Herald*, 22 February 1938.
4. Phillip Adams, interviewed by Dan Torre and Lienors Torre, November 2019.
5. For more on the history of Australian animation see, Dan Torre and Lienors Torre, *Australian Animation – An International History* (London: Palgrave, 2018).
6. John Gardner, *On Writers and Writing* (Berkeley: Counterpoint, 1994), p. 248.

Chapter 1

THE GENEALOGY OF GRENDEL

An article published in *Vogue Australia*, which coincided with the 1981 release of *Grendel Grendel Grendel*, identified three different Grendels: 'Grendel Mark I' (the original *Beowulf* poem), 'Grendel Mark II' (John Gardner's novel, *Grendel*) and 'Grendel Mark III' (Stitt's animated feature film, *Grendel Grendel Grendel*).[1] Although such a ranking was intended to foreground the importance of the animated film, it did effectively highlight an evolutionary trajectory of the Grendel character – from terrifying monster, to sympathetic beast, to loveable anti-monster.

This chapter describes the evolution and genealogy of the character Grendel as he has been depicted in a variety of *Beowulf* inspired narratives, spanning a wide range of media and eras. It begins with a discussion of the original *Beowulf* epic and traces its development in popular literature. It further considers how the *Beowulf* story and the character of Grendel have evolved through their cinematic iterations as well as the character's appearances in other forms of popular culture such as comics, video games, novels and a major opera production.

Gardner's novel stands out as one of the most significant retellings of the *Beowulf* poem. It has garnered high praise for his innovative use of the literary form and its explication of the subtleties of Grendel's quest for identity and philosophical meaning. Arguably, Alexander Stitt working within the medium of animation also produced a significant, but vastly underrated, contribution to the genealogy of Grendel, and one that is worthy of serious study.

The Beowulf *poem*

Beowulf is a 3,182-line poem that is set in sixth-century Scandinavia. It was written, perhaps as early as AD 700, by an anonymous English poet. The genesis of the narrative emerged from the oral story-telling traditions of the Anglo-Saxons (a tale which might have been handed down over generations) before being adapted to the written word. The original written form of the poem would then have been transcribed numerous times over the centuries, until finally again being hand-copied in about AD 1000 – resulting in what is now the oldest (and only) known copy of the poem. Narrowly surviving a devastating fire in 1731, this now very worn and damaged manuscript resides in the British Library (see Figure 1.1).

Set within the realm of King Hrothgar, the poem describes three major battles between a foreign warrior named Beowulf and three different monsters: Grendel, Grendel's mother and a great fire-breathing dragon. The poem also details much of the politics and social interactions of the era. Importantly, it is set against a backdrop of conflicting, yet overlapping religious beliefs – the historic pagan religions of the north (which were waning) and the rapidly spreading Christian religion.

The poem describes how, prior to the arrival of the troublesome monsters, King Hrothgar presided over a prosperous and expanding kingdom. To mark his success, he builds a great meadhall, which he names, Heorot. It is a place in which the King and his warriors come together to drink mead (an alcoholic drink made from fermented honey and water) and listen to stories and songs performed by the scops (minstrels) which often detail their heroic adventures. However, the loud nightly revelry begins to disturb, and increasingly to anger, a troll-like monster named Grendel, who lives just beyond the outskirts of the kingdom. Grendel begins to terrorize and frequently to attack the meadhall. This continues for some twelve years, when finally a heroic warrior from the friendly northern kingdom of Geatland hears of King Hrothgar's troubles and, along with a small group of warriors, sails across the sea to offer his services to the King. Very happily the King accepts, and Beowulf and his men soon battle Grendel. Because the monster is impervious to weapons, Beowulf resorts to brute strength and cunning and thus manages to enact a fatal blow by ripping off Grendel's arm at the shoulder socket. Consequently, Grendel's mother emerges from her underground lair in order to avenge her son's death, attacking and killing one of the King's closest comrades. Beowulf follows her to her lair and kills her. While there, he also finds the body of Grendel and cuts off the head, which he brings back triumphantly to King Hrothgar. Beowulf is richly rewarded; then returns to his Geatland. Because of his great fame, he is soon made King and rules successfully for fifty years. But when a great dragon begins to trouble his land, he sets out (now an old man) to battle it. With the assistance of his loyal warrior (and nephew), Wiglaf, he succeeds in killing it. However, the dragon also fatally wounds Beowulf. He is given an elaborate funeral, being remembered as a great hero and a great King. Wiglaf, who is now heir to the throne, is set to follow in Beowulf's footsteps.

The poem is written in Old English (Anglo-Saxon) and is unreadable to most without a translation into a modern language. The text follows the traditional Anglo-Saxon poetry form, which would have been performed for an audience and therefore would follow a number of compositional rules that facilitated its oral performance (such as patterns of alliteration and stressed syllables, and

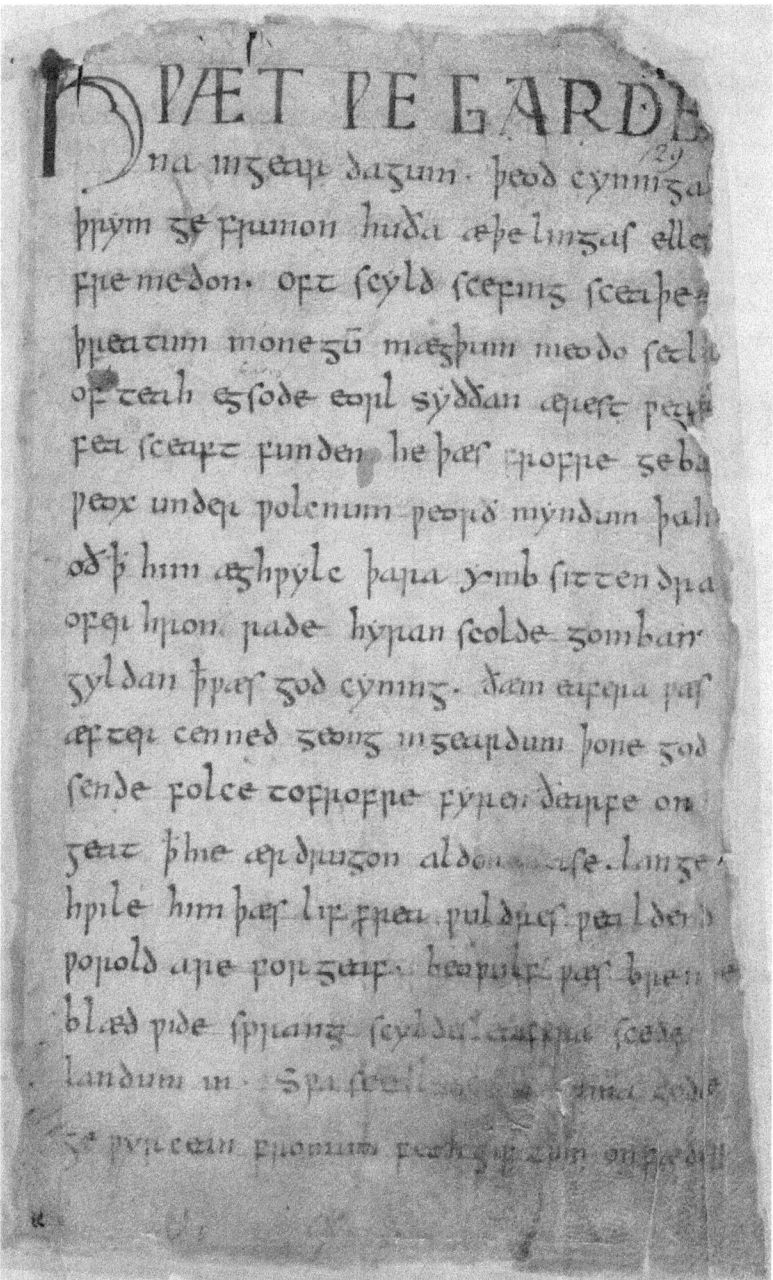

FIGURE 1.1 The first page of the oldest surviving manuscript of the original *Beowulf* poem (this surviving copy was transcribed in *c*. AD 1000).

frequent use of kenning). In homage to the poem, kenning (two-part poetic descriptions) was also extensively used in Gardner's novel; and used also in Stitt's animated feature.

The first complete translation of the *Beowulf* poem was made by Grimur Jonsson Thorkelin and published in Latin in 1815. Two decades later, in 1837, the first complete modern English prose translation, *A Translation of the Anglo-Saxon Poem of 'Beowulf'*, was made by John Kemble. Many additional translations soon followed, both in prose and in verse form, in English and in several other (mostly European) languages. A number of simplified and abridged retellings of the Beowulf story (mainly aimed at children) appeared around the turn of the century. Several notable examples featured detailed illustrations (including those of the monster Grendel). These included *Beowulf, Told to the Children* by Henrietta E. Marshall, illustrated by J. R. Skelton (1908); and *Myths and Legends – The British Race* by Maud Isabel Ebbutt, illustrated by J. H. F. Bacon (1910). In Marshall's publication, Grendel was depicted as a giant, somewhat Neanderthal-like, hairy man (see Figure 1.2a); while Bacon's version depicted Grendel more akin to a swamp-monster, with scales, shark-like teeth and an over-sized head (see Figure 1.2b).

Despite the increasing number of translations, the *Beowulf* poem failed to be taken seriously in academia. Up until the 1930s the poem's significance centred

FIGURE 1.2 The character of Grendel as conceived by earlier visual artists: (a) an illustration by J. R. Skelton in *Beowulf, Told to the Children* by Henrietta E. Marshall (1908); (b) an illustration by J. H. F. Bacon in *Myths and Legends – The British Race* by Maud Isabel Ebbutt (1910).

primarily on the fact that it was the oldest surviving long-form poem written in 'English', also for the historical insights that it suggested. Beyond this, its *literary* value was seen as tenuous and many scholars, it seems, were embarrassed by the poet's inclusion of fanciful monsters and dragons. J. R. R. Tolkien sharply criticized those scholars who saw the poem only as a place in which to search for historical insights, rather than for its poetic and literary merits.[2] In 1936, he delivered to the British academy what has become an oft republished lecture, 'Beowulf: The Monsters and the Critics', in which he advocated that the poem should also be heralded as a highly creative literary work. Tolkien asserted, 'Beowulf is in fact so interesting as poetry, in places poetry so powerful, that this quite overshadows the historical content'.[3] Tolkien also suggested that the monster Grendel is of equal significance to Beowulf, and to those that would be distressed by such a claim, he assures them, 'We do not deny the worth of the hero by accepting Grendel.'[4] Not only did Tolkien advocate the recognition of *Beowulf* and its monsters, he also used it as a source in his own creative writing. For example, the creature known as Gollum in *The Hobbit* and *Lord of the Rings* reflects the characteristics of Grendel. However, unlike the original poem, Tolkien's Grendel-like creature (Gollum) is also worthy of some sympathy as he is merely possessed by the power of the cursed ring and is therefore not fundamentally evil or monstrous.

One of the most prominent of the recent English language translations is Seamus Heaney's *Beowulf* (1999). Heaney's translation has proven to be extremely popular and is credited with spawning the production of a number of *Beowulf*-themed films that appeared in the early 2000s. Another significant publication is J. R. R. Tolkien's long-awaited translation, *Beowulf: A Translation and Commentary*. This text was actually translated in 1926, but was not published until many decades later by his son, Christopher Tolkien, in 2014. The book also includes a previously unpublished *Beowulf*-themed fairy tale, 'Sellic Spell' (which Tolkien had originally written in the 1940s).

In 1961, Rosemary Sutcliff published her very popular adaptation of the poem. Originally titled, *Beowulf – Retold by Rosemary Sutcliff*, it was renamed for the later paperback edition (1966) as *Dragon Slayer – The Story of Beowulf*. The book was aimed primarily at children and subsequently adopted by many primary schools as an introduction to the *Beowulf* poem. It is a slim novel of less than ninety pages and tells the story in a concise and easy to read manner. It covers the whole of the epic poem – but being aimed at children, it does place strong emphasis on the scenes with the monsters (and omits many of the poem's more tangential sections). Although it is not at all sympathetic to Grendel, the monster does feature in one of the most memorable scenes in the book, giving him (almost) equal billing with the hero Beowulf.

A significant reworking of the *Beowulf* poem can be found in William Hamilton Canaway's *The Ring-Givers* (1958). His novel seeks to 'demythologize the legend'[5] by focusing on the political and economic landscapes of the era. There are no real monsters in Canaway's novel; Grendel is simply a very tall human, who is starving and thus compelled to attack the kingdom.

Beowulf realized as soon as he saw the form in the light of the nearest torch that this was no troll. True enough, he was black, but with filth ... it glanced about, seeking the meat it craved. It was this lack of fresh meat that had made Grendel mad.[6]

In this novel, as with the original poem, the role of the singer or 'scop' is also extremely important; ultimately he is the vital tool of propaganda used in supporting Beowulf and his kingdom and effectively ostracizing Grendel. Although rarely mentioned, *The Ring-Givers* clearly provided inspiration to a number of subsequent authors.

John Gardner and Grendel

Although many Beowulf scholars had previously acknowledged that there are elements within the original poem which might suggest that Grendel and his mother deserve a certain degree of sympathy, it was John Gardner's novel *Grendel* that most radically advanced a revised treatment of these characters.

John Gardner (1933–82) was an American author, scholar and professor of medieval literature and creative writing. He grew up on a farm, experiencing a strong religious upbringing (his father was a Christian minister). However, he had a very tragic experience at the age of eleven when he accidentally killed his younger brother by driving over him with a cultipacker that he was pulling with a tractor. As would be expected, this incident left a lasting scar and he mentioned it frequently in interviews and thematically wove it into his writings – in particular in his short story, 'Redemption' and his first published novel, *Grendel*.

His most popular fictional novels included *Grendel* (1971), *The Sunlight Dialogues* (1972), *Nickel Mountain: A Pastoral Novel* (1973) and *October Light* (1977). He wrote a number of influential, non-fictional texts on such subjects as writing and medieval literature, including *The Life & Times of Chaucer* (1977) and *On Moral Fiction* (1978); and the posthumously published, *On Becoming a Novelist* (1983) and *The Art of Fiction* (1984). He also wrote several children's books, a radio play and the libretto for an opera. Gardner died in a motorcycle accident in 1982 at the age of forty-nine.

His most celebrated work, by far, is *Grendel*. At the time of its publication it attracted strong critical acclaim and seemed to have a very profound impact on many of its readers (including director Alexander Stitt). Although it is a reworking of *Beowulf*, the novel is also a philosophical analysis of what it means to be human, representing a poetic and a darkly lyrical experience. It features an internalized narrative told from Grendel's perspective, and often runs in non-chronological order.

The novel begins with Grendel disdainfully observing the base activities of animals in nature, thereby distancing his character from the animal world. He then shifts his attention to the human race and watches with equal derision as Hrothgar's kingdom expands. One day, a Shaper (Gardner's term for a minstrel or scop) arrives whose songs and poetry have a profound 'shaping' effect on the humans, and an even more profound effect on Grendel. From these songs, Grendel learns that he is considered to be a descendant of Cain (the biblical figure that killed his own brother) and thus cursed for eternity. Soon after this Grendel has a metaphysical vision whereby he meets a dragon. The dragon is a philosophical yet whimsical creature that extensively quotes (uncredited) the American philosopher, A. N. Whitehead. It attempts to clarify for Grendel his monstrous identity and his purpose in life. Inspired by the dragon, Grendel begins to act more monstrously, regularly attacking the King's meadhall.

In Grendel's quest for meaning, he attempts to emulate the Shaper, but when the Shaper suddenly dies, Grendel is left to struggle with his own feebly poetic interpretations of the world. Finally, a nameless stranger arrives. The reader understands that it is Beowulf, who has come to kill Grendel, but neither his name nor intentions are ever spelled out. In a final showdown, Beowulf manages to rip off Grendel's arm. Fatally wounded, Grendel flees into the forest and collapses. Speaking aloud to the animals that have come to watch him die, he pronounces, 'Poor Grendel's had an accident'; then adding with emphasis, '*So may you all*'. This final statement doubles as a curse that is on one hand directed towards the animals watching him suffer, but also towards the reader who, from his perspective, is probably the more monstrous one.

The novel spans just the first third of the original poem – up to the point where Grendel is killed by Beowulf. But Gardner cleverly brings in elements from the other two thirds of the poem. At the end, for example, rather than having a real dragon for Beowulf to fight, Gardner brings in a dragon character which is a figment of Grendel's imagination. Gardner assumes that the reader will be familiar with the original Beowulf narrative and thus see these connections. 'Though a reader can appreciate *Grendel* without knowing *Beowulf*, an awareness of the epic reveals the ingenuity as well as the irony of Gardner's improvisation and parody.'[7]

Grendel has become a regular part of the curriculum in North American high school and university literature courses. Quite often, Gardner's novel will be taught in tandem with the *Beowulf* poem. The novel not only makes the poem more accessible, but its themes have proven to be very relatable to contemporary young readers:

> *Grendel* is both a coming-of-age story and a philosophical search for the meaning of life. Like most teens, Grendel is smarter than his mother, and being sensitive, insecure, and introspective, he feels isolated and lonely. He seeks human companionship, only to be violently rejected by humans. And he views authority figures as deeply flawed, if not thoroughly corrupt. In other words, he passes through some of the stages of teenage angst: experiencing moments of self-loathing, suffering an identity crisis, rejecting authority, and rebelling against conformity.[8]

The impact of this novel has continued to grow. *Grendel* has now come to be regarded as an important twentieth-century literary classic.

John Gardner was also a large admirer of 'cartoons'. These included the classic animated films of Walt Disney, but also the broader 'cartoon-like' storytelling of such authors as Charles Dickens. 'For me', he once noted, 'Disney and Dickens were practically indistinguishable. Both created wonderful cartoon images, told stories as direct as fairy tales, knew the value of broad comedy spiced up with a little weeping.'[9] He further remarked that he placed greater value on the symbolism found in Disney animated films compared to 'those realistic writers who give you life data without resonance, things merely as they are'.[10] In his essay on the subject of cartoons Gardner draws a direct link between Grendel and animation:

> I seem incapable of writing a story in which people do not babble philosophically, not really because they're saying things I want to get said but because earnest babbling is one of the ways I habitually give vitality to my short-legged, overweight, twitching cartoon creations. And needless to say, from artists like Dickens and Disney I get my morbid habit of trying to make the reader fall into tender weeping.[11]

Although, on one hand it is deeply puzzling as to why any director would seek to make an animated film out of such a complex and non-conventional novel as *Grendel*, it does seem that Gardner viewed animation as an ideal vehicle for many of his visionary writings.

Gardner was, of course, a respected scholar in medieval literature – and as he began to devote more of his efforts to creative writing, he stated, 'I found in medieval culture and art [...] exactly what I needed as an instrument for looking at my own time and place [...] medieval ideas and attitudes gave me a means of triangulating, a place to stand.'[12] Clearly, for Gardner, when it came to writing *Grendel*, the historic realms and literary spaces of the Beowulf epic narrative were also a very effective zone with which to critique modern-day society – which, at that time, was in the throes of the Vietnam War. For director Alexander Stitt, animation provided a similar safe space from which adroitly to critique contemporary society.

Eaters of the Dead

Eaters of the Dead, published in 1976, is a novel by Michael Crichton that also significantly alters the original *Beowulf* narrative. According to the author, the novel was 'conceived on a dare' when, in 1974, a university professor suggested to Crichton that *Beowulf* was one of the 'great bores' of literature – required reading that was much too tedious to enjoy. Crichton disagreed with this labelling, arguing that 'Beowulf was a dramatic, exciting story' and, to prove his point, he straightaway set about writing a novelization of the poem.[13] But

Crichton soon adopted a secondary intention, which was to argue that Beowulf had originally been based on actual events, and that these events 'had been embellished over centuries of oral retelling, producing the fantastic narrative we read today'.[14]

Crichton's novel is unique in that it purports to be a translation of a newly discovered ancient manuscript written by Ahmad Ibn Fadlan, a tenth-century Arab writer. In fact, the first two chapters of the book are direct translations from the actual ancient manuscript penned by the real-life Ibn Fadlan (who really was an Arabic writer from the tenth century). The rest of the novel is fiction, although written in a similar style, and describes Fadlan's imagined travels into Scandinavian territories where he encounters a Viking leader named Beowulf (here called 'Buliwyf').

In his telling of *Beowulf*, Crichton effectively declaws the monsters in the poem, indicating how their mythical status might have evolved from the mundane into the fantastic. For example, in his novel the monster 'Grendel' is revealed to be a tribe of surviving Neanderthal humans called the 'Wendol'. Similarly, the purported sightings of a fire-breathing dragon are also debunked; these 'dragons' turning out to be simply groups of torch-wielding Wendol journeying through the fog. Crichton's novel suggests that monsters are simply manifestations of irrational fears and fanciful storytelling, while it is the very real barbaric acts committed by humans which are truly monstrous.

Crichton played it very straight, professing the text to be a factual account, writing it in a similar style to the Ibn Fadlan manuscript and incorporating numerous and very pedantic footnotes. Thus, at the time of its publication many believed it to be an historical non-fictional text. It was such a convincing approach that a great many librarians of the time catalogued the book under the non-fictional category of 'Viking history'.[15]

Crichton never acknowledged that he had been influenced by other contemporary literary sources. However, it is difficult to imagine that he was not strongly influenced by Gardner's *Grendel* (which had been published just a few years earlier), but it is even more probable that Crichton was also greatly influenced by the earlier W. H. Canaway's novel, *The Ring-Givers* (1958). Canaway's novel is very similar to Crichton's in that it also seeks to 'demythologize the legend'.[16] Crichton's *Eaters of the Dead* was made into the movie, *The 13th Warrior*, in 1999. It was directed by John McTiernan and starred Antonio Banderas as Ibn Fadlan.

Another important aspect of *Eaters of the Dead* is that it provides a number of interesting observations of early Scandinavian culture. Alexander Stitt found Crichton's novel very compelling in this way, and cites it as one of several contributing influences to his animated feature. One section that Stitt clearly found intriguing – and one that he took to comic extremes in *Grendel Grendel Grendel* – was Crichton's lengthy description of the Viking's obsession with their noses.

Grendel Grendel Grendel

Alexander Stitt's feature-length animated musical adaptation of Gardner's novel was released in 1981, exactly ten years after the publication of the novel. Stitt's film is a very loose adaptation; however, it does follow the general structure of the novel and most of the events and much of the dialogue are retained. In addition to directing the film, Stitt also wrote the screenplay adaptation, wrote the lyrics to the songs and designed all the characters, layouts and backgrounds. The use of traditional cel-animation (with its starkly flat expanses of bright colours, cute characters, stylized movement and musical numbers) is, at first glance, the polar-opposite to the complexities and nuances that Gardner's book evokes. But upon closer study the ingenious brevity of the design and animated movement does convey a parallel level of intellectual complexity, irony and creative prowess.

The tone of the film is alternatingly irreverent and deeply serious. The promotional material for the film reflects this tone, thus summarizing it:

> We are in Scandinavia, once upon a time in AD 515, where we are introduced to Grendel. He is charming and urbane. He's also green, spotty and twelve feet four inches tall. Which is a worry. When he accidently bumps into the local king – Hrothgar – and his loyal subjects Wiglaf and Dung, the poor little humans are scared off, quick-smart. Wiglaf falls foul of a couple of villains, and is fairly severely stabbed. Hrothgar and a new recruit, the noble hero Unferth retaliate by stabbing the villains back more severely. A wandering minstrel, The Shaper, arrives in the kingdom and ingratiates himself by composing a much-embroidered version of the encounter. Hrothgar acquires a wife, and The Shaper sings a special song to celebrate the marriage. Listening outside, Grendel assumes that he is one of the 'dark damned half' of mankind mentioned in the song, and disrupts the proceedings by begging to be taken in and 'forgiven'. He's misunderstood by the warriors and driven off – but not before he's been obliged to kill a few of them. Grendel has a dream, in which he visits the all-knowing Dragon who advises that he, Grendel, exists, was created, simply to frighten the little humans, to go bump in their night. Grendel is not totally convinced, but decides to follow the Dragon's rules by dropping in on the kingdom from time to time to eat one or two of the tasty warriors. On one of Grendel's visits, the noble hero Unferth challenges him. Grendel toys with him by simply throwing apples at him – it's more fun than killing him. Unferth is furious. Hrothgar is irritated, and decides to do something about ridding his kingdom of the monster. He sends a message for help across the sea to Beowulf – famous warrior-lord and friend of the family. Beowulf arrives and sets a trap for Grendel, should he visit the mead-hall that night. Grendel, of course, does just that, and encounters Beowulf. In the ensuing battle, Grendel loses an arm before beating a hasty retreat. Minutes later, we find Grendel outside, lying in the snow. 'Poor Grendel's had an … accident', he says.[17]

Another piece of promotional material provides an even more irreverent, and much briefer, summation of the film:

> King Hrothgar gets a nice little kingdom going. The noble hero Unferth swims through the pool of firesnakes. The Dragon tap-dances. Wiglaf gets his head bitten off. The Queen screams a lot. And poor Grendel has an accident.[18]

Although ostensibly the film is told from Grendel's point of view, at the same time it provides the viewer with an overtly critical perspective of human society, religion and politics in a way that the novel does not. A good deal of the film follows Grendel as he observes the absurdity of human society – in this way he is a bit like Lewis Carroll's character, Alice (who encounters characters and situations that are increasingly strange and puzzling). Ultimately, Grendel becomes, as the Dragon said he would, 'man's anti-man'. But, of course, Grendel has 'an accident' before he can truly fulfil his purpose – that is, Beowulf rips off his arm and leaves him to die under the stars.

The film features sequences of voice over narration provided by Peter Ustinov as Grendel, and some brief monologues in which Grendel espouses his thoughts to his off-screen mother; however, a substantial portion of the narrative is revealed through conventional action and dialogue. Most of the characters in the film are performed with working-class, Yorkshire accents, while Grendel is given an urbane Londoner accent. *Grendel Grendel Grendel* is also a musical, showcasing seven songs as performed by the various characters.

Importantly, Stitt chose to tone down a lot of the monstrous characteristics of Grendel, and instead employed humour to highlight the monstrous absurdity of human nature (see Figure 1.3). Not only does Stitt's film show the 'human' side of Grendel, it also manages to discredit nearly all of the 'humanity' in the humans. Upon its Australian release in 1981, one reviewer noted:

> Alex Stitt and his associates have created a work that stands on its own feet as entertainment, a work which is considerably lighter in tone than Gardner's book, but remains faithful to the story line as Gardner reshaped it. The script, also by Stitt for whom this whole project has obviously been an enormous labor of love, has simplified Gardner's prose style artfully, keeping an eye on the movie audiences who are going to be delighted both by the vocal characterisation and the occasional pungent colloquialism.[19]

Stitt's Grendel, though adapted from Gardner's novel, can also trace its roots to some of Stitt's earlier animated works, most notably his very successful and very long-running animated advertising campaign known as *Life. Be in It*. This campaign was funded by the Victorian State Government (Australia) to encourage fitness and health. Ironically, the series of animated commercials featured a lazy, overweight character named Norm, who spent all of his time sitting in front of the television, drinking beer. His catchphrase became,

FIGURE 1.3 Image of Grendel, the (almost) loveable monster, from *Grendel Grendel Grendel* (Alexander Stitt, 1981).

'Warm the tele, and cool the tinnies [cans of beer]'. But the whole point of the commercials was to encourage viewers to turn off their televisions, go outside and exercise, and eat good food (and by extension, drink less beer!). Even though the ads had a positive effect, the anti-healthy Norm became a huge celebrity. People loved Norm (even though they probably knew they shouldn't) and by his doing *nothing*, he effectively encouraged people to *do things*. Stitt's Grendel is a similarly overweight character that people have found very likable (even though they probably shouldn't), and by his being monstrous, he effectively encourages people to *not be monstrous*.

Although *Grendel Grendel Grendel* suffered considerably at the box office, it did enjoy brief theatrical runs in Australia and New Zealand, several theatrical runs in various European markets, and a very limited release in America. Furthermore, it also enjoyed a fairly wide home video release in a number of international markets and was screened multiple times on cable television in North America. The film in more recent years has had both authorized and unauthorized releases on DVD and is currently available for streaming online. While no sales figures are publically available, it is quite probable that the film's overall reach and impact have been much more substantial than have been previously acknowledged.

In the mid-1990s, New Zealand film director, Vincent Ward (director of *What Dreams May Come* [1998]), began preliminary work into making a live-action version of Gardner's novel. He contacted Alexander Stitt (and producer Phillip Adams) in order to purchase their, still-current, film rights to the book. Although the project never came to fruition, Ward's film was intended to be a more balanced blending of Gardner's novel and the original *Beowulf* poem.

More Grendel films

Beowulf (Yuri Kulakov 1998). It was almost twenty years after Stitt's animated feature that the next animated version of the *Beowulf* story was produced. Broadcast on the BBC in 1998, *Beowulf* is a brief, 27-minute-long animated film. The screenplay was written by Murray Watts and directed by Yuri Kulakov. It is a Welsh and Russian co-production and was animated in studios located in both Moscow and Cardiff. Derek Jacobi narrated the film, Joseph Fiennes playing the voice of Beowulf, Michael Sheen that of Wiglaf.

This animated version harkens back to the original poem and does not display any sympathy for Grendel, who is represented as a large black, faceless, shadowy figure. The warrior's sword blades simply slice through Grendel's shadowy form as if it were a thick mist. But in his epic battle Beowulf does manage to rip off Grendel's arm. Later, Beowulf follows the wounded Grendel to his cave and battles Grendel's mother. Finally, with the aid of an enchanted sword, Beowulf cuts off the heads of both Grendel and his mother and carries them back to show Hrothgar; but as he holds them aloft, they dissipate as if they were actually made of an enchanted, inky black mist.

There is one particularly interesting animated treatment in the final battle between Beowulf and the dragon. In a somewhat surreal scene in which the dragon and Beowulf find themselves in a greyish void, Beowulf's shadow grows and transforms into a giant version of himself. This large Beowulf shadow form laughs sinisterly as it shape-shifts into the dragon. Beowulf manages to defeat the dragon, but he himself is also wounded and soon dies. This one scene appears to mirror Gardner's approach (and to some degree Stitt's) of conflating the characters of the dragon and of Beowulf. Also, the frequent innovative use of shadows does, to some degree, echo Stitt's intriguing and frequent use of shadows and silhouetted forms in his animated feature (see Chapter 5).

Beowulf (Graham Baker, 1999). The next major cinematic version of the Beowulf story was the feature-length film, *Beowulf*, directed by Graham Baker and released in 1999. This (mostly) live-action film diverges greatly from the original poem, and for the first time reveals the identity of Grendel's father. The film stars Christopher Lambert as Beowulf, Grendel being represented as an animated visual-effects creature. Grendel's mother is a shape-shifting creature who can take the form of a terrifying animated monster, or a beautiful (live-action) seductress woman. In her human form she mates with King Hrothgar and, unbeknown to him, she bears a child whom she names, Grendel. Many years later, she returns to the kingdom and confronts Hrothgar:

> GRENDEL'S MOTHER: The one you call the beast, he's your son, Grendel.
> HROTHGAR: Impossible! That thing's not human!
> GRENDEL'S MOTHER: He's half. That's why he's so handsome.

Here, by making Grendel half-human (and of half-noble blood) his monstrousness is inherently diminished. Contra wise, it is revealed that Beowulf is also not entirely human – being the son of a human mother and the god Baal. The film's trailer highlights this fact as it proclaims, 'A man, more than mortal, born half of heaven and half of hell, is their only salvation'. Even though the film is clearly told from the perspective of Beowulf, the genetic make-up of the 'hero' and the 'monster' becomes extremely confused. In fact, the film's catchphrase, 'Beowulf – unleash your dark side', seems to celebrate the monstrous nature of the 'hero' Beowulf.

Beowulf & Grendel (Sturla Gunnarsson, 2005). *Beowulf & Grendel* is an Icelandic and Canadian co-production, which was directed by Sturla Gunnarsson, written by Andrew Rai Bereins and released in 2005. The film spans the first two-thirds of the original poem, ending just after Beowulf kills Grendel's mother. This film, which includes both the names of Beowulf *and* Grendel in the title, takes a decidedly sympathetic approach to the character of Grendel. The film clearly draws inspiration from Gardner's novel, but seemingly from Stitt's animated feature as well.

This movie also reveals the identity of Grendel's father – in this case he is portrayed as a giant hairy man. The opening prologue sequence entitled 'A Hate is Born' portrays Grendel's father playing happily with his son in a grassy meadow. The young Grendel looks essentially like a child-version of his father. Suddenly, King Hrothgar and his men launch an attack, killing Grendel's father. From his hiding place, a very distraught Grendel witnesses the horrific event. It is from this that Grendel's 'hatred' towards Hrothgar and his kingdom stems.

The 'hero' Beowulf is depicted in a decidedly non-heroic manner. When he first arrives on shore, he does not travel on a mighty ship accompanied by warriors, but swims in, alone and half-drowned with 'his shins and thighs burdened by lamprey eels attached to his flesh'.[20] Beowulf's arrival is witnessed by a fisherman. Then, in what could be interpreted as a slight acknowledgement to the Australian animated film, the fisherman says, 'G'day' and Beowulf responds, 'G'day'. After a while, and over supper, the fisherman begins to poke fun at Beowulf's status as a 'hero', asking, 'So … what's it like being a hero? Quelling things with axes and that sword of yours … in – what – a kinda bloody madness?'

When Beowulf encounters Grendel, he repeatedly tries to fight with him, but is unsuccessful. Grendel also seems to poke fun at his 'hero' status. In scenes that clearly reference Gardner's novel (and Stitt's film), Grendel denies him a chance to be a hero, merely throwing small stones at his helmet then walking away. (These scenes mirror both Gardner's and Stitt's versions, in which Grendel throws apples at Unferth, mocking him and refusing to fight.) In this film, Grendel is only interested in seeking revenge on those that killed his father, namely the Danes – and King Hrothgar in particular.

The film also introduces a new character named Selma,[21] who is an outcast of Hrothgar's kingdom and generally regarded as a witch. Selma, in a way, becomes a Wealtheow-type character who, by fulfilling her role as 'a servant of common good', bridges the chasm between the monstrous Grendel and the monstrous humans. She even gives birth to Grendel's child (who she keeps hidden away). She, unlike the other humans, is also able to understand Grendel's language (which is an early form of 'Old Norse/Icelandic'). In an exchange between herself and Beowulf she attempts to explain that Grendel has a very human side.

> BEOWULF: Grendel?
> SELMA: Grendel, your troll. Weirdly enough he has a name, it means 'grinder'
> BEOWULF: Of bones?
> SELMA: No of teeth. He was born with bad dreams.

Thus, Selma attempts to explain that the word 'grinder', Grendel's namesake, actually describe his fragile, human nature. But Beowulf immediately interprets it to mean that he is a violent and monstrous killer. Beowulf's minstrel singer, Thorkel, later composes a song which cements this interpretation of Grendel: 'Born of scum and swampy things, lurking in his mother's moss, the mark of Cain came to his brow, of evil and a sea hag born, Grendel, *grinder* of lost men's bones.' At the conclusion of Thorkel's song, two of Beowulf's men debate its meaning:

> CREW MEMBER: Cain? What's that?
> BRECCA: A man who killed his brother in the Christian tale.
> CREW MEMBER: What's Cain got to do with Grendel? Did Grendel kill his own brother too?
> BRECCA: No, I think Thorkel was saying that Grendel is like Cain – a killer.
> CREW MEMBER: We all are!
> BRECCA: Yeah, well …
> CREW MEMBER: Thorkel's tale is shit!

Clearly, like Gardner's novel, this film encourages one to sympathize with the character Grendel. It also, by referring to the singer's tale as 'shit', references a passage in Gardner's novel in which Grendel refers to the Shaper's song about Cain as 'Bullshit!'[22] Similarly, in Stitt's film, Grendel indignantly decries, 'Am I one of the dark-damned half? A child of this awful brother? But … they are the ones who murder each other!'

Robert Zemeckis' Beowulf

The most successful Beowulf film to date is the 2007 animated film, *Beowulf*, directed by Robert Zemeckis. With a budget of US$150 million, it grossed well over US$200 million (and also spawned a simultaneously released video game). This film, written by Roger Avary and Neil Gaiman, spans the entirety of the original *Beowulf* poem, but also marks a substantial reworking of the story. Zemeckis' *Beowulf* unmistakably draws influence from Gardner's novel (1971), Stitt's animated feature (1981) and Baker's live-action *Beowulf* (1999).

All of the central human characters were performed by major Hollywood stars. Not only were the actors' voice talents utilized, but their likenesses were also infused into the 3D digital character designs. Additionally, the film incorporated the Hollywood actors' motion-capture performances to form the basis of the characters' animated movement. The film features Anthony Hopkins as King Hrothgar, Angelina Jolie as Grendel's mother, Ray Winstone as Beowulf, John Malkovich as Unferth, Robin Wright Penn as Wealtheow and Crispin Glover as Grendel. Intriguingly, the same actor, Ray Winstone, performs both Beowulf and the Dragon (and the Dragon's human incarnation). This echoes the approach that Alexander Stitt took in his production, *Grendel Grendel Grendel*, in which the voice actor, Arthur Dignam, performed both Beowulf and the Dragon characters. For Stitt, this provided an opportunity to actualize Gardner's lyrical and thematic conflating of the characters of Beowulf and the Dragon. For Zemeckis, it provided an opportunity to underscore the fact that, in his film, Beowulf was actually the Dragon's father.

The film begins with drunken celebrations at King Hrothgar's newly constructed meadhall. The distant noise of their partying so agitates Grendel, who is depicted as a grossly deformed giant, that he is compelled to attack the hall. He kills a number of the revellers; but when Hrothgar challenges Grendel, demanding that he fight him, Grendel retreats, fleeing the hall in an agitated fury. Returning to his cave, his mother chides him for going to the meadhall where the humans live. His mother is revealed to be a mysterious sea-creature that can also take the form of a beautiful woman. The woman's form is that of a 'nude Angelina Jolie', her nakedness only partly obscured by a fluid gold paint-like substance. Grendel's mother is clearly intended to resemble a domineering seductress; her very long braided hair resembles a whip-like tail, and her bare feet are designed with built-in stiletto heels. It is soon revealed that King Hrothgar is Grendel's father. Many years previously he had made an accursed deal with Grendel's mother – in exchange for providing her a son, he would be guaranteed a long and successful reign. As a consequence, his wife, Queen Wealtheow, who has found out about this union, refuses to sleep with the ageing King, and thus will not provide *him* with an heir to his throne.

Grendel leads a miserable existence; he is hideously deformed, has the mental capacity of a child and is in continuous pain.[23] But Grendel's mother tenderly cares for him – caresses him and sings him gently to sleep. Despite his monstrous nature and truly repugnant appearance, Grendel does attract a certain amount of pity. By contrast, his father, King Hrothgar, is shown to be a very unsympathetic character, full of avarice and lechery.

When Beowulf first arrives in Daneland he brings with him his most loyal warrior, Wiglaf. Interestingly, in the original poem Wiglaf does not make an appearance until its very end. But because Wiglaf epitomizes all that is loyal, the writers thought that it would make sense to have him at Beowulf's side throughout the entire film. Remarkably, this is a similar strategy to what director Alexander Stitt had done some twenty-five years earlier when he wrote his screenplay – however rather than have the loyal figure of Wiglaf attached to Beowulf (who only makes an appearance at the very end of his film), he chose to attach the loyal Wiglaf to King Hrothgar.

In Zemeckis' film, when Beowulf declares to the King, 'I am here to kill your monster!' Hrothgar replies with a sardonic tone, 'So, you will kill *my* Grendel for me, will you?' (By emphasizing the word '*my*' Hrothgar is also acknowledging the fact that, as Grendel's father, the monster does in fact paternally *belong* to him.) Beowulf then, in line with the sexually charged themes of the movie, announces that he will fight Grendel naked and promptly strips off his clothes. He then successfully defeats Grendel by ripping off his arm. Soon after, Grendel's mother, in order to avenge her son's death, attacks the hall, killing dozens upon dozens of people. Beowulf follows her to her cave but, instead of fighting, Grendel's mother appears in her golden clad, nude female form and offers him a proposition: 'I shall make you the greatest king that ever lived. As long as you hold me in your heart and this golden horn remains in my keeping. You will forever be king.' Beowulf, dazzled by her beauty, quickly relents, thereby accepting the same cursed proposition that had been offered to Hrothgar many years earlier. Upon Beowulf's return to the kingdom, King Hrothgar immediately senses what must have transpired. He is absolutely elated, for now he will be free of the monster's curse. Thus, after hurriedly bequeathing everything (including his wife) to Beowulf, he leaps off the castle wall to his death.

Some thirty years later a dragon appears in King Beowulf's realm. The dragon turns out to be Beowulf's son, the offspring of himself and Grendel's mother – it is actually a shape-shifting creature that, in addition to being an incredibly powerful fire-breathing dragon, can also take the form of a young man. The now aged Beowulf, with the support of his loyal Wiglaf, engages the dragon in battle. Beowulf manages to mortally wound the dragon, but in a mirroring of Grendel's earlier fate, Beowulf also suffers the fatal loss of his arm in the battle. Thus, the two end up lying side by side on the sandy beach – an aged Beowulf, and the dragon, which has transformed back into the form of a human. The two, father and son, die together, meaningfully touching hands. After Beowulf's death, Wiglaf is then set to become the new King. But as he stands at the water's edge, Grendel's mother emerges, seductively beckoning to him. It is thus implied that Wiglaf will also mate with her, providing her with yet another monstrous son.

In many animated films, the identity of the celebrity voice-actor becomes an important marketing point (and often plays an influencing role in the character's design and personality). But in Zemeckis' *Beowulf*, the identity of the superstar extends dramatically into the visual realm as well. Thus, Grendel's mother photo-realistically captures the likeness of Angelina Jolie, King Hrothgar mirrors Anthony Hopkins and Unferth imitates John Malkovich.

Much of the focus of the marketing of this high-budget film was on the technical achievement of the motion-capture, and on the 'photo-realistic' visuals of the characters and environments. Zemeckis had used a similar process for his earlier motion-capture animated film, *The Polar Express* (2004), but *Beowulf* used a more sophisticated capturing system: 'The setup featured 16 digital video cameras to capture valuable performance reference and 228 motion capture cameras – four times the number used in *The Polar Express*.'[24] Additionally, small electrodes were attached to the actors' faces to capture facial expressions and eye movements.[25]

Despite all of these technical advancements, the characters still frequently fall into what is known as the 'uncanny valley' – a space in which the animated characters look very real, but do not look quite real enough to avoid appearing unsettling to the viewer. As with many 3D animated films that seem to fall into this 'uncanny valley', when the character is presented as a still image it can look very convincing and life-like. Our uneasiness usually arises when movement is introduced to these photo-realistic characters. This phenomenon ultimately has to do with the disconnect that occurs between the image and the animated movement (see Figure 1.4).

The fact is that, no matter how may motion-capture sensors might be placed on an actor, these sensors will struggle to capture every nuance of movement. Furthermore, the movement that *is* captured is rarely applied precisely or

FIGURE 1.4 Characters from the 3D animated film, *Beowulf* (Robert Zemeckis, 2007), which incorporate both the vocal talents and the movement and likeness of well-known Hollywood actors. From left to right: Ray Winstone as Beowulf; Anthony Hopkins as King Hrothgar; Robin Wright Penn as Queen Wealtheow. Although relatively photo-realistic in their depiction, these animated characters often appear somewhat zombie-like in their movement (thus bordering on the monstrous).

accurately enough to the 3D model. Thus, one tends to end up with a figure that looks more real than its movement can convey; and the character will often appear somewhat zombie-like, as if it were not fully alive. But if the photo-realism of the character is reduced, thus allowing the corresponding movement to exceed the complexity of the form, then the uncanny or troubling effect will most probably be diminished.[26]

Because of the uncanny valley effect, the humans in Zemeckis' film look zombie-like, at least part of the time. Although this was not intended by the filmmakers, by its very nature Zemeckis' *Beowulf* transforms all of the human characters into zombie-like monsters. This state of monstrousness is further compounded by the fact that most of the humans are also presented as lecherous, morally depraved and violent characters. By stark contrast the characters in *Grendel Grendel Grendel* have an entirely different effect upon the viewer. Because Stitt rendered his film in a very simplified and cartoony manner, the monsters of his film all look, at least to some degree, inherently endearing.

To coincide with the cinematic release of Zemeckis' *Beowulf*, a high-budget video game, *Beowulf – The Game*, was released by Ubisoft. The video game utilizes some of the film's dialogue recordings and a number of its visual assets. The game promises that players will 'battle fierce enemies and slay giant monsters as you play through 30 years of Beowulf's life not seen in the movie'. The introduction to the accompanying game pamphlet reads,

> you are Beowulf, legendary Norse warrior with the strength of 30 men – arrogant, carnal, self-serving, and lustful for gold and glory. You journey to Denmark to destroy a bloodthirsty beast that is wreaking havoc on the frigid land. But evil persists, and you succumb to its promise of easy power, propelling yourself onto to the Danish throne. As King, you must face the monstrous consequences of your actions ... lead your Thanes into battle, crush your enemies, and slay the Titans of a dying age that threaten to annihilate your kingdom.[27]

This third-person action adventure game begins with a series of brief adventures until Beowulf meets Grendel's mother who, enamoured by him, grants him extra powers. Beowulf is then summoned by King Hrothgar to fight Grendel. Beowulf defeats the monster and becomes King. The remainder of the game play then takes place during the thirty-year span of Beowulf's reign as King, which is not depicted in the movie (or the original poem).

Grendel is not given much sympathy in this game being merely an obstacle that Beowulf must overcome in order to advance to the next level. However, Beowulf must also fight his own 'inner monsters' as he progresses through the game. Within the gameplay the player is presented with a sliding scale system which rates the Beowulf character as either more 'carnal' or more 'heroic' depending on what actions are taken – and thereby how Beowulf's legacy will be remembered.

Grendel's appearance in other media

The first major Beowulf-themed comic book was a bi-monthly series published by DC titled *Beowulf – Dragon Slayer*. It was intended to be a long-running series but, due to poor sales, the series was dropped after just six issues, which ran from May 1975 to March 1976. The comic received a lot of initial publicity as it was written by Michael Uslan, a university lecturer who is credited with having devised and taught the first university course on comics in North America.[28] In the first issue of the comic book, Uslan wrote

> when DC first announced its interest in developing some new titles, we searched for a subject that would not only be a fast-paced comics-magazine, but would also have specific educational value. For the field of education is the place where comics can do the most good in the years to come. And so came Beowulf, Prince of the Geats![29]

In the second issue, Uslan revealed that one of his sources of inspiration for the comic book was John Gardner's novel, *Grendel*. This is most evident through his inclusion of a character called 'The Shaper' (a character that was invented by Gardner), and some of Grendel's initial attributes also seem to be derived from the novel. Although the first issue does reference the original *Beowulf* poem quite directly (and by extension some aspects of Gardner's novel), by the third and subsequent issues the narrative had veered off into very divergent territory as battles ensue against vampires, a minotaur, space aliens and even Satan himself. In a strange sequence in issue six, Grendel unknowingly saves Beowulf's life when he defeats Satan (who was in the midst of remotely attacking Beowulf). As absurd as the narrative became, it did effectively blur the lines between monster and hero. The comic book's narrative ends very abruptly, as the decision to cancel the series was made during the production of what became its final issue.

Another comic book series, Matt Wagner's *Grendel*, has very little to do with the original *Beowulf* narrative, merely borrowing the monster's namesake. In this series, the character Grendel is a deadly, human ninja-like assassin who is contracted to kill various unsavoury characters. As one author notes:

> Though his protagonist is an assassin, and an amoral character at best, Wagner uses Grendel to lay bare the seedy underside of America; Grendel may transgress the values of modern American culture, but, at the same time, he exposes the hypocrisies and vices of that culture.[30]

There is also an ongoing character named Argent who serves as Grendel's nemesis. But rather than being a human character, as is Grendel, he is depicted as a wolf-man hybrid creature. Thus, in a role reversal of the *Beowulf* epic, Grendel is depicted as a human, and the stand-in for 'Beowulf' is depicted as a monster. The comic book series first began in 1982 and has run on and off until the present day.

In recent years, following in John Gardner's footsteps, a wave of novels has emerged which seek to tell the *Beowulf* epic from alternate perspectives. There have been several that have articulated the poem specifically from the mother's point of view, including Ralph Bourne's *Grendel's Mother* (2009), Susan Signe Morrison's *Grendel's Mother – The Saga of the Wyrd-Wife* (2015) and Maria Dahvana Headley's *The Mere Wife* (2018). Donnita L. Rogers has written a trilogy titled *The Women of Beowulf*, comprising three separate novels, *Faces of Fire* (2013), *Fanning the Flames* (2015) and *Cloak of Ashes* (2016), which give voice to the many female characters. Even the Danish Queen is given her own perspective in Ashley Crownover's *Wealtheow: Her Telling of Beowulf* (2008). These texts, building upon Gardner's groundbreaking novel, seek to give voices to many of the disenfranchised characters of the original poem. Some of these novels, such as Headley's *The Mere Wife*, also present a very sympathetic (although very complex) representation of Grendel.

In 2006, Gardner's novel was adapted into an opera titled *Grendel – Transcendence of the Great Big Bad*. Elliot Goldenthal was the composer, Julie Taymor and J. D. McClatchy the librettists and the bass-baritone Eric Owens played Grendel. Opening in Los Angeles in 2006, the opera was an extremely extravagant production with an estimated budget of US $3.1 million (more than five times that of Stitt's animated feature). The production was a long time in the making; Goldenthal and Taymor both read Gardner's novel in the 1970s, and initially conceived the idea for the opera in the mid-1980s (soon after the release of Stitt's animated musical feature). Adapting Gardner's very nuanced and philosophical novel to an opera proved to be a challenge (as it had been for Stitt's animated version). As noted by librettist McClatchy, 'Opera is not a particularly subtle art form. It's not going to stand for philosophical analysis.' As a result, their production evolved into a very liberal adaptation in which they focused on Grendel's desire to fit in. Echoing the primary theme of Stitt's animated film, Eric Owens (who played Grendel) noted that the opera expressed how 'society needs these monsters [in order] to band together'. In a similar tactic to that used by Alexander Stitt in his animated feature (in which Grendel spoke with a high-brow London accent, while the humans spoke in working-class Yorkshire accents), Grendel sings his operatic lines in contemporary English, while the humans sing theirs in the Old English of the *Beowulf* poem. Such an approach, according to Taymor, 'forces the audience to identify with the outsider, with the monster'.[31]

Notes

1 Lee Tulloch, 'Lee Tulloch Talks to Grendel and Friend, Grrumph!' in *Vogue Australia* (January 1981), p. 64.
2 John Grigsby, *Beowulf & Grendel* (London: Watkins Publishing, 2005), p. 4.

3   J.R.R. Tolkien, *The Monsters and the Critics and Other Essays* (London: HarperCollins, 2006), p. 7.
4   Ibid., p. 17.
5   Kathleen Forni, *Beowulf's Popular Afterlife in Literature, Comic Books, and Film* (London: Routledge, 2018), p. 43.
6   W.H. Canaway, *The Ring-Givers* (London: Michael Joseph, 1958), p. 57; and quoted in Forni, *Beowulf's Popular Afterlife*, p. 44.
7   John M. Howell, *Understanding John Gardner* (Columbia, SC: University of South Carolina Press, 1993), p. 62.
8   Forni, *Beowulf's Popular Afterlife*, p. 45.
9   John Gardner, *On Writers and Writing* (Berkeley: Counterpoint, 1996), p. 243
10 Ibid.
11 Ibid., p. 248.
12 Ibid., p. 247.
13 Michael Crichton, *Eaters of the Dead – The Manuscript of Ibn Fadlan, Relating His Experiences with the Northmen in A.D. 922* (New York: Random House, 1993), p. 182.
14 Ibid.
15 David Lonergan 'Fooling LC', *Behavioral & Social Sciences Librarian* 16, no. 2 (1998), pp. 63–72.
16 Forni, *Beowulf's Popular Afterlife*, p. 43.
17 Promotional press kit, *Grendel Grendel Grendel*, 1981.
18 Ibid.
19 Ivan Hutchinson. 'Grendel Will Get You', *The Sun*, 18 June 1981, p. 48.
20 Andrew Rai Berzins, *Screenplay Beowulf & Grendel*, 2005, www.beowulfandgrendel.com/script (accessed 2 November 2019).
21 The name Selma is an anagram of Salem, a city in Boston, USA, that in 1692 was the site of the notorious witchcraft trials.
22 John Gardner, *Grendel* (New York: Alfred A. Knopf, 1971), p. 54.
23 Mary Ann Cooper, '"Beowulf": Transforming an Ancient Epic into a High-Tech Blockbuster in *Boxoffice*', November 2007; 143, 11; pg. 19.
24 Jody Duncan, 'Beowulf All the Way', *Cinefex*, no. 112 (2007), p. 46.
25 Ibid., 47.
26 See Dan Torre, *Animation – Process, Cognition and Actuality* (New York: Bloomsbury, 2017).
27 Promotional material, *Beowulf – The Game*, Ubisoft, 2007.
28 Chris Bishop 'Beowulf: The Monsters and the Comics', *Journal of Australian Early Medieval Association* 7 (2011), pp. 73–93.
29 Michael Uslan, *Beowulf: Dragon Slayer*, illustrated by Ricardo Villamonte (New York: DC Comics, 1975–6).
30 Michael Livingston and John William Sutton, 'Reinventing the Hero: Gardner's "Grendel" and the Shifting Face of "Beowulf" in Popular Culture', *Studies in Popular Culture* 29, no. 1 (October 2006), pp. 1–16 (p. 5)
31 Jeff Lunden, Grendel: An Operatic Monster's Tale, 11 July 2006, www.npr.org (accessed 1 May 2019).

Chapter 2

SCENES OF *GRENDEL GRENDEL GRENDEL*

Grendel Grendel Grendel is a significant and a unique (but relatively overlooked) animated film. It is also a disarmingly complex film, and many of its themes and events can go unnoticed on first viewing. As such, this chapter provides a useful and detailed scene-by-scene summation of the animated feature's narrative. Each of the film's seventy-odd scenes (sixty-eight plus the introduction and end credit sequence) is described. This chapter also provides lyrics to several of the songs as well as transcriptions of key sections of dialogue. Additionally, a number of frame grabs from the film are also included, which help to provide further context and explication. Although many of these scene summations also include some critical analysis and direct comparisons to Gardner's book and to the original *Beowulf* epic – the foremost purpose of this chapter is to provide a very detailed and practical impression of the film, which in turn serves as a basis for subsequent chapters' more in-depth analysis.

Stitt's film is a *broad* adaptation of John Gardner's book *Grendel*, which is a complete retelling (essentially a parallel novel) of the original *Beowulf* epic. Alex Stitt writes in the introduction of the film's tie-in book, *The Grendel, Grendel, Grendel Film Picture Book*:

> For the sake of Mr Gardner's readers and reputation, I hasten to add that it's a very free adaptation. Many of the complexities and subtleties of his *Grendel* defy reworking into ninety minutes of animation. *Grendel Grendel Grendel* must be regarded as a separate entity that I, as the designer and director, Bruce Smeaton as the composer, Phillip Adams as the producer and dozens of animators, painters, actors, musicians and technicians found satisfying to fashion alongside Mr Gardner's inspirational work.[1]

In one interview, Stitt acknowledges that

> the whole thing is an adaptation of Gardner's book, but I haven't tried to adapt it faithfully in any way, so the purists will hate it. Out of the attitudes and emotions that Gardner has given the characters, I have selected and toned them down a bit.[2]

Arguably, it is quite misleading to label Stitt's film as merely a *simplification* of the novel – even although it achieves this on several levels. But the movie also generates many of its own 'complexities and subtleties' which ultimately would defy the printed page of a novel. These stem from Stitt's ability as a designer and a director, his deep understanding of Gardner's novel and the original *Beowulf* epic, and of the inherent qualities of the animated form. Furthermore, Stitt draws upon a number of additional sources, thereby imbuing the film with his own interpretations and world views. The end result is an animated film that proves to be far more complex than its minimalist animated graphics suggest.

In both the book and the film, the narrative is told from the perspective of Grendel. However, the film places greater emphasis on the human's position, and there are moments where the perspective shifts (but not entirely) towards the human inhabitants of Hrothgar's kingdom. Grendel, however, is never far away and is often seen lurking in the shadows or slinking away into the night after a scene of human activity has concluded, thus plausibly maintaining 'the monster's point of view'. This shift in perspective was a pragmatic alteration for Stitt to make since the character of Grendel rarely speaks in the novel – it is primarily 'narrated' and structured through his internal thoughts. And being a non-human 'monster', these thoughts can prove to be rather convoluted and schizophrenic. Although there are aspects of dark humour and even moments of levity, Gardner's Grendel is, on the whole, a dark, brooding, troubled and desperate character. The reader tends to identify with him for much of the novel, simply because it is told from his point of view, rather than because he is particularly *likeable*. Arguably, in this way, we are forced to identify with our own 'monstrous' nature. Stitt, on the other hand, wanted viewers truly to *like* Grendel; Stitt noting, 'the heavier or darker side of Grendel's nature [is] glossed over or almost lost entirely'. And this omitted monstrous nature is replaced with a more civilized one: 'He's cultivated and thinks of himself as being very worldly, even though in many ways he's quite innocent.'[3] Because of this streak of innocence, one can also draw some parallels with the main character of *Alice in Wonderland*; for Grendel also journeys through a strange world, attempting to figure out just what he is doing there. But thanks to voice actor Peter Ustinov, Grendel is also imbued with a number of other increasingly complex layers. Stitt noted, 'Ustinov is a bit untidy, terribly urbane and also a bit cheeky and mischievous. That's how people think of him and that's what we want them to think about Grendel.'[4]

Adaptations (especially if they are substantially altered *reinterpretations*) do tend to benefit from a knowing audience – that is, an audience that is well versed in the original source material. John Gardner's book assumes that the reader is familiar with the original *Beowulf* poem. Stitt's film also assumes that the viewer is familiar with the generalities of the original *Beowulf* story (and to some degree, of John Gardner's novel). Of course, both Gardner's book and Stitt's film do stand on their own, but viewers will probably gain a richer experience if familiar with both source materials. Ultimately, these three accounts of the *Beowulf* story (the original poem, Gardner's novel and Stitt's animated feature) form, when placed together, an intriguing, trilateral construct of 'Beowulfiana' (to borrow J. R. R. Tolkien's original term).[5]

In the following scene-by-scene break down of the film, each scene is divided and numbered as they appear in the original storyboards and screenplay for the film.

Introduction

At the commencement of the film, producer Phillip Adams presents a three-minute long introduction.[6] Although characterized as a 'live-action' sequence, in actuality, only the initial twenty seconds are composed of any *filmed* footage. This live-action portion features Adams, dramatically backlit, stepping through a doorway and walking up to the camera (see Figure 5.8), at which point he proclaims:

> Monsters! From the minotaur to the bogeyman; from the dragons of legend to the creature from the Black Lagoon, monsters have haunted the human imagination, going bump in our night. It's almost as though we needed monsters, those metaphors for death, as aphrodisiacs for life; to unite us in our common struggle against the implacable fates.

The camera pans away, and Adams continues his narration as a series of still images (both historic and contemporary) play across the screen. Adams effectively outlines a number of the central themes of the film, namely that even though Grendel is branded as a monster, he is not quite so monstrous after all. To underscore this point, he describes how important monsters have been in human culture and the surprisingly positive role they have thus played in facilitating our societal achievements. Furthermore, Adams notes that in our post-Vietnam era, 'Our version of Grendel is seen through twentieth century eyes when perhaps we are a little suspicious of the military hero and more inclined to see humanity in a monster.'

The final portion of the introduction features a sequence of still photographs which provide a behind-the-scenes glimpse of the film's production. Displayed are dozens of images of storyboards, character design sheets, drawings, cel paints, the animation camera and editing bays, and a shot of animation director, Frank Hellard, at work. There are also numerous still photos from the voice recording sessions featuring the actors Peter Ustinov and Keith Michell, and the music recording sessions featuring composer Bruce Smeaton, along with a number of studio musicians.

Although this introductory sequence certainly complements the overall themes of the movie, its visuals (often historic black-and-white etchings and photographs) are in stark contrast to the strikingly vibrant colours and graphic-designed imagery of the animated film. Similarly, its tone (scholarly) also differs wildly from that of the film (whimsical). Nevertheless, the introduction does provide some suitable insights into the motivation of the filmmakers and clearly signifies to the audience that what they are about to view is not your average cartoon, but instead is an intelligent and 'grown up' feature film. Adams concludes his introduction with the words 'Ladies and Gentlemen, it is with pride that we introduce the lonely, loveable monster who has been living and dying for fifteen centuries with our very best interests at heart.' And, it is after this rather poetic and multifarious, introduction that the animated film begins.

Scene 1

The opening scene provides an introduction into Grendel's vibrant world, which is composed of brilliantly coloured trees and rocks (greens, yellows, pinks and blues), all flatly rendered. Some elements are intermittently adorned with large polka-dots or striped patterning. There are, of course, no edge lines or black interior line work visible within the background imagery. The characters also are designed in vibrant solid colours, accentuated occasionally with patterning – creating a generally designed homogeneity.

The film commences with the intertitle 'Tuesday morning, Scandinavia, 515 AD'. This, simultaneously precise (Tuesday morning) yet somewhat less determinate (Scandinavia, 515 AD), caption helps to establish the generally whimsical tone of the film. Two men, Basil and One-eyed Arthur, enter the scene. (These are both original characters created by Stitt for the film and not found in Gardner's book or the *Beowulf* epic.) The two men notice a very large footprint on the forest floor, determining it to have been left by the 'Big Boogy' (i.e. their rather infantile description of the monster, Grendel) and they run away in terror.

Scene 2

Standing on a hillside, King Hrothgar and his men witness the fleeing Arthur and Basil (see Figure 2.1 and Figure 4.8). In response, Dung says, 'Lookit them yobbos! Looks like they've just seen the Great Boogy'. But King Hrothgar quickly dismisses references of a 'Boogy' as 'superstitious hobble-gobble'. To this strong, royal dismissal, Dung replies admiringly, 'You really understand things!' Quickly asserting his seniority, Hrothgar retorts, 'That's why I'm your king!'

However, Grendel (the Great Boogy) does indeed exist, and the camera promptly pans across the landscape to a large stone monument that is, coincidentally, engraved with an image of the monster. Suddenly, Grendel, himself, ascends into frame, striking a pose identical to that of the engraving (see Figure 2.2).

This opening sequence introduces King Hrothgar and his rather incompetent band of warriors, one named Dung, another named Wiglaf. In the original poem, Wiglaf, rather than being associated with King Hrothgar, is one of Beowulf's warriors. This altered role of Wiglaf's character was utilized by Stitt to represent an 'everyman' soldier, one who was very reliable, but also quite unremarkable. Dung, on the other hand, is an entirely new character,

FIGURE 2.1 King Hrothgar with his loyal subjects, Wiglaf and Dung, watch as One-eyed Arthur and Basil run away after discovering Grendel's giant footprint (*Grendel Grendel Grendel*, Alexander Stitt, 1981).

FIGURE 2.2 Grendel makes a surprise appearance (*Grendel Grendel Grendel*, Alexander Stitt, 1981).

found neither in Gardner's novel nor in the epic poem. He is an idiotic character, named with an appropriately demeaning moniker, who provides comic relief throughout the film. Stitt humorously underscores their general unprofessionalism by directing the voice actors to speak with exaggerated northern England, working-class accents.

Scene 3 – Credits sequence / Scene 4

The opening credit sequence (see Figure 2.3) runs for approximately three minutes and is composed of both illustrative motion graphics and detailed credits information (as well as conventional character animation). It also features the movie's theme song *A Song for Grendel*, which is sung from the perspective of Grendel's Mum (the film's character name for the mother), essentially as a sentimental lullaby to her son. Stitt desired the song to convey a combined sense of 'innocence and fear'.[7] However, given the context and the chosen visual graphics (and the very fact that it is a lullaby to a monster) it also conveys a strong sense of humour and irony. The singer, Julie McKenna, delivers her vocals as a torch song – evoking the syrupy theme songs of contemporaneous James Bond movies (which also would typically convey contradictory moods, set against the incongruous backdrop of an action spy thriller).

The visual design of the credit sequence oscillates between hand-written text, which provides the actual details of those involved in the production, and animated graphics that exemplify the meaning, mood, and particularly the irony, of the theme song's lyrics. Some of these graphics merely portray moving patterns and shapes of flat colour; others concretize the meaning of the words

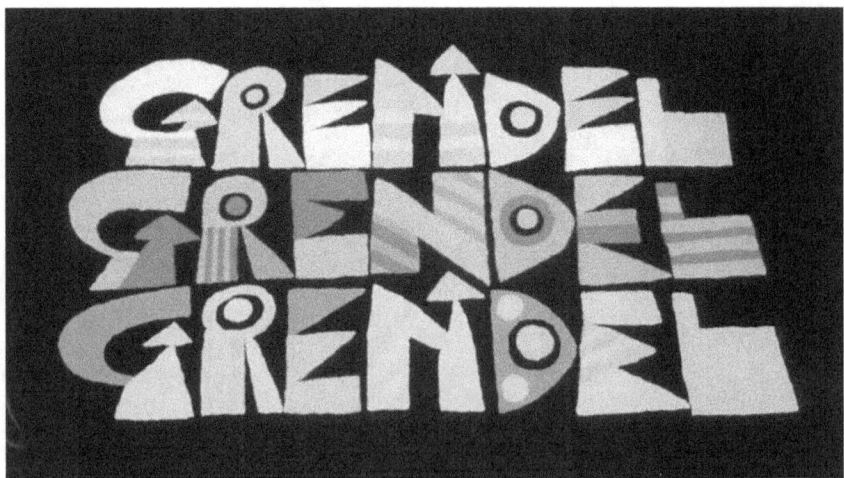

FIGURE 2.3 Title sequence (*Grendel Grendel Grendel*, Alexander Stitt, 1981).

in graphic form. A number of key words are also playfully depicted as large text-based graphics (see Figure 3.9), animatedly spelling out such words as: 'Grendel', 'Mother', 'Twelve feet four', 'Fang' and 'Claw', all in sync to the song lyrics (printed below).

Grendel, Grendel, Grendel.
Your mother loves you, Grendel.
Standing there, all twelve feet four
Or more of you,
Mother loves every hair, scale, tooth nail,
Fang and claw of you.

Grendel, Grendel, Grendel (Grendel).
Grendel, Grendel, Grendel (Grendel).

Your mother needs you, Grendel.
List'ning nightly at the door for you,
Mother loves every grunt, groan, howl, moan,
Wail and roar from you.

Grendel, Grendel, Grendel (Grendel).
Grendel, Grendel, Grendel (Grendel).

But other people, Grendel
May not even like you, Grendel.
The feel, the size and scale of you
The smell, the eyes and wail of you
Are all too much, and much too scary.
Perhaps if you weren't so
Green and hairy
Someone other
Than just your mother
Could love you,
Grendel, Grendel.

This opening theme song serves to invert the monstrous reputation of Beowulf's dreaded adversary. Through a syrupy love song, which evokes a mother's tender love, Grendel is swiftly declawed and transformed into an identifiable and much more sympathetic character.

A second intertitle appears, informing that it is now, 'Some years later'. A despondent Grendel treads through the landscape. Despite the undying love of his mother, Grendel is feeling very much alone. Even the creatures of the forest fear him and keep well away. A brief reprisal of the theme song ensues:

But other creatures Grendel
May be less pleased with you Grendel
The jaws, the fangs and growl of you,
The claws, the smell and scowl of you
Are all too gross, most alarming
If only a part of you were charming
Perhaps another, besides your mother
Could bear you Grendel
Grendel Grendel Grendel (Grendel)

During this final stanza, Grendel strolls along a rocky seashore (see Figure 2.4) and with a heavy sigh, reclines on the boulders. A bird lands upon his nose, mistaking it for a rock. Grendel is delighted by the arrival of the bird, but when he moves, the bird realizes its mistake and quickly flies away, leaving Grendel all the sadder. In another sequence, two crows feed on the carcass of a dead creature, then begin fighting over the entrails. In turn, a large wild pig arrives, scaring the smaller birds away. When Grendel happens by, the pig in turn is scared away. Grendel sadly shakes his head; he is clearly at the top of the food chain, and it is a very lonely place to be. Grendel peers into a pool of water and angrily hurls a stone at his reflection, shattering it into increasingly obscured ripples. He is wholly distraught by his isolation and the inequity of his treatment; rarely does he engage in monstrous behaviour (compared to the actions of wild animals and humans) yet, quite unfairly, he is continually labelled as monster.

FIGURE 2.4 Grendel takes a melancholic stroll through the countryside and inadvertently frightens the wildlife (*Grendel Grendel Grendel*, Alexander Stitt, 1981).

Later, Grendel encounters an array of large stone monuments, many of which pejoratively depict Grendel engaged in monstrous acts. Slowly, his melancholy turns to anger as he becomes aware of more and more of these offensive human-made objects. He carefully contemplates his place in the world as he stands among the monuments, staring up at King Hrothgar's newly built meadhall. What follows are a sequence of shots which emphasize both Grendel's outrage and Stitt's unique design aesthetic. Beginning with an impressive, rotating-animated-camera, and a rapid time-lapse transition from day to night, Grendel storms towards the hall. Then, rendered through a designed use of limited colour and dramatic lighting, Grendel smashes down the meadhall door. A battle ensues as Grendel attacks the people inside; glimpses of the violence are made visible through the windows, which are represented as isolated squares among an expanse of night-time blackness.

After this rare glimpse of his monstrous side, Grendel carries off two dead bodies. When daylight comes, Grendel is again quite pensive as he rests upon a hillside. With distant detachment, he watches the humans perform an elaborate ritual involving the burning of their dead on a large funeral pyre. Finally, he gets up, taking the bodies with him and leaves – walking off into the distance (and over the rise) in what will become his signatory retreat. This particular animated action will be reused many times throughout the film (see Chapter 5).

These events closely parallel those described in Gardner's novel showing, in particular, Grendel's deep-seated loneliness. But in the novel, Gardner also focuses on describing Grendel's disdain for all social beings. For example, Grendel encounters some mating sheep; being an outsider with no prospect of social interaction, and being neither human nor animal, such displays of intimacy greatly disturb him.

> 'Why can't these creatures discover a little dignity?' I ask the sky. The sky says nothing, predictably. I make a face, uplift a defiant middle finger, and give an obscene little kick. The sky ignores me, forever unimpressed. Him too I hate, the same as I hate these brainless budding trees, these brattling birds.[8]

Similarly, the original poem also portrays Grendel as an outsider. His first appearance is marked by his increasing agitation by the boisterous noise emitting from the socializing humans in King Hrothgar's meadhall.[9] In all iterations of the *Beowulf* story, Grendel is described as an outsider, not only excluded from human society, but from virtually all social interaction.

Later, Grendel returns home to his cave (see Figure 2.5a). The space is depicted in a very stylized manner, but includes some gently gruesome imagery of skulls and bones. The cave is also full of colourful animated plant life – which seems to mirror Gardner's repeated representation of personified plant life in his novel. Additionally, a number of rather cute, little black fuzzy creatures scuttle about the cave. These creatures are Stitt's more gentle depiction of what Gardner's

FIGURE 2.5 (a) Grendel enters into his mother's cave; (b) Grendel carefully washes his hands as he speaks to his off-screen mother (*Grendel Grendel Grendel*, Alexander Stitt, 1981).

novel portrays as Grendel's ancient relatives – in fact Gardner describes these as more monstrous than even Grendel or his mother, 'I understood the emptiness in the eyes of those humpbacked shapes back in the cave.'[10] Contrastingly, Grendel's mother is rarely seen in Stitt's film. In their cave, she is always indicated as an off-screen, silent character. Nevertheless, Stitt does seek to humanize her by giving her the affectionate (and very Australian) name of Grendel's Mum.

As Grendel enters the cave, he speaks to his mother in the rich, urbane, English-accented voice of Peter Ustinov.

> Mother? I'm home mother. Where are you, dear, In your pit? I've got some nice legs for you. And now don't – ooh, you don't smell any better do you? – don't

gobble them up and get indigestion. Would you like me to talk to you for a while dear? Oh, I know you can't understand me, but I think that you like it when I talk to you, don't you? I dropped in on the King last night, I don't think you've seen their great meadhall have you? Quite interesting architecturally. Makes me wonder sometimes why we put up with this stinking cave. I wouldn't get you to move, though, would I mother? Anyway, I smashed the door down again and grabbed a couple of the closest warriors. Heh, heh! It's lucky that. It's always the lovely plump ones who aren't fast enough to get away. Oh the shouting and the screaming and the praying! Very satisfying. Fun and games, mummy, fun and games. Fun and games.

While Grendel speaks to her, he meticulously washes his hands in a sink, drying them carefully with a hand towel (see Figure 2.5b). These are of course very civilized actions, not ones expected of a monster.

Grendel continues, speaking to his mother, now reminiscing of when he was a child and the first time he ventured out of their cave and into the wide world:

When I was a young sprout I played games all the time. Explored this cave. Every bit of it. While you were asleep, of course. I remember the first time I found my way out through the pool of fire snakes. I didn't go very far. Not that first night. But after, other times, I played my way out farther and farther into the night and into the world, and marvelled at the cold mechanics of the stars.

Again, Grendel's tenderness and eloquent speech belies his monstrous character. Stitt's main objective in these opening scenes is to demonstrate the humanness of monsters and the monstrousness of humans. But, in addition to the human's overtly evil acts (murder, etc.), he also seeks to highlight their silliness and irrational logic.

Scene 5

A flashback to the time when Grendel was a young child is depicted in this sequence. Voice actor Peter Ustinov alternates between narrating in his 'adult Grendel' timbre and speaking as a Young Grendel, affecting his voice to bear a lighter, higher pitched tone. 'Dark chasms! Seize me! Seize me to your dark, foul, black bowels and crush my bones!' the young Grendel calls out to the sky; then, as a bolt of lightning strikes very nearby, he playfully quips, 'Missed me!'

Grendel wanders the night, enjoying this time of innocence, just prior to his first confrontation with humans. He encounters a frog, declaring in French 'Grenouille au naturel'; adding, 'No wonder those little leaping amphibians enjoy a certain gastronomical reputation'. In this youthful flashback, Grendel also displays his, as of yet, undeveloped singing and dancing skills. He dances awkwardly and mumbles out a few lines of what will eventually become his theme song. He sings these hopelessly out of tune: 'Who's the beast who looks so swell, G-R-E-N-D-E-L. What's his purpose can't you guess, N-E-M-E-S-I-S.' This is, in fact, the very same song that he will reprise and sing with show-stopping confidence at the end of the film, just before his final battle with Beowulf. But as he sings, clumsily dancing around, Grendel falls off a cliff and becomes wedged in a tree – stuck between two large branches. It is an unfortunate accident, and Grendel cries out into the black night, 'Poor Grendel will hang here and starve to death. Poor Grendel.'

Scene 6

The next morning, Grendel awakens, still stuck in the tree (see Figure 2.6a). He hears human voices – but this being the first time that he has encountered them, he is a bit confused. In the novel, Gardner writes:

> I opened my eyes and everything was blurry [...] Then voices, speaking words. The sounds were foreign at first, but when I calmed myself, concentrating, I found I understood them: it was my own language, but spoken in a strange way, as if the sounds were made by brittle sticks, dried spindles, flaking bits of shale.[11]

Here the author describes the contrasts in dialect between Grendel and the humans – a point that Stitt made light of by having the humans speak in northern England accents, while Grendel (Peter Ustinov) speaks in an urbane London accent.

The three men, King Hrothgar, Wiglaf and Dung, stand at the base of the tree, as they try to figure out what exactly Grendel is. This is a flash-back scene that takes place prior to the first appearance of, and before there had been any sightings of, the Great Boogy. The men debate whether it is some kind of growth that is killing the tree or if it is the spirit of the tree. It doesn't cross their minds that he is an entity of his own.

> WIGLAF: I think it's a growth of some kind, King. Some beast-like fungus.
> DUNG: Here. There's sap running all over. Eee. Just like blood. I'd say that tree's a goner.
> WIGLAF: Ah, maybe we could try to cut the fungus out?
> KING: Nay – could be it's some kind of oak-tree spirit. Better not mess wi' it. [...] I think we should make friends with it.
> WIGLAF: How?
> KING: Give it something to eat.
> WIGLAF: What's it eat?
> KING: Pig. Oak-tree spirits eat pig. Get it a pig, Wiglaf.

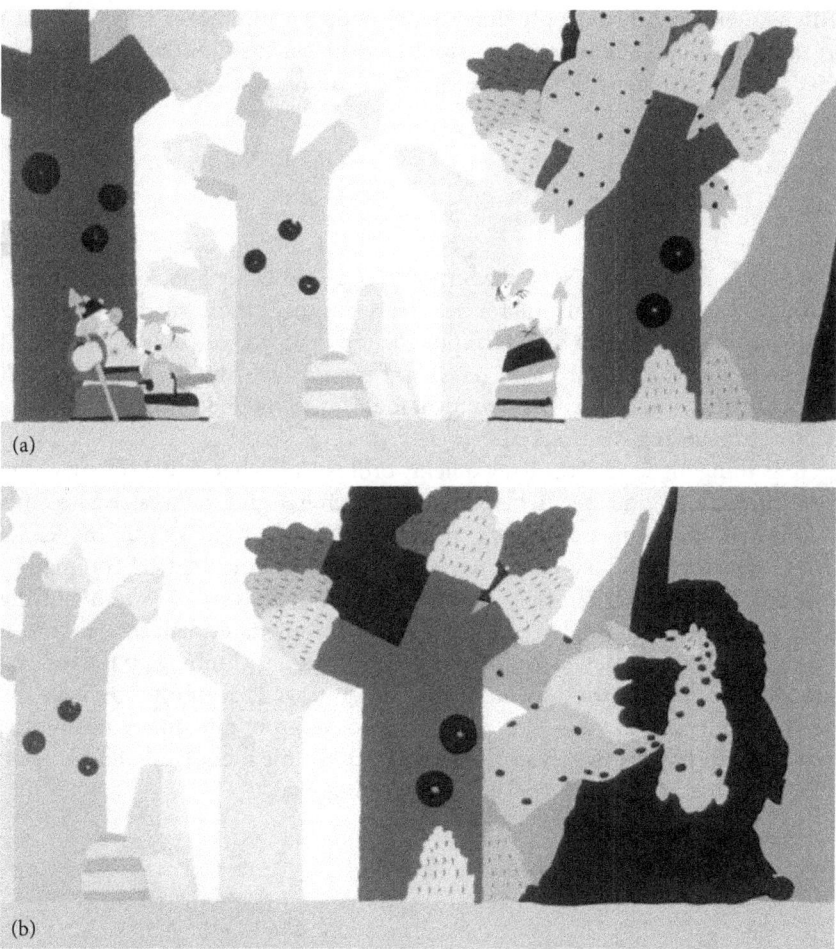

FIGURE 2.6 (a) King Hrothgar, Wiglaf and Dung ponder Grendel's form, which is stuck in a tree (b); Grendel's Mum (her character name in Stitt's film), depicted as a black silhouette, carefully rescues Grendel (*Grendel Grendel Grendel*, Alexander Stitt, 1981).

Grendel is hungry and likes the King's suggestion very much, so he begins grunting in agreement. But the sudden, loud monstrous noises and movements startle the men. Soon after, Grendel's Mum appears to rescue her son and the men run away in terror. In the novel, Gardner describes his mother's arrival as such:

> She came roaring down like thunder, screaming like a thousand hurricanes […] Then her smell poured in like blood into a silver cup, filling the moonlit clearing to the brim, and I felt the two trees that held me falling, and I was tumbling, free, into the grass.[12]

This sequence marks the only time that Grendel's Mum makes an appearance in the film – and she is curiously rendered in black silhouette, a treatment that is inconsistent with the other brightly coloured elements of the scene (see Figure 2.6b).

Scene 7

The fleeing King is soon separated from Wiglaf and Dung and, as he stumbles through the forest, he falls into a bear trap. Stunned, the King comes to, and finds he is at the bottom of a deep pit. Having managed to elude Grendel and Grendel's Mum, King Hrothgar has now been captured by the man who will eventually become his primary political foe. 'You're not a bear then', comes the deep commanding voice of Unferth.

Regaining his senses, the King quickly orders Unferth to help him out of the pit. Unferth is not inclined to help him, so the King begins to threaten him. This is followed by attempts of bribery, and finally an offer to make him the King's '2-I-C' (a contemporary colloquial expression meaning 2nd in command). Unferth, however, sardonically retorts that he is already a '1-I-C'! Finally, the King offers to make him his heir. 'All right. Just remember that, though, or I'll have your royal marbles', warns Unferth. As the King is climbing up the rope he says, 'You've made a wise decision, Unferth. You won't regret it. You have the undying gratitude of your King'. But, once above ground he immediately sees that Unferth has previously captured and tied up his men, Dung and Wiglaf. 'Christmas!' exclaims the shocked King (see Figure 2.7).

FIGURE 2.7 Unferth, after capturing Wiglaf and Dung, reluctantly rescues the King from a bear trap in the forest (*Grendel Grendel Grendel*, Alexander Stitt, 1981).

The exclamation of 'Christmas', being a clever euphemism for 'Christ!', is used frequently throughout the film. It not only avoids problems with censorship (complying with the film's G-rating, in which the irreverent use of 'Christ' might appear incompatible) but also suggests the impending spread of Christianity into Scandinavia's previously pagan culture. This shifting of religious dominance is an important underlying theme in the original *Beowulf* poem.

Scene 8

This scene features an absurd verbal exchange between the King and his men, which further showcases the foolishness of the warriors and the ungenerous nature of the King.

> KING: Luckily for you two, Unferth's on our side now. He's our second-in-command.
> WIGLAF: But that's me. I'm second-in-command.
> KING: You've just been promoted to third-in-command.
> DUNG: Does that mean I get to be fourth-in-command now, then?
> KING: No, Dung. You're still eleventh.
> DUNG: But there aren't eleven of us, are there?
> KING: There might be, one day.
> DUNG: I never thought of that!

Grendel is a witness to this bickering and begins to perceive the growing rivalry between the humans. While the general buffoonery of the humans provides comedy for the viewer, it also serves to highlight Grendel's inverted world view – a world where the humans behave more like violent children, and monsters more like grown-ups.

Scene 9

This scene marks a return to conventional narrative time. Although Gardner's novel is prone to jump back and forth in time, such flashbacks are minimized in Stitt's film. After witnessing many years of the human's conflicting inhumane and ridiculous behaviour, as well as some occasionally intelligent inclinations, Grendel is beginning to contemplate his own complex relationship to humanity. In his cave, Grendel muses aloud to his mother:

> Yes, that was the first time I came across those strange little creatures. Men! A bit like us, really, weren't they, Mother? In a grotesque sort of way, that is. They had a language, too, just as I have. And maybe Mother had, a long time ago. And – very strange this – I understood them, though they didn't seem to

be able to understand me. Nervy, silly little creatures they were. But, just the same, I knew I'd have to watch them.

Grendel's musings clearly articulate some of the notable differences between himself and the humans, but at the same time hint at some possible connections.

Scene 10/11

Initially set within an expansive white space, this interlude sequence depicts a hunter on horseback pursuing and subsequently killing a deer. As the hunter hunches over the carcass, Wiglaf sneaks forward, shoots him with an arrow and runs off with the deer. Grendel then saunters up and collects the dead human (presumably so as not to let it go to waste).

However, to further complicate this absurd chain of events, Wiglaf is ambushed by two other humans, One-eyed Arthur and Basil, who want the deer for themselves. Wiglaf resists telling them to 'Piss-off!' Arthur, retorts, 'Piss-off is it? Who do you think you are then?' 'I'm Wiglaf, I'm with the King and his lads!' At this, the two stab Wiglaf, and abscond with the deer. Moments later, the King, Unferth and Dung, find the wounded, yet still alive Wiglaf. They decide to seek revenge and plan an attack on One-eyed Arthur and Basil.

Scene 12

In this scene, the King is again shown to be cunning and opportunistic, but equally ineffectual in battle. Unferth leads the attack, killing Basil and Arthur and in the foray, Unferth mistakenly bumps the King's nose with the handle of his axe (see Figure 2.8). Importantly, this very minor incident of 'friendly fire' will later be greatly embellished and the King will be exalted for his extreme fortitude and bravery during this battle. After the battle, the King greedily collects their swords, boots and other valuables (while simple-minded Dung is over-joyed to be allowed to take home a pair of used socks).

Grendel, who has again been observing the human violence, sneaks in and collects the dead bodies of Basil and Arthur. It appears that he is able to consume countless humans, but rarely ever has to kill them himself: the humans take care of such monstrous acts for him. However, the deer (the cause of the series of murders) remains on the spitfire, uneaten – another wasted life.

Scene 13/14

The trio (Dung, Wiglaf and the King) are gathered at the table, lit by candlelight. While reminiscing their recent battle, the King decides that they need a singer

FIGURE 2.8 King Hrothgar's nose is accidently bumped by Unferth; a minor event that later will be greatly exaggerated and heralded as a great act of bravery (*Grendel Grendel Grendel*, Alexander Stitt, 1981).

in order to properly celebrate their great warrior deeds. He, therefore, promotes Dung to the role. However, Dung, being tone-deaf and small-minded, proves to be both a terrible lyricist and singer. Outside the hall, a silhouetted Grendel listens to the din and quickly clamps his hands over his ears.

As Grendel slinks away, he helps himself to a couple of the King's pigs. The King had, after all, offered Grendel a pig earlier when he was trapped in the tree; and in this instance Grendel does not consider that he is stealing, but merely following through in his acceptance of the King's generous offer. In Stitt's film, Grendel frequently misunderstands conversational context and nuance and tends to interpret things quite literally. When Dung steps out and sees that someone has stolen the pigs, rather than suspecting Grendel, the blame is immediately attributed to a neighbouring tribe. 'Must have been those lads on the next hill', says the King. 'We'll do 'em!' he promises. And, a few days later, they do, 'do 'em'. That is, they violently attack their neighbours in order to seek revenge. Of course, seen through Grendel's eyes, such retaliations appear utterly absurd – particularly since the King had, earlier, seemed quite happy to gift his pigs to Grendel.

Scene 15

Grendel, again observing the human's ongoing violence and stupidity, muses:

> So it went. Little groups of these men, ragged little bands roamed the forest all through that year, fighting at every chance. And all through the next year,

and the next. They killed cows. They killed horses. They killed each other. I would listen to their noise. Secretly watch their battles. I began to be more amused than frightened of them. It didn't matter to me what they did to each other. Sometimes a hut was burned. Any survivors would crawl off to a neighbour and beg to be taken in. They'd hand over whatever they had left – any cows and pigs – any of the things they used to prod or hit each other – any pretty things or shiny things – and in return they'd be allowed to sleep in the cowshed and eat the worst of the food. The king and his lads did best of all out of it.

As Grendel narrates, a montage of frenzied and violent activity is depicted, illustrating Hrothgar's expanding kingdom.

Scene 16/17

It is Unferth who continually leads the kingdom to victory, while the King remains in the safety of his meadhall and eagerly awaits the spoils of war. This becomes a constant source of friction between Unferth and the King, manifesting in petty squabbles. In this scene, the King, seated on his throne, is trying on a newly acquired gold crown, when Unferth walks in:

UNFERTH: What's that funny hat?
KING: It came in with some poor dispossessed persons that arrived today.
UNFERTH: Hasn't got any horns on it. It's not a hero's hat.
KING: It's a king's hat, Number Two. They give it to me as a tribute. Real gold, it is.
UNFERTH: Won't stop many spears though; or swords.

In response, the King sticks out his tongue, blowing a loud raspberry at Unferth as he leaves. This childish behaviour serves two purposes – maintaining a light-hearted cartoony aesthetic for the film, and revealing how Grendel has come to understand their senseless actions. Summing up their ridiculous behaviour, Grendel narrates:

The king's growing wealth attracted enemies. They'd come in the night, thundering up on horseback, leaping the pig-fences, scattering the livestock as the doors banged open and the king's warriors tumbled out of their meadhall. Then they'd stop and face each other, waving their prodders and shouting their lungs out. Terrible threats! Things about their fathers and their father's fathers. And even about their mothers. Things about justice. And honour. Then they would fight. The king and his growing band won every time, and took more tributes. Within a dozen years there was nobody left strong enough to challenge them.

Grendel is bewildered by the human's highly contradictory actions: on one hand, childish stunts; on the other hand, monstrous exploits involving widespread carnage.

Scene 18

This scene introduces the Sculptor, a character that is unique to the animated feature (he does not appear in Gardner's novel nor the original *Beowulf* epic). As the scene opens, the Sculptor is in the midst of carving a portrait of the King out of a large stone slab. But the King is displeased with his work.

> KING: I don't think you got the nose quite right, Sculptor. Don't you think Sculptor's got nose wrong, Dung?
> DUNG: I think Sculptor's got nose wrong, King. I don't think nose is very well sculpted at all.

Then, perhaps as a result of the criticism, the Sculptor taps a bit too hard with his chisel, knocking the entire nose off. 'Great Boogy', exclaims the King in dismay. Stitt uses this opportunity to integrate another exaggerated reference to the supposed anxiety that the Norsemen had of having their noses cut off – even partially (perhaps emblematic of a deeper fear of castration and loss of masculinity).[13] Here, the Sculptor has figuratively (but quite visibly) cut off the King's nose, which is perhaps a rather bad omen.

Later in the film, in Scene 21 (and correspondingly later in Gardner's novel), there will arrive a character known as the Shaper. He, through his storytelling, his songs and poetry, will greatly influence and in a sense 'shape' the human's minds. Following Gardner's lead, Stitt also places strong emphasis on the Shaper character and what he represents. According to Stitt, 'the Shaper, in fact, is an analogy of the story itself, representing as he does a character like the one who would have first performed the *Beowulf* poem'.[14] But as *Grendel Grendel Grendel* is told through the visual medium of animation, the idea of a *visual shaper* also emerges in Stitt's film. This takes the form of the Sculptor who, along with his assistants, can be seen continually etching, carving and sculpting large stone monuments, which increasingly populate the film's backgrounds. These monuments tend either to glorify the King and their God, or to denigrate the Great Boogy (Grendel) – thus perpetuating the human's fear of monsters.

At the conclusion of this scene, the King, wishing to increase his regal realm, announces his latest ambitious vision. 'I'm going to build a grand hall. One that's worthy of me and my kingdom. With grand sculptures and that', he proclaims. Importantly, the building of this grand meadhall will not only create a dynamic performance space in which the Shaper will sing his influential songs, but also provide a space for the impending battle between Grendel and Beowulf.

Scene 19

This scene depicts a montage of labourers hard at work building the King's meadhall. Grendel narrates the frenzied activity:

> So the King sent off to far distant realms for axmen, woodsmen and carpenters, for metalsmiths and gold workers, for masons, builders, carters and workers, to build a magnificent meadhall. For weeks their uproar filled the days and nights. And from behind the vines and boulders, I watched it all.

Importantly, this sequence also includes the construction of a grand, larger than life, stone statue of the king. It is sculpted in three-dimensions, and features an exaggerated (and fully intact) nose. The statue, a potent symbol of the King's absurd narcissism, is then mounted atop a huge pillar at the entrance to the new meadhall.

Scene 20

King Hrothgar's new meadhall is now complete. Unfortunately, the sounds emerging from the hall are being belted out by Dung, who is still the kingdom's official singer. The sound of his voice echoing among the spacious walls of the meadhall and out through the open windows can be heard far and wide. He belts out what seems to be his only composition, 'This feller, he shoved his sword into our Wiglaf, he did! Sooooooo, we done him!' Grendel, who is some distance away, covers his ears and cringes at the horrifying cacophony. Grendel's flinching actions serve as a humorous reference to the original *Beowulf* epic in which the monster becomes increasingly agitated by the celebratory noises emanating from the newly built meadhall. In that version, Grendel is so disturbed by the joyous noises of human society – a grouping that he is noticeably excluded from – that he is driven to attack. But in Stitt's version, Grendel, who possesses a rich musical timbre, is merely horrified at Dung's butchering of accepted musical conventions.

Scene 21

The character known simply as the Shaper approaches the meadhall. Significantly, he is blind and accompanied by a young mute assistant, the Shaper's Boy. Upon seeing them, Grendel slinks down behind the rocks so as not to be detected.

Dung continues to sing his cacophonous tune, and even the Shaper is disturbed by it. 'Great Boogy', he decries. 'Did you hear that, Boy? A desperate need of a shaper, no mistake!' Then, because he is blind and the

Boy is mute, he places his hand on top of the Boy's head and asks, 'Tell me Boy, is it a grand hall we're coming to?' The Boy nods and the Shaper, feeling the affirmative movement of his head, continues speaking, 'Yes. Yes. A grand hall. This will be Hrothgar's kingdom they speak of. We'll do well there. Lead me, Boy'.

The Shaper and the Boy represent a most unconventional pairing – one is blind and the other is mute. From this first encounter, it also becomes clear that (to both the viewer and to the eavesdropping Grendel) that the Shaper is driven, at least in part, by greed.

Scene 22

Standing at the meadhall door, the Shaper melodically strums his instrument; his assistant knocks at the door. Wiglaf opens the door and brashly exclaims:

> WIGLAF: Wotter we got here, then? Ay-oop. Singer?
> SHAPER: Shaper.
> WIGLAF: Shaper is it, then? Come in. Bit of shoosh, lads. Here's a real singer.

As the Shaper and the Boy are hurriedly ushered into the meadhall, Grendel stealthily creeps nearer in order to eavesdrop at the windows. He is about to witness one of the most poignant recitals that he has ever encountered.

Scene 23

Inside the meadhall, the King greets them.

> KIN: So, you're a singer then?
> SHAPER: Shaper. We professionals say shaper.
> KING: A professional in need of a job by the look.
> SHAPER: Not as much in need of a job as you are in need of a shaper.
> KING: Well put Shaper, well put.

Eager to hear the new singer, and even more eager to have him replace Dung, the Shaper is invited to perform. The Shaper then very quickly ascertains the political landscape, and standing at the head of the hall announces, 'My lords, noble warriors. I will sing you the song of the revenge of Wiglaf. I will sing of your noble and heroic king'.

But at this point, Dung quietly interrupts the Shaper, proudly reminding him that the 'King got his nose thumped'. This interjection not only adds to the reoccurring and absurd reverence to their noses, but also humorously overlooks

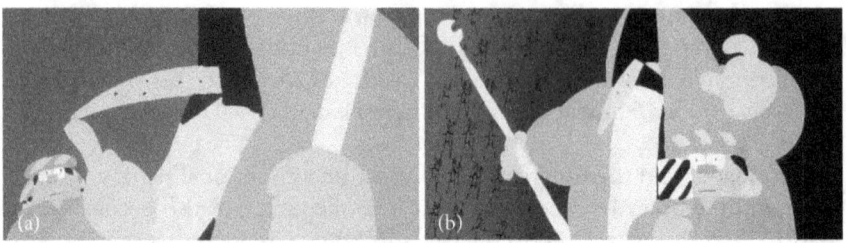

FIGURE 2.9 (a) The Shaper gently touches his own nose in a display of empathy for the King's injured nose; (b) the Shaper and the Shaper's Boy sing of the King's bravery (*Grendel Grendel Grendel*, Alexander Stitt, 1981).

the fact that it was Unferth who had accidently bumped the King's nose during battle. 'Nose?' queries the Shaper in reply. With a slight chuckle, he pauses, and gently fondles his own large nose (see Figure 2.9a). Taking full advantage of this new bit of information about the King, the Shaper resumes his introduction, 'Of your gallantly *wounded* king and his glorious victory' (see Figure 2.9b).

As the song begins, Unferth sits in the corner, brooding. He knows that it was he that had won the battle for the King (and virtually every battle since). He also knows that he deserves the glory, not the opportunistic King. He realizes that he is, in a sense, being written out of history. The Shaper sings:

You meadhall gatherers,
King-loved warriors,
Listen to the story of the Thanes.
See the King-blessed warriors,
Prideful skirmishers,
Gather in the early winter rains.
Swords glisten. Mouths bitter.
Eyes glisten. Spears glitter. Listen!
They listen, as their King revives
Their former bitter anger.
They pledge to give their very lives
As Wiglaf's proud avengers.

Honour the King.
Honour we'll bring to the king.
Honour is king.

Their journey takes them to the place
Of Wiglaf's assignation.
Their mission brings them face to face
With Satan's congregation.

Swords clatter. Mouths tighten.
Blood spatters. Eyes brighten. Imagine!

The day is done, the King has won,
Surviving bitter blows,
And proudly bears the battle-scars
Upon his noble nose.
Honour the nose!
Honour the scar that it shows!
Hail to the nose.
Hail to the King,
Death to the foes of the King.
Long live the King!

In response to the song, the King loudly applauds and exclaims, 'Great Boogy! Did we do all that?' In quick reply, Dung asserts, 'We must have!' Unferth also appears greatly moved by the Shaper's song, and also seems now to believe that perhaps the King is a deserving hero after all.

But it is Grendel, who is listening outside, who appears to be the most enthralled by the Shaper's song. To emphasize the point, a great meteor streaks across the sky, underscoring the huge significance in the Shaper's epic storytelling.

Scene 24

Grendel is so intensely moved by the Shaper's song that he walks off into the night, whistling its tune. In the novel, Gardner describes the effect that the Shaper had on Grendel most strongly.

> I too crept away, my mind aswim in ringing phrases, magnificent, golden, and all of them, incredibly, lies. What was he? The man had changed the world, had torn up the past by its thick, gnarled roots and had transmuted it, and they, who knew the truth, remembered it his way – and so did I.[15]

By contrast in Stitt's film, the complexities of Grendel's inner monologue are primarily expressed through the animated effect of a meteor streaking across the sky and through Grendel's blissful whistling as he retreats into the night, heading home to his mother.

Scene 25/26/27

It is morning and Dung rings the alarm bells, warning that foreigners are approaching the kingdom. He informs Unferth that the foreigners are presently camped in the nearby valley. Unferth and Dung, supported by a small group of soldiers, go down to pay the foreigners a visit.

Unferth approaches the Foreign King and demands that he and his people immediately leave the vicinity. Amusingly, the Foreign King speaks with a hyperbolic British accent that is very strongly reminiscent of the iconic British actor, Terry-Thomas.[16] It is unclear as to whether Stitt had hoped to employ Terry-Thomas for the film but, coincidentally, he had co-stared with Peter Ustinov in Disney's animated feature, *Robin Hood* (Wolfgang Reitherman 1973), which had been released just a few years earlier. In this performance, the Australian actor, Barry Hill, delivers his Terry-Thomas sound-alike with an added vocal affliction (a substitution-speech-disorder) in which he replaces the letter 'r' with the letter 'w' (thus the word 'ring' is pronounced as 'wing').

As Unferth approaches the foreigners, he demands, 'Who's in charge here?' Soon, the leader of the group emerges from a tent, and calmly says:

FOREIGN KING: I am old bean. What seems to be the twouble?
UNFERTH: Have you heard of the great King Hrothgar. This is his kingdom you're in and I've come as his official representative with his official message which is 'Push off!'
FOREIGN KING: I say! That's a bit wugged isn't it? We just wanted to have a bit of a west here.
UNFERTH: Defying the King are we?
FOREIGN KING: No, no. Not at all. I wouldn't dweam of it. How about some twibutes, wings, and bwacelets, and twinkets, like that.

After a number of threats from Unferth and his men, the Foreign King, desperate to avoid conflict, announces:

Look stop them and let us be and I will suwwender a very special tweasure to you. Come and see. If you will let us go on our way, I will give your king, my sister to take as his bwide. She will be a symbol of unity between your twibe and my twibe. Her name is Wealtheow, which means 'holy servant of common good'.

Unferth is absolutely mesmerized by Wealtheow's beauty. Immediately (but somehow not surprisingly), the King appears to claim the young woman as his bride, declaring – 'Right here! I'm your lord and sovereign, and husband to be. Welcome to the family: I'm the King. I'm royally pleased to accept your lovely gift – along with the gold and that' (see Figure 2.10).

The lust and greed of the lecherous King Hrothgar are palpable as he quickly begins pushing everyone, except for Wealtheow, out of the tent. It is evident that he plans to consummate their relationship – immediately. But, disturbed by the Kings impatience, the Foreign King insists, 'I say, do you have a pwoper

FIGURE 2.10 King Hrothgar meeting his new wife, Queen Wealtheow, as Unferth and the Foreign King look on (*Grendel Grendel Grendel*, Alexander Stitt, 1981).

pwiest to pweside at the ceremony?' The King thinking quickly responds, 'Uh, of course. Dung! Dung here is our head priest'. Although Dung has no religious expertise, he is exceedingly pleased to be promoted to this new role.

Scene 28

Dung quickly presides over King Hrothgar and Wealtheow's wedding, while Grendel narrates his observations:

> So, the Old King accepted the Young King's gift, along with some other things – swords and cups, some servants and so on; and both sides made speeches – all long-winded, tediously poetic, mostly lies – and then, with a lot of hand-shaking and a last few touching observations, the foreigners went away.

Then, Grendel, talking to himself, reveals that he is also quite smitten by the new Queen.

> Soooo … what do you want to do tonight Grendel? Oh, I don't know, Grendel. What do you want to do tonight? Well, I believe there is a good show at the meadhall. Splendid new singer. The meadhall, eh? You wouldn't be thinking that you might catch a look at that pretty new queen, now? No, no, no. I just enjoy a good tune, that's all. Isn't that curious? I did enjoy that shaper's tune. Imagine them conceiving something that I like? Well, I hadn't thought them

capable of it. [...] Have they changed, do you think, or have I? Mind you, they murder each other and no less for it.

Grendel is now decidedly conflicted by how he feels about the humans. On one hand, he is repulsed by the species' constant treachery, but on the other hand he has been moved by both the Shaper's glorious music and the incredible beauty of Wealtheow.

Scene 29

Stitt's film, unlike Gardner's novel, overtly explores many of the political developments and tensions within Hrothgar's kingdom. In this scene, as Grendel looks on, it is announced that the King and Queen plan to have a son, an heir who will then inherit the kingdom. Unferth is greatly angered by this news, as the King had previously promised everything to him (as a reward for having saved him from the bear trap).

Scene 30

The Shaper is called up to sing a song to mark the occasion of the announcement of Hrothgar's planned heir. Grendel rushes up near to the windows of the meadhall, so as to not miss a word or note of the Shaper's mesmerizing song. With ceremonial display, the Shaper sings 'The Creation Song', a song that not only heralds the rise of Christianity and the establishment of rigid societal conventions, but one that also defines the origins of evil as expressed through the narrative of the 'brother-killer', Cain.

God saw the darkness, and he made it right.
God halved the darkness into day and night.
God saw the garden, and he made it fresh.
God halved the garden into clay and flesh.

God saw his image, and he gave it life.
God halved his image into man and wife
Man, wife united to create two sons.
God halved his kingdom for the chosen ones.

God's love was Abel's to perpetuate.
Cain halved his feelings into love and hate.
God-fearing Abel loved his brother so.
Cain halved his brother with a bitter blow.

Cain bore the fury of both God and man.
God halved his children into loved and damned.
Now and forever, all the beasts of Cain
Live halved from grace, in foul, black pits of pain.

There are some striking visual compositions and scenic layouts in this sequence which underscore some of the Shaper's claims. For example, when he sings, 'God halved his image into man and wife', the Shaper is, at that moment, precisely positioned so that his body appears to forge a wedge between the seated King and Queen (see Figure 2.11). Most importantly, the Shaper's song warns the audience that Grendel is a descendant of the accursed Cain.

Scene 31

Grendel, upon hearing 'The Creation Song', and taking the lyrics to heart, becomes quite emotional and cries out in disbelief, 'Halved us from grace? Us? Me? Am I one of the dark-damned half – a child of this awful brother? But they are the ones who murder each other! Can I be' Grendel stops mid-sentence as he notices a watchman signalling for backup. Almost immediately, dozens of Guards begin to attack Grendel. But he does not wish to fight these men; he would much prefer to live peacefully with the humans, and to prove that he

FIGURE 2.11 The Shaper sings 'God halved his image into man and wife'. These words, along with the Shaper's strategic positioning, suggest the burgeoning rift in the relationship between the King and Queen (*Grendel Grendel Grendel*, Alexander Stitt, 1981).

is not one of the awful followers of Cain. To announce his good intentions, Grendel cries out, imploringly, 'Friend? Friend? Friend?' to the attacking soldiers. But with each utterance of the word 'friend', the men increase the ferocity of their attacks. Soon his cries turn to anger, and he is forced to shift his hopeful queries of friendship into angry assertions of his monstrous identity. He cries out the word, 'friend!' once more. Then, he conflates the word 'friend' with his own name, calling out the word, 'Griend!' and finally, in his loudest voice yet, he howls, 'Grendel!' and then turns, and flees into the night. He has been forced to accept his monstrousness – he is, Grendel.

Scene 32

The King emerges from the meadhall after Grendel has run away, demanding to know why they did not stop the monster. 'Who was on guard then? Who's fault is it? Bloody hell! Where is your devotion to your king!' Hrothgar cries in frustration. The Shaper then emerges, coyly declaring, 'Perhaps, the fault is a lack of devotion to the *King of the Gods*'. In order to correct this lack of religious devotion, he announces that he will lead a lengthy ceremony in the morning in order to 'appease the King of the Gods'.

Rather than be troubled by Grendel's deadly attack or the Shaper's ominous words, Unferth appears to be much more concerned with what the King had earlier announced regarding his heirs. He rebukes the King, 'That speech in there about sons and heirs. I'm your successor, remember?' The King, thinking quickly, replies disingenuously, 'Oh, aye! That was just for the lass'. Unferth is not entirely convinced, but he decides to not pursue the point any further.

This scene demonstrates that not only are political tensions rising, but that the Shaper has found a means to increase his own power through an increased assertion of religious command. Ironically, it will soon be revealed that the 'King of the Gods' that the Shaper refers to is in fact, the Dragon God.

Scene 33

This scene represents a pivotal moment in both the film and the novel. Grendel is attempting to come to grips with his new-found knowledge about the chosen (the humans) and the damned (himself and the other descendants of Cain). He cries out:

> God have pity! God have pity! I yelled that a hundred times that night, hammering the ground in the middle of the forest where I had fled, slamming the ground so hard that a seam split open twelve feet long. Why hadn't they been able to understand that we could all live together?

By emphasizing that he truly wishes to peacefully co-exist with the humans, Grendel becomes less of a monster – while the humans, fuelled as they are by their unyielding system of beliefs, appear more monstrous.

Contrastingly, in the novel, Gardner is much less direct in his portrayal of Grendel's desire to 'get along' with the humans. He does, however, attempt to illustrate how Grendel is certainly less monstrous than the humans. He does this, through an interesting commentary on the use of profanity.

> I slammed the earth with such force that a seam split open twelve feet long. 'Bastards!' I roared. 'Sons of bitches! Fuckers!' Words I'd picked up from men in their rages. I wasn't even sure what they meant, though I had an idea: defiance, rejection of the gods that, for my part, I'd known all along to be lifeless sticks. I roared with laughter, still sobbing. We, the accursed, didn't even have words for swearing in![17]

Here, Gardner demonstrates, through language, that Grendel is less monstrous than the humans. In contrast to the humans, who habitually use offensive language, monsters have no conception of such derogatory words. These strictly human utterances are, ironically, the very words that have caused Gardner's novel, *Grendel*, to be banned in some locals in the United States.[18]

The next morning (in the animated film) Grendel is seated on a nearby hillside, 'dabbing mud into my various cuts and wounds' and watching the Shaper performs his ritual in order to 'appease the King of the Gods'. Grendel laments the loss of good meat as they throw the dead bodies onto the funeral pyre – and derides their rituals:

> Then, according to some lunatic theory, they threw on golden rings, old swords, serviceable helmets – and chanted heroic catch-cries, as if they'd won some great battle. I laughed at myself, had I really been all that anxious to be accepted by them? Midnight foolishness. I went home to my ugly, loving mother.

At this point in the animated film, Grendel appears to be abandoning hope of any peaceful co-existence with mankind. However, in Gardner's novel, Grendel has not yet given up on the humans. He is still mesmerized by the Shaper's words, but also troubled by them. He recognizes that much of what the Shaper says is 'a cold-blooded lie', but on the other hand his words are so profound that he was willing to accept them, even if it means that he 'must be the outcast, cursed by the rules of his hideous fable'.[19] In effect, Grendel would be content with bearing the curse of Cain, just so long as he could continue to be part of this human, Christian narrative. It is a sentiment that Stitt does not elucidate clearly at this point in the film, but a semblance of this will play out in the following scenes.

Scene 34

This scene features Grendel's first encounter with the dragon, arguably one of the most vibrant characters in both the book and the film. However, the Dragon does not actually exist in Grendel's world, but is merely a figment of his imagination. In the movie, Grendel prefaces his visit to the dragon with the statement, 'That night, in the safety of my cave, I had a dream, or perhaps a journey.' In a similar manner, Gardner's novel describes this metaphysical journey: 'I made my mind a blank and fell, sank away like a stone through earth and sea, toward the dragon.'[20] Stitt adds in his *Grendel Grendel Grendel – The*

FIGURE 2.12 (a) Grendel meets the Dragon, who (b) momentarily morphs into a red block (*Grendel Grendel Grendel*, Alexander Stitt, 1981).

Book of the Animated Feature Film that Grendel subsequently 'finds himself in a great, black pit, or in space, or nowhere. But wherever he is, he is there with a dragon – bright red and as big as a mountain'.[21] This ambiguous black space serves as a perfect setting for a surrealistic, animated dream.

Upon his arrival, the Dragon greets him, 'Ah, Grendel you've come. We've been expecting you'. Understandably, Grendel is quite startled by these unfamiliar surroundings and especially by the enormity of the Dragon (see Figure 2.12a). The space is also daunting, being composed of pure blackness save for the large mound of gold coins that initially comprises the ground plane. The Dragon warns Grendel, 'Stand around the side, boy. I get a cough sometimes and', at which point the Dragon coughs out huge flames and billows of smoke, causing Grendel to cower in fear, and chatter his teeth. The Dragon and Grendel continue to converse:

DRAGON: Now you know how they felt when they saw you, eh? Scared enough to pee in their pants! Uh, you didn't did you? Good! That's valuable stuff you're standing on.
GRENDEL: [attempting to refocus the conversation] You have a point, about how they must feel when they see me. I mean, it's one thing to eat one of them from time to time – it keeps their numbers down for one thing – but it's quite another to give them heart attacks, for no...
DRAGON: Fiddle sticks!
GRENDEL: Pardon?
DRAGON: Why not frighten them? Stupid, stupid, stupid, the whole kit and caboodle. Why did you come here? Why bother me? Don't tell me, I know. I know everything. That's what makes me so sick, and old ... and tired.

As the Dragon says this, he transforms from his bright-red dragon form into a large two-dimensional red square (see Figure 2.12b). Realizing that he has offended the Dragon, Grendel quickly apologizes, 'I'm sorry', which provides just enough deference so as to bring the dragon out of this block form, and return him to his normal, dragon-shape. Wearily, the Dragon continues, 'I know you're sorry ... You're sorry right now for this one frail flicker-flash in a long dull fall to eternity. I'm not impressed.'

After spending a great deal of time explaining his superiority to other creatures (supported by an array of clever animated antics), the Dragon leans in close to Grendel as if to let him in on a profound secret – 'I know why you were invented in the first place.' He proceeds to explain:

They're half right with their mumbo-jumbo. They've stumbled onto a half-truth; good and evil, positive and negative. There's a fundamental involved here, Grendel. For everything that's cold, there's something hot. For everything that is, there's something else that's not. Light must have its darkness, good must have its bad. For everything subtracted, there's something else to add.

The Dragon launches into a song and dance routine that attempts to explain to Grendel why he exists and what his purpose is. It is a lively and humorous scene in which the lyrical meanings are often punctuated with instances of metamorphosis and graphic playfulness. The Dragon sings:

For everyone who's rich,
Another ten are poor.
For everyone who never was,
There's one who was before.
For every positive, a negative
Is knocking at the door.
For every entertainer, there's a bore.
Need I say mooooore?

For every entertainer
For every entertainer
For every entertainer, there's a bore.
Bore, encore, encore!

For everyone who fails,
Another will succeed,
And every act of charity
Supplants an act of greed.
For every deity, the laity
Is slaving at the yoke,
And every hollow laugh demands a joke.

For every answer, there's a question.
To each exception, there's a rule.
For every sound, a silence.
For every sage, a fool.

For everyone who's mean,
Another one is nice.
For everyone who's virtuous,
Another's full of vice.

For every synonym, an antonym
Is waiting round the bend,
And every bright beginning has an end.

Every bright beginning,
Every bright beginning,
Every bright beginning has an end.

The final two stanzas are, in fact, sung as a duet during which the Dragon leads Grendel in a choreographed dance routine. At its conclusion the Dragon proclaims, 'A splendid way of making the point, wouldn't you say, dear boy?' Grendel rather dizzy and confused replies, 'What point?' Rather impatiently, the Dragon exclaims:

> DRAGON: What point? The point dear Grendel is that you are man's anti-man, piety's pie-in-the-eye, ignorance's bliss. In short, dear Grendel, you are here, you exist, simply to go bump in their night.
> GRENDEL: But the Shaper said…
> DRAGON: Illusion. Tripe. Mere sleight-of-wits. *You* are the reality. You will drive them to poetry, science, religion in their efforts to explain you.
> GRENDEL: You want me to scare them to…
> DRAGON: It's not what I want. You'll do it anyway.
> GRENDEL: Aren't you making me do it, by telling me to?
> DRAGON: No, no, no. We dragons don't cause anything. I told you that.
> GRENDEL: But if you hadn't told me…
> DRAGON: I had to tell you. I knew I would.
> GRENDEL: I suppose that's right.
> DRAGON: Of course, it is.

At this point, the Dragon begins to fade away, leaving Grendel alone. As the Dragon dissipates, he manages to say one final, but incomplete, sentence.

> DRAGON: And for everyone who's right, another one is…
> GRENDEL: Left?

Grendel is indeed 'left' alone. The Dragon, the mounds of gold, the black void have all vanished and Grendel finds himself once again in his familiar world. The Dragon has imparted a great deal of information, but Grendel seems to be none the wiser.

Scene 35

Grendel happens upon two sculptors who are carving figures and runes into large stone monuments. The runes are, in fact, 'mock-runes' that Stitt devised, which are basically English language words but with all vowels removed (and if a word begins or ends with a vowel, an added '+' is used to denote that a vowel has been removed). The pseudo-runes (in translation) read, 'Great Dragon God, protect Hrothgar from Grendel the Great Boogy'. The accompanying image depicts Grendel, holding up two helpless humans (one in each hand) above his head. In an attempt to emulate this depiction, Grendel grabs the two hapless sculptors and holds them up above his head. But then he hesitates, unsure as to whether or not he is doing it properly, and consults the diagram. Realizing that he does not have it quite right, he then swaps each of the humans to opposite hands and again holds them up high above his head. Still uncertain, he consults the image once again and further alters his pose and grip of the hapless humans (see Figure 3.5). Finally, deciding that it is not worth the effort, he drops them to the ground and walks off smiling, musing, 'Little do they know that they are better than that'.

Grendel is easily influenced by what he overhears (as is evident by his reaction to various extracts of overheard conversation and to the Shaper's songs). It is now clear that he is also becoming easily swayed by the imagery that the Sculptors devise.

Scene 36/37

In all the iterations of the *Beowulf* narrative, Grendel is depicted as an outsider, belonging neither to the human race nor to the animal kingdom. In this scene, as Grendel continues on his journey through the landscape, he happens upon a wild deer. The deer flees when it catches sight of Grendel, causing Grendel to grumble aloud, 'All the blind prejudice! All the unfairness of everything – I've never killed a deer in my life.' Then he playfully quips, 'After all cows have more meat, and they are easier to catch!'

FIGURE 2.13 The Priests offer a sacrifice to the Great Dragon God (*Grendel Grendel Grendel*, Alexander Stitt, 1981).

As Grendel continues to wander, he encounters the humans who have captured and killed the deer. He is mystified as to why these humans, instead of eating the animal, would rather use it to conduct some sort of improvident religious ceremony. Two of the humans, Dung and Wiglaf, also find this religious ceremony to be rather ridiculous (but for slightly different reasons).

> WIGLAF: I don't know, seems like we got more priests than heroes these days.
> DUNG: Aye, the great Boogy's attracting them like flies.
> WIGLAF: How do they expect a dead deer to do them any good? I remember when we used to do it properly – sacrifice a couple of live virgins. Religion is sick these days.

Through this humorous exchange, the men are also referencing the tensions that play out in the original *Beowulf* poem between the growing influence of Christianity and the waning authority of paganism. Of course, here, the animated film simultaneously takes aim at contemporary religious institutions.

Scene 38

This scene takes place at the King's castle where Queen Wealtheow emerges onto the balcony. She does not see Unferth standing there and mutters to herself, expressing her unhappiness with the King: 'Great Boogy, what a smelly old bore that … ' at which point she sees Unferth and quickly says, 'Oh, forgive me, my lord. I was unaware that you … ' Unferth swiftly replies with acrimony, 'I'm not your lord!' and walks away. It has become quite clear that the Queen is unhappy in her forced marriage, and that Unferth is equally unhappy, muttering, 'He'd have you with child and have me out. Fine way to treat a hero. He's your lord, not Unferth.' At which point, the Shaper, who had been lurking in the shadows, chimes in:

> SHAPER: Not, Unferth?
> UNFETH: Ah, it's nothing. I meant nothing.
> SHAPER: When shall I sing the song of Unferth, then?
> UNFERTH: Eh?
> SHAPER: Unferth, means nothing. Unferth, does nothing. If Unferth treads no steps, there is no song.
> UNFERTH: And what's that supposed to mean, then?
> SHAPER: Nothing. It also means nothing.

It has become clear that the Shaper is sowing what could be described as the first seeds of treason, and is exploiting Unferth's evident dissatisfaction with the King. Grendel, of course, also witnesses this brewing conflict.

Scene 39

That evening, the Shaper again sings loudly his venerating ballad to the King, particularly towards the King's nose (and again, providing another humorous reference to the Viking obsession with noses that was suggested in Michael Crichton's parallel novel, *Eaters of the Dead*).[22]

> Honour the nose!
> Honour the scar that it shows!
> Hail to the nose.
> Hail to the King, death to the foes of the King.
> Long live the King!

The King sits upon his throne, nose upheld prominently, basking in the glory of it all.

Scene 40

Dung rushes in announcing that the Great Boogy has returned. Unferth, followed by Dung and the King, then go outside to find that Grendel has captured Wiglaf and is holding him upside down (in a similar manner to the previously described depiction on the stone monuments, see Scene 35). The men are stunned. However, Unferth yearning to be a hero calls out, 'Foul monster! I am Unferth, son of Ecglaf. Are you right with your god? – or devil? – for I am about to send you to him. Prepare for … ' At which point Grendel, instead of fighting Unferth, casually bites off Wiglaf's head. By contrast, Gardner's novel describes this event in a much more graphic manner:

> As if casually, in plain sight of them all, I bit his head off, crunched through the helmet and skull with my teeth and, holding the jerking, blood-slippery body in two hands, sucked the blood that sprayed like a hot, thick geyser from his neck. It got all over me.[23]

Much of the novel's violence and graphic nature is toned down in the movie. For example, the actual action of biting off the head occurs off-screen (accompanied by a loud 'crunching' sound effect), and when Grendel holds aloft the headless soldier, just a few highly stylized drops of blood are visible. This graphic act is further alleviated in the film by the ensuing squabbles between the King and his men. Upon witnessing it, Unferth exclaims, 'Christmas', and the King, in a rather petulant tone, demands, 'Why didn't you stop him, Unferth?' In response, Unferth snaps, 'Why didn't *you* stop him?' Feeling that it is time to leave, Grendel then saunters off into the night, performing his trademark retreat towards the horizon (see Figure 4.12).

Scene 41/42

Back in his cave, among a forest of highly stylized and vaguely personified plant life, Grendel confides to his mother,

> Well, I couldn't resist it really. There they were, smugly damning all of their enemies to hell. I simply did what the Dragon said I should – said I *would*? – and gave them something to worry about. Mind you, I wish I'd taken his helmet off first. I think I've broken a tooth.

Grendel continues speaking; however, his tone shifts to that of a narrator. His descriptions are set against a montage of human activity:

> That was the start of this silly business – this war, they call it – that's been going on for a dozen years now. To stop them from becoming too smug, I'd drop in from time to time and eat one or two. Why? Oh, who knows why? I hated the greedy little king, now becoming dottier by the year, doting on two really beastly children that the Queen had borne him. I despised Unferth, the great hero, who clearly loved the Queen, hated the King, and continued to issue pompous challenges, mostly to me, without ever being willing to act. I teased him by ignoring him and killing others who raised their swords to me with far less fury. I envied the Shaper, his poetry, but despised his mystic meddling. It seems to me, that – as the dragon would have it – I was following some natural law by giving them a challenge far above their petty domestic squabbles. Shaking them up a bit during this 'one frail flicker-flash in the long dull fall to eternity!' End quote.

As Grendel speaks, also visible is an array of tombstones, each with an inscription (written in 'mock-runes') of a soldier that has been killed by Grendel. For example, 'DNG'S FRND WGLF 3RD +N CMMND KLLD BY GRNDL FRDY JLY 13TH YR 527'. By the conclusion of this lengthy monologue, Grendel appears to be rather unhappily resigned to playing the role of the monster. To demonstrate this, he storms up to the meadhall crying out, 'Here I am. Grendel! Wrecker of meadhalls, ruiner of Kings!' but then he adds with a heavy sigh, 'Poor Grendel'.

FIGURE 2.14 Grendel refuses to fight Unferth, and instead humiliates him with apples (*Grendel Grendel Grendel*, Alexander Stitt, 1981).

Scene 43/44

It is evening and Grendel returns to once again attack the meadhall. The King, as usual, cowers upon his throne. In a very condescending manner Unferth announces, 'Don't worry. I know what to do, even if you don't', and he heads off to confront the monster. Desperately hoping for a deadly fight with the monster, Unferth finds Grendel in the meadhall and quickly challenges him, calling out bravely, 'Great Boogy, prepare to die! No longer will you murder men as you please in this hall. This one, red hour makes your reputation or mine. Dread creature! Foul monster!' But Grendel has heard this all before, many times and has realized that the most effective way to torment Unferth is to refuse to fight him. Thus, he endeavours to humiliate him by gently throwing apples at him, particularly aiming for his nose. No matter how much Unferth attempts to battle Grendel, he is simply further pelted with apples (see Figure 2.14).

In Gardner's novel, this scene also becomes the moment in which Unferth realizes that Grendel understands and can speak the human language. This, in particular, has an unsettling effect on Unferth. Gardner describes this scene with a beautifully contrasting verbal exchange, during which Unferth yells out insults, and Grendel responds in calmly flowing, condescending, but erudite speech.

> 'Dread creature–' he said.
> 'But no doubt there are compensations,' I said. 'The pleasant feeling of vast superiority, the easy success with women.'
> 'Monster!' he howled.

'And the joy of self-knowledge, that's a great compensation! The easy and absolute certainty that whatever the danger, however terrible the odds, you'll stand firm, behave with the dignity of a hero, yea, even to the grave.'[24]

Here, Gardner effectively uses language to show the difference between the rather primitive human and the much more verbally evolved Grendel. By contrast, Stitt uses Grendel's pantomimed, animated actions to illustrate the chasm between the characters of Unferth and Grendel. For example, at the conclusion of the 'apple-fight', while Unferth fumes, Grendel bows deeply to Unferth in a very courteous, but mocking farewell.

Scene 45

Stitt uses this scene to further articulate the rift that is widening between Unferth and the King. The King enters the meadhall after Grendel has left and, finding Unferth prone to the ground and covered in apples, laughs hysterically. As Unferth rises and begins to stomp off, he slips on the scattered apples and humiliatingly falls again – this time in front of the Queen as well.

Scene 46

Unable to control his rage, Unferth pursues Grendel into the night following him all the way to his cavern – even swimming the long distance through the underwater passage full of fire snakes. This travelling sequence is accompanied by the strange unconventional sounds of a waterphone performance (see Chapter 4). Unferth, half-drowned, pulls himself onto the cave floor and, with a pitiful attempt at heroism, calls out in a weak and faltering voice (all the while, wheezing and coughing):

> Unferth has – cough – come. It will be sung. The Glorious Song of Unferth. The Shaper will sing that Unferth went down through the burning lake and gave his life in battle with the – cough – Great Boogy. Know you, that a hero stands here unafraid to die. For mark me well, one of us will die this night.

Grendel who had been listening to all of this with a bemused smile on his face arises and walks towards Unferth.

Scene 47

In this scene Unferth, overcome with shame, is carried upside down by Grendel, back towards the meadhall. Unferth complains aloud:

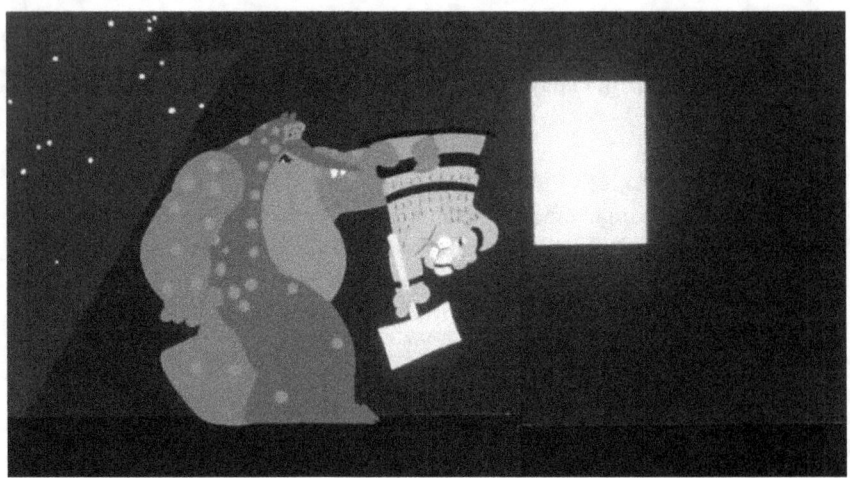

FIGURE 2.15 Grendel again refuses to do battle with Unferth, and instead carefully returns him to the meadhall (*Grendel Grendel Grendel*, Alexander Stitt, 1981).

> It's all very well for you then, making a fool of me in front of everyone. You don't understand that all a hero's got is his reputation. And where's mine now? Buried! Under all those bloody apples!

Once back at the hall, Grendel merely deposits the hapless Unferth in through the window, much to the astonishment of the King and his men (see Figure 2.15).

In the novel, Grendel's mother also plays a role in Unferth's humiliation. She is described as desperately wanting to kill and eat the human, but Grendel, wanting to deny Unferth a hero's death, continually blocks her efforts. Furthermore, when Grendel returns Unferth to the meadhall, Gardner describes how Grendel quickly kills two of the night watchmen so that he 'wouldn't be misunderstood'. This action serves to further humiliate Unferth, to make him 'crazy with shame that he alone is always spared, and furiously jealous of the dead'.[25]

Scene 48

In this scene, King Hrothgar stands at the seaside, bidding farewell to a messenger (who has been dispatched to plea for Beowulf's help). 'God watch you!' the King calls out to the vanishing ship. At this moment Unferth approaches, but does not see who the King is calling to, and assumes that the King is showing signs of senility. 'Talking to the sea, now then, are we?' he chides the King. Hrothgar, not wishing to reveal his plan to Unferth just yet, responds playfully,

'Why not? Some of us talk to the Great Boogy, and not very fruitfully at that. Ha! Ha! Ha! Shouldn't have mentioned fruit, should I?'

Not happy that the King has once again ridiculed him over the apple-fight incident, Unferth storms off. He unknowingly walks past the hidden Grendel and mutters aloud, 'Potty! He's gone completely potty. Potty old fool'. It is unclear if Grendel has witnessed the entirety of this verbal exchange, but he has certainly heard Unferth assert that *someone* is 'potty' or crazy. Accordingly, taking this snippet of conversation on board, Grendel wanders off along the seashore.

Scene 49

This scene features Grendel singing a song as he dances and traverses the seashore. The song fulfils a number of purposes, one of which is to declare that he, Grendel, is crazy – an assertion that has perhaps been encouraged by Unferth's recent declaration (from the previous scene) that *someone* was 'a potty old fool'. It is also a very playful retelling of several passages in Gardner's book in which Grendel's increasing isolation is described, as well as his gradual acceptance of his monstrous nature. A significant portion of the song lyrics which he sings in the animated film was derived from the novel's following passage:

> Balance is everything, riding out time like a helmless sheep-boat, keel to hellward, mast upreared to prick out heaven's eye. He he! (Sigh.) My enemies define themselves (as the dragon said) on me. As for myself, I could finish them off in a single night, pull down the great carved beams and crush them in the meadhall, along with their mice, their tankards and potatoes – yet I hold back. I am hardly blind to the absurdity. Form is function. What will we call the Hrothgar-Wrecker when Hrothgar has been wrecked? (Do a little dance, beast. Shrug it off. This looks like a nice place –oooh, my! – flat rock, moonlight, views of distances! Sing! [...] Grendel is crazy, O, O, O![26]

Additionally, this animated sequence also references another inspirational source, Lewis Carroll's, *Alice through the Looking Glass* (a referencing which is further explored in Chapter 3).

At the commencement of this scene, Grendel prefaces his soliloquy-song by playfully addressing an array of carved figures, which have been etched into the cliff side (see Figure 2.16). Speaking to the carvings, as if they were his attentive audience, he announces, 'Today dear friends, closest only friends. Today is my birthday. I'm so glad you could all come. We will have a party.' Subsequently, Grendel bursts into song. He dances, spins and traverses the rocky shore. As he sings, a group of oysters join in and sing several of the lines with him:

FIGURE 2.16 Grendel, standing near the Sculptor's rock carvings, sings his 'Soliloquy' (*Grendel Grendel Grendel*, Alexander Stitt, 1981).

And now I'm larger than anything else is.
When they made me, they spared no expense.
I'm bigger by half than a pig or a calf, and even
Compared to a bear I'm immense.
Poor me. Poor, poor me.

Too big for a comforting pat on the head.
Too big for a table. Too big for a bed.

Who'd wed me?

And I'm plainer than everyone else is.
A stye in your eye, dear beholder.
My nails are a mess, and my scales, I confess
Are cracking and yellowing as I grow older.
Poor me. Poor, poor me.

A shave and a haircut? Some eau de Cologne?
Why doll yourself up when you're dining alone?
Like poor me?

Here, Grendel picks up and samples one of the oysters – tossing it into his mouth. As he swallows it, his eyes momentarily swirl and flash red, before returning to normal.

 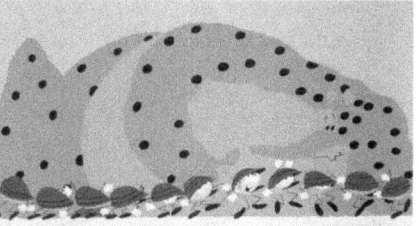

FIGURE 2.17 Grendel interacts with the oysters while singing his 'Soliloquy' (*Grendel Grendel Grendel*, Alexander Stitt, 1981).

And it's driving me crazy!
I'm losing my balance.
I'm just riding out time like a rudderless boat.
Silly old goat! Crazed as a loon.
Mad as a snake. Touched by the moon.

Grendel runs madly towards the camera, leaping into the air and landing in a prone position. A line of oysters, hurry towards him, singing:

Barmy old shatterpate. Silly old goose.

As Grendel sings his reply, the oysters pick him up, carry him along the beach, then run off, leaving him alone once again (see Figure 2.17b). Grendel continues:

Rattle your screws – there's enough of them loose.
Silly me.
I'm as silly as everyone else is.
As crazy to love as to hate.

Off screen the oysters sing their final refrain:

They hate you and hurt you,
why don't you just finish them off?

In reply, Grendel sings the final portions of the song:

Yet I wait.
Conserving the game.
After all, what will we call the king-wrecker
When the king has finally been wrecked?

Grendel's crazy, don't you know?
Grendel's crazy. Fe. Fi. Fo.

Scene 50

Grendel soon encounters another absurd religious ceremony – where yet another hapless deer is being sacrificed. This time the ceremony is clearly directed to the 'Dragon God'. This is a detail that ironically demonstrates the hypocrisy of the humans – they abhor the monster Grendel, but in turn worship the monster Dragon. It is also a detail that serves to further conflate Grendel's imagined dragon with the real world. Stitt describes the scene:

> A circle of giant stones surrounds one even larger stone, engraved with an image of the Great Dragon God. The carcass of a deer, intended to persuade the God to dispose of Grendel, lies at the base of the stone.[27]

The Shaper calls out to the heavens, 'Great Dragon Spirit. Defend our people and kill our enemy. The terrible world rim-walker, the foul night stalker, the Great Boogy!' As the ceremony concludes, it begins to snow and the priests quickly head for shelter.

Afterwards, in a rather humorous display of political pettiness, Dung pushes one of the priests out of the way saying, 'Back there, Number Twelve!' – this being a reference to an earlier scene in which the King had 'promoted' Dung to eleventh in command. Much to Dung's dismay at the time, there had only been three commanders – but the King, in his denigrating way, had assured him that there might one day be eleven or more men in their circle. Clearly the kingdom has expanded, Dung now enjoying seniority to at least one other person (Number Twelve) in Hrothgar's kingdom.

Scene 51/52

Now that the sacred religious site has been deserted, Grendel approaches. He speaks to the stone monument in a gently patronizing manner: 'Well, well. The Great Dragon God. Delighted to meet you. Permit me to introduce myself: Grendel; wretched, hideous monster, in person. The one and only, at your service!' He then bows in an exaggerated manner, and in doing so, accidently knocks down the stone monument. It crashes into the snow. The Shaper, having heard the crash of the falling stone monument, returns to the sacred circle to investigate. Despite his blindness, he ascertains that it was the holiest of the monuments that has fallen, and he places a profound religious significance to this event.

Grendel hovers closely behind the Shaper, watching and listening carefully to every word as the Shaper cries out, 'This is sacred ground! Oh! The Dragon God has fallen! The kingdom will follow! Oh, the king will die. *Now the king will die!*' Upon hearing the Shapers repeated proclamation that 'the king will die', Grendel, prone to narcissism and literal interpretations assumes it to mean that *he*, Grendel, will be involved in the King's death.

Scene 53

An early snowstorm ravages the kingdom. But rather than being concerned with the arrival of unseasonal weather, the King appears obsessed with what the ocean might bring. 'It's now all up to the sea. Trust the sea, Unferth', he says. This outward display of foolishness makes Unferth increasingly uncomfortable; he replies, 'Come on King, it's snowing. See? Snow. Come on back before you freeze to death'. But getting no response from the King, Unferth leaves, shaking his head, convinced that Hrothgar has gone insane, 'Why bother telling him. Barmy old bugger'.

Scene 54

Although the King appears ambivalent towards religion, as with many leaders, he uses it to advance his cause and to maintain power over his subjects. It does not matter to him whether it is the old pagan religion or the emerging Christian faith (or their equivalences). To underscore this sentiment, when he gets back to the privacy of his castle he remarks to Queen Wealtheow, 'Priests under your feet everywhere. Any road, you see one sacrifice, you've seen 'em all'.

Not far away on the castle balcony, Unferth's anger towards the King is brewing. He mutters to himself, 'that old goat who's losing his marbles. But one day perhaps' The Shaper, who had overheard, approaches him, and interrupting, says:

SHAPER: One day very soon!
UNFERTH: What's that? Is that treason your talking Shaper?
SHAPER: Treason, in some ears your words might ring of it.
UNFERTH: My words? Listen Shaper, a hero is loyal, devoted.
SHAPER: Portents. Listen, I speak of signs. Portents of the …
UNFERTH: Sounds like you're planning something.
SHAPER: No, no the signs.
UNFERTH: What signs?
SHAPER: The Great Boogy is a sign. The early snow is a sign. And there is something else, just now at the sacred circle, the Dragon-God, the King's

own sign, fell to the ground. The King will fall Unferth. And we will need a strong leader to protect us all.
UNFERTH: How will the king fall?
SHAPER: Who knows? Perhaps the Great Boogy. Or perhaps to appease the dragon God, we should …
UNFERTH: We!?
SHAPER: When the King is dead, Unferth, you will protect us.

However, the King has overheard Unferth and the Shaper's plotting, and he suddenly yells out, 'Hot water!' which signifies both an urgent order for his servant to bring him hot water for his bath, but also a warning to the plotters that they *are in hot water*. The King then looks at the camera (breaking the fourth wall) and says, 'They'll keep' with a knowing tap of his nose.

Scene 55

The King is called into the meadhall where he finds a distraught Shaper helplessly observing the King's spoilt young boys as they wreak havoc with his musical instruments. Instead of reprimanding his children, Hrothgar insists that the Shaper sing them all a song about the Great Boogy. Although the Shaper is deeply annoyed by the chaos that the King's children have caused, he is much too shrewd to let his irritation be observed by the King. Instead he performs a song which he knows will both confound and also further stoke tensions between the King and his chief political rivals.

Scene 56/57

This scene features an expertly constructed and cleverly animated song routine, sung by the Shaper and co-performed with his young assistant, the Shaper's Boy. It is one of the liveliest musical numbers in the film, also bursting with humour, irony and litotes (ironic understatements). The original *Beowulf* epic is also very rich in its use of irony, and scholars have discovered ninety-four well-defined examples of litotes in the original poem. John Gardner also uses a great deal of ironic understatements in *Grendel*, such as when Grendel refers to himself as a 'respected guest' at the meadhall (whereas he is more accurately described as a terrifying monster). Grendel also describes how he has 'knocked politely on the high oak door' (by contrast, Grendel did not knock politely, but in fact routinely smashed down the meadhall doors); most significantly, the final words that Grendel utters, 'Poor Grendel's had an accident', dramatically understate the fact that he was fatally wounded in a vicious battle.[28]

Alex Stitt, acutely aware of Gardner's frequent use of irony (well before other scholars had published these observations) also dedicated an entire musical number to the theme, which he titled 'We Know a Lovely Monster'. However, because irony is clearly lost on the simple-minded King, the interludes between each stanza are filled with queries and discussions (as outlined below). The Shaper begins his song:

We know a lovely monster
Who often comes to call.
We eagerly anticipate
His visits to our hall-o,
His visits to our hall.

At this point in the song, during a pause between stanzas, the King asks indignantly of his advisor, 'What's all this "lovely monster" talk?' The assistant replies, 'I expect that the reference is ironic, my Lord.' The King, still not comprehending and clearly confused, replies searchingly, 'Oh!?' However, the song continues:

An amicable monster,
Beloved by one and all.
We listen as his gentle tap
Demolishes the wall-o,
Demolishes the wall.

After further pondering what his advisor had said, the King implores, 'what's "ironic?"' Then, in a hyper-speed patter (lasting just two seconds) the assistant elucidates: 'Irony is the conveyance of meaning by words who's literal meaning is the opposite of what is actually meant.' After a slight pause, the King, although still none the wiser, replies with false confidence, 'Oh!' And with this, the song resumes again:

An entertaining monster,
An asset at a ball.
He rhumbas quite adroitly –
With a tendency to maul, though,
A tendency to maul.

The King, starting to become annoyed with this difficult to understand 'irony' nonsense, murmurs, 'He's too clever for his own good, that Shaper!' The song continues again:

A gentlemanly monster,
Perhaps a trifle tall.

> *Removal of a foot or two*
> *May benefit us all-o*
> *May benefit us all.*
>
> *An ambidextrous monster,*
> *Whose claws are none too small.*
> *Removal of an arm or two*
> *Might benefit us all-o,*
> *May benefit us all.*

Here, the Shaper is clearly foreshadowing how Grendel will die – through the ripping off of his arm. But at this moment the King is much more concerned with his own political monsters (and his own survival as King), rather than the threat of Grendel. Thus, he begins to plan and plot his political survival, murmuring to the rhyming pattern of the song lyrics while carefully eyeing Unferth, 'Removal of a friend or two might help, an' said all!' The Shaper continues:

> *We know a lovely monster*
> *Who often comes to call.*
> *Removal of his apples*

At this mention of the word 'apples', the audience erupts into laughter. It is both a double-entendre (a suggestion of the removal of his 'manhood') and, of course, a reference to Unferth's earlier humiliation that involved Grendel throwing apples at him instead of engaging in a battle. Unferth, reminded of his dishonour, glares about angrily.

> *Might benefit us all-o,*
> *Might benefit us all.*

At the conclusion of the song, the King's sons call out tauntingly to Unferth: 'Have an apple Unferth!' says the first boy. 'Yes, have an apple Unferth!' cries the second. At this public display of ridicule, Unferth erupts into a tremendous rage and attacks the two children with his axe – narrowly missing them. In turn, the King is outraged and reassures his children, 'Don't worry, daddy will fix him up!'

This song sequence was expertly animated by Frank Hellard, and includes some of the film's most innovative animated choreography (see Figure 2.18). The Shaper and the Boy move in ways that not only exemplify the literal, but also the ironically implied meanings. For example, when the lines, '*We listen as his gentle tap, demolishes the wall-o*', are sung, the Shaper gently taps the Boy,

FIGURE 2.18 The Shaper and Shaper's Boy perform 'We Know a Lovely Monster' (*Grendel Grendel Grendel*, Alexander Stitt, 1981).

who then falls to the ground. But because of the very stylized use of animation the Boy does not fall over in a realistic manner – instead his form is treated as if it were a solid block of wood, which teeters gently, before tipping over to the ground. But this action also exemplifies the ironic understatement that Grendel does not *gently tap* the wall, but, in fact, *smashes* through it, frequently killing people in the process. Such a complexity of performance not only adds layers of humour, but also underscores the confusion experienced by the small-minded King Hrothgar as he views the act.

Scene 58/59

Grendel, who was listening to the 'We Know a Friendly Monster' song outside the meadhall, no doubt also had some difficulty in understanding the subtleties of the Shaper's use of irony. He had obviously heard the song lyric, that Grendel was 'loved by one and all'; he is now convinced that, given his obsession with the Queen, that she also must be one of the people who love him.

Thus, Grendel sneaks off into the night and heads towards the royal palace. There he spies Queen Wealtheow standing, naked, in her window (see Figure 2.19a). Without much hesitation, Grendel enters the building. The Queen screams out in terror: Unferth quickly responds to the cries, and arrives to save her. Unferth enters the Queen's chambers and finds Grendel standing near her bed, where the Queen sits, naked and screaming (see Figure 2.19b). In her defence, Unferth raises his battle-ax, and takes a mighty swipe at Grendel. To accompany this action, an impressive animated camera move follows the swinging of the axe. But, instead of striking Grendel, the axe knocks over the candelabra, plunging the room into utter darkness. What follows is, literally, ten seconds of pure blackness. During the visual blackout, Unferth shouts, 'Let her alone, monster! She's done nothing. Your quarrel is with me and the King. Kill us now. You're going to do it one day: get it over with!' Grendel of course does not engage with Unferth, nor does he touch the Queen. Instead, he makes his exit by leaping from the upper story window.

In the original storyboards (version 1, see Chapter 4), when Unferth first challenges the monster, Grendel simply reaches out and gently 'shoves a hand into Unferth's face' tauntingly bumping his nose. Grendel then retreats out of the window, while 'Unferth gingerly tests his nose' to make sure that it is undamaged. This again would have been another comedic reference to the kingdom's over-the-top obsession with noses.

Grendel's uninvited entrance to the Queen's chambers had the potential to be a most monstrous incident; yet, Grendel does not actually harm anyone and quickly leaves the scene. In the novel, Gardner spells out in very graphic detail Grendel's original intentions, but then describes how Grendel suddenly changes his mind.

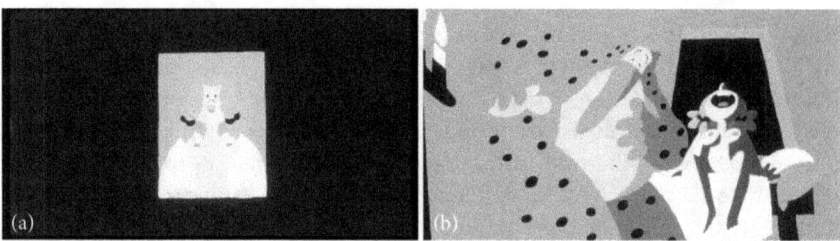

FIGURE 2.19 Queen Wealtheow in the nude (a) as she appears at her window and (b) in her chambers (*Grendel Grendel Grendel*, Alexander Stitt, 1981).

I would kill her and teach them reality. […] Nothing alive or dead could change my mind! I changed my mind. It would be meaningless, killing her. As meaningless as letting her live. […] I let go her feet. The people stared, unbelieving. I had wrecked another theory.[29]

Although in the novel, Grendel had every intention of doing harm, he swiftly realizes that there is greater advantage in the disrupting of the human's perception of his monstrous nature, than in actually being monstrous. Stitt, on the other hand, makes Grendel's intentions much more ambiguous – fuelled by a misunderstanding of the Shaper's ironic song, and a misreading of what he thought was the Queen's welcoming stance at her window. He also uses this scene as yet another opportunity to further humiliate Unferth through Grendel's refusal to engage in battle.

Scene 60

As Grendel leaps from Queen Wealtheow's window, he falls through an increasingly abstract space comprising colourful geometric shapes (reminiscent of windows), which slide upwards through the black void. He lands for a *second* time in the Dragon's lair (in the novel, Grendel visits the dragon just once). Here again, as the Dragon and Grendel speak, Frank Hellard's expert animation talents are on display – particularly in his exploitation of animation's capacity for micro-second visual allusions and referencing.

> DRAGON: [awakens] What are you doing here?
> GRENDEL: What do you mean what am I doing here, I thought you knew everything.
> DRAGON: Shh! [the Dragon instantly transforms into a small red circle, then resumes his dragon form, now sitting astutely on a chair.] Yes, well of course I do, but not when I'm asleep which I was.
> GRENDEL: Well?
> DRAGON: Well what?
> GRENDEL: What am I doing here?
> DRAGON: All pigs eat cheese. The king is a pig. Do pigs eat kings? Or something … [He impatiently taps his fingers, then quickly stands up]. Games, my boy, games, games, games. No total vision, no total system. Merely vague schemes with a vague fibre-resemblance [Dragon momentarily transforms into a red block, and then back again]
> GRENDEL: Oh, is that why I'm here?
> DRAGON: Must have something to do with it, why do you think you are here?
> GRENDEL: I want to ask you a question.
> DRAGON: Exactly, I know you do!

FIGURE 2.20 The Dragon impersonates Humphrey Bogart as he speaks with Grendel (*Grendel Grendel Grendel*, Alexander Stitt, 1981).

At this point, the Dragon quickly transforms into a cigarette-smoking, Humphrey Bogart-inspired character, Rick Blaine (specifically, Humphrey Bogart performing the detective in the movie, *Casablanca* [Michael Curtiz, 1942]), and says, 'Ok, Sweetheart, go ahead and ask' (see Figure 2.20). After numerous other transformations, the Dragon makes meta-reference to the greater *Beowulf* narrative:

> DRAGON: Ah yes, inevitable, the whole thing. Did you know Grendel that my death is inevitable? A certain man will kill me absurdly. A terrible pity. Loss of a remarkable form of life. Conservationists will howl.

This is, of course a reference to the original poem, in which Beowulf kills the Dragon (but also is fatally wounded in the process).

The Dragon concludes the scene with a riddle, 'When the White Wolf flies, with the help of Grendel's good right arm, a new lord will rule.' This riddle cryptically prophesies not only the arrival of the warrior Beowulf, but also of how Grendel will eventually die – by having his arm ripped from its socket. The Dragon laughs heartily at this inside joke: 'That's a good one. Grendel's good right arm. Heh!' At which point the Dragon levitates upwards and out of the scene.

Scene 61

Grendel finds himself alone again in the landscape by the sea. He complains:

> Riddles. Stupid old goat. All you want is a simple answer to a simple question and all you get is abuse and riddles. When the white wolf flies indeed. Well, I think dragons are very much over-rated.

Just then, Beowulf's ship, bearing a large sail with a depiction of a white wolf, comes into view. However, Grendel, walking away, narrowly misses seeing this important clue which would help to provide an answer to the Dragon's confusing riddle. Beowulf has arrived.

Scene 62

The Shaper is in bed, unwell and evidently dying. An attendant observes, 'I've seen him looking better'. To this, the King quips, 'You won't be seeing him looking any worse', as he surreptitiously hides a bottle of poison in his cloak (see Figure 2.21). The King then ominously blows out the candle, adding, 'Must have been something he ate.' Clearly, the King has murdered the Shaper. In

FIGURE 2.21 King Hrothgar poisons the Shaper (*Grendel Grendel Grendel*, Alexander Stitt, 1981).

Gardner's novel, rather than the Shaper being poisoned by the King, he merely dies of old age and is mourned by a woman who had become secretly involved with him. However, Stitt appeared interested in further underscoring how these humans, while participating in their insidious political rivalries, would happily engage in all sorts of monstrous acts.

Scene 63

This scene marks the arrival of Beowulf to Hrothgar's kingdom. In the original epic, Beowulf is not only the main protagonist and hero, but is also the poem's namesake. However, in Gardner's novel, by waiting to bring Beowulf in until the final two chapters, Gardner denies him any opportunity to establish himself as a hero. In fact, Beowulf is not even mentioned by name in the novel. By contrast, Stitt does allow Beowulf a greater presence in the movie (and he is mentioned by name), but he also makes Beowulf into an ungracious and very condescending character.

The scene opens with Dung announcing to the King that a foreign ship with a white wolf on its sail has just arrived on their shores. 'Good', replies the King, 'He's come'. Almost immediately, King Hrothgar begins barking orders:

> KING: Get the place organised! We're about to have company.
> DUNG: What company?
> KING: The son of Edgetho, grandson of Hrethel, great-grandson of Swerting – Beowulf, the king of the Geats, that's who!
> DUNG: Oh, it's double-dutch to me!

Dungs 'double-dutch' comment is intended as a humorous reference (albeit a slightly geographically incorrect one) to Beowulf's heritage. Although Beowulf is not from 'Dutch' speaking Holland, he is from nearby Geatland (part of modern-day Denmark). Significantly, this is also the first time that Beowulf is mentioned by name in the movie.

Scene 64

The doors to the meadhall open through the use of a distinctive cinematic wipe effect, revealing Beowulf and his warriors (see Chapter 5 and Figure 5.8c). These are a tough, yet scruffy looking lot. The King and Beowulf converse:

> KING: Beowulf! Beowulf, my boy, it was good of you to come.
> BEOWULF: [patronisingly] Yes, yes, it was.
> KING: [taken aback] Uh. I'm King Hrothgar. I knew your father.

BEOWULF: Hrothgar, yes. I believe he mentioned you.
KING: Won't you and your, uh, warriors come into our humble hall.
BEOWULF: Yes, oh, yes, indeed we will. But, it's not all that humble, surely.
KING: Well, no, I.
BEOWULF: Nothing like the splendour of my own, that is to be sure, but comfortable wouldn't you say?

Beowulf speaks with a posh, upper-class British accent. Such well-articulated speech mirrors the original Beowulf character, who was also surprisingly well spoken. Scholars of the original poem have suggested that it was largely due to Beowulf's eloquent use of language that he was initially allowed entry into Hrothgar's kingdom.[30] Stitt, by imbuing his Beowulf character with a posh Londoner accent, humorously elevates him above most of the other characters in the film (who speak in working-class or north England accents).

As Beowulf enters into the Kings meadhall, he remarks with condescending civility, 'Ah! Charming. Yes, indeed, charmingly provincial' (see Figure 2.22). Hrothgar, who is following behind, looks rather offended by these comments. Unabashed, Beowulf continues, speaking to the King, as one might to a servant, 'Ah! My dear old fellow. Some food would be appreciated. Please tell the chef not to go to any trouble. Something simple for me and some raw meat for my *noble* companions.' (By choosing to refer to his ragtag team of warriors as *noble*, Beowulf further insults the King by undermining his nobility.) Beowulf then introduces his warriors: 'May I present Gruf, Grim, Shaggy Arthur, Pigfat, Shabby, Blood-Axe, Coal-Eater, Bog the Short, Torg and, of course, Troll.' Conspicuously, the one called Troll is quite monstrous in appearance – and is

FIGURE 2.22 An arrogant Beowulf arrives at Hrothgar's meadhall (*Grendel Grendel Grendel*, Alexander Stitt, 1981).

FIGURE 2.23 Beowulf, with Troll, dines at the meadhall (*Grendel Grendel Grendel*, Alexander Stitt, 1981).

highly reminiscent of Grendel's character design (albeit smaller, and coloured purple instead of green)[31] (see Figure 2.23).

Unferth is very unsettled by the arrival of Beowulf and his men, and he approaches the King, demanding:

UNFERTH: What have you done? Who is that?
KING: That's Beowulf the famous hero, I knew his father.
UNFERTH: What's he want?
KING: I asked him to come here to kill the Great Boogy.
UNFERTH: You barmy old coot! You can see he's a lunatic.
KING: He's famous!
UNFERTH: I can look after Great Boogy. We don't need outsiders poking their noses-
KING: You've been looking after the Great Boogy a bit too much, and visa versa!
UNFERTH: Get rid of him!
KING: I'm king here Unferth, not you!

Beowulf quickly breaks into their argument to suggest that they bring in some music. This proves to be a very awkward request since the King has just killed the Shaper. Unferth then turns angrily to Beowulf:

UNFERTH: And you, you best be off before our monster shows up! He'll have you for afternoon tea.

BEOWULF: Very amusing!
UNFERTH: He's twelve foot high and green and hairy. Horrible claws and fangs! He bites heads off.
BEOWULF: My dear cousin. Monsters are my business. Not to put too fine a point on it, big horrible hairy ones are just my cup of tea.

In this scene, Stitt draws attention to the acute tension between Unferth and Beowulf. However, these feelings are further developed both in Gardner's novel and in the original epic, in which Beowulf seizes the opportunity to rebuke and humiliate Unferth by drawing attention to the fact that he had killed his own brother. By doing so, he equates Unferth with the accursed lineage of Cain (and by extension, Grendel). Although Stitt omits this narrative element in this particular scene, he does make an ongoing point to illustrate the hypocrisy of arbitrarily dividing people between the descendants of Cain and those of Abel. Despite all their pious talk, these humans appear quite prone to murdering each other, brothers and all.

After their heated exchange, Beowulf turns his attention to his drink and proceeds to insult (very subtly) the King's prized mead; then his food; and finally, the King himself.

BEOWULF: Speaking of which – Mead of sorts, is it? Extraordinary. Troll!
TROLL: Urg, Uh? Uh?
BEOWULF: Troll, fetch us a cask of the '93, dear boy.

FIGURE 2.24 The pious priests are deeply insulted by Beowulf's 'heresy'; note the strategic placement of Beowulf's sword in the foreground, mockingly suggesting the Christian cross (*Grendel Grendel Grendel*, Alexander Stitt, 1981).

>   TROLL: Urg, ah!
>   BEOWULF: Ah, luncheon. Let us all sit down and enjoy a charming rustic meal. Ah, Robgar …
>   KING: Hrothgar!
>   BEOWULF: Yes, of course, you sit here, […] and I shall sit here, by the door, to protect you all from monsters.

With that, Beowulf thrusts his sword violently into the table top which, because of its placement, forms a very dramatic representation of the Christian cross. With this religious symbol, prominently on display, Beowulf proceeds to insult all of the priests at the table (see Figure 2.24).

>   PRIEST: God, protects us from monsters!
>   BEOWULF: Ah, then it seems that he must be falling down on the job, eh? Not to worry, I'm here now to help him out.
>   PRIESTS: Heresy!
>   BEOWULF: I always say, never discuss religion or politics over dinner. Bad for the digestion.
>   PRIEST: If the monster claims lives, it's God's will. You speak heresy!
>   BEOWULF: Heresy is determined by which end of the sword you're at. Now, don't be boring or I might have to sort a few of you out. Beowulf's good at that, sorting out the troublemakers.

Just as the conversation is beginning to get out of hand, Queen Wealtheow enters the meadhall conveying her calming presence (something that her character is well known for in virtually all iterations of the *Beowulf* narrative). Beowulf is instantly rapt by her beauty:

>   BEOWULF: Hello, who have we here?
>   KING: This is me better half – the first lady of the realm.
>   BEOWULF: Well, well, what a lucky fellow you are to be sure, Hobgar
>   KING: Hrothgar.
>   BEOWULF: What is your name dear heart?
>   QUEEN: I'm called Wealtheow. It means servant of common good.
>   BEOWULF: I'd say uncommonly good. The old boy really doesn't deserve you, you know.

Beowulf's lascivious comments towards the Queen are punctuated by a lustful stare. However, this look is achieved, merely through a very subtle animated glint in his, nearly non-existent eyes. This exceptional bit of limited animation effectively underscores Beowulf's true character.

In Gardner's novel, the arrival of Beowulf is primarily presented through Grendel's increasingly anxious perspective. Grendel's attention fixates on this unsettling and frightening new stranger. This is also the first time in the novel in which Grendel begins to conflate the Dragon and Beowulf together. In this way, Grendel observes, 'He had a strange face that, little by little, grew unsettling to me: it was a face, or so it seemed for an instant, from a dream I had almost forgotten.'[32] By referring to his dream, Gardner is actually pointing to Grendel's recent dream-encounter with the Dragon. Like the Dragon, this stranger *appears* to be able to shape-shift right before Grendel's eyes:

> And again, I found something peculiar happening to my mind. His mouth did not seem to move with his words, and the harder I stared at his gleaming shoulders, the more uncertain I was of their shape.[33]

As he continues to stare, Grendel finds it increasingly difficult to understand even the basic form of Beowulf, imagining that from his shoulders there might, at any moment, emerge dragon wings. With a great deal of subtlety, Stitt also hints at Gardner's literary conflation of Beowulf and the Dragon, by designing his Beowulf with a bright red cape that is attached by exaggerated shoulder spikes (which can be interpreted as the budding wings of a dragon).

Scene 65

Grendel is seated in his cave, contemplating a stone carving of the Dragon. He speaks alternately to the Dragon-carving and to his (off-screen) mother. In a direct follow on from the previous scene, in which Beowulf had declared to Wealtheow, 'The old boy really doesn't deserve you, you know', Grendel mimics:

> He doesn't deserve her, you know, Mum. And she has such a desperate existence in that place with that foolish old man. Perhaps that's why the dragon says I will kill him, one day. [Then speaking directly to the stone carving of the dragon] You did say I'd kill him, didn't you? That's what it seems like you said. What's a flying white wolf? The early snow? It's snowing out there already, Mum. Perhaps I can bring her winter to an end. Kill the king. Bring her home. Here. A new lord will rule. That's what you said, dragon. Would she be better off with me as her new lord? She couldn't be worse off, anyway. Do you fancy a daughter-in-law, mother? She's inclined to scream a lot.

Grendel is quite confused, both by the Dragon's prophecy and by his own observations of human events. He assumes that the Dragon has advised him, through his riddle, that he is destined to become the new ruler of the land. He is however, unaware of Beowulf's pending arrival, and he assumes that it is he who will become king and make the beautiful Wealtheow his Queen.

Scene 66

With the Shaper dead, the Shaper's Boy is compelled to carry on in the role of the kingdom's official singer. On that final evening, just prior to Grendel's demise, he sings the lullaby-styled song, 'The Moon Is Rising'. It serves as a highly restrained prelude to the imminent battle between Beowulf and Grendel.

This is the first time that the Shaper's Boy is heard to speak in the film; previously it was assumed that he was the Shaper's *mute* assistant. The *female* voice actor who performs this song is the same singer who performs the opening credit's theme song. This was a rather odd choice, as the theme song is intended to be from the perspective of Grendel's Mum. In parallel with the opening song, this final song is also performed as a gentle lullaby, and is somewhat incongruous with the accompanying scenes of murder and escalating tensions between Beowulf and Grendel. The Shaper's Boy sings:

The moon is rising on his final evening in the
world he shares with you and me.
The monster, the Great Boogy, doesn't know that
he is walking to eternity.
For Beowulf has told us so, and Beowulf must surely know.

The promise of our visitor is we will no more
live in dread as formerly.
The many evenings we have waited for his hated
tread are now no more to be.
For Beowulf has laid his plan, and Beowulf is
more than man.

Grendel at this point is seen walking across the landscape, and he interjects his own lines into the song. He becomes illuminated by a staged-spotlight and, as he sings, the letters of 'G-R-E-N-D-E-L' and 'N-E-M-E-S-I-S' are spelled out in designed font above him (see Figure 3.6a).

Who's the beast who looks so swell?
G-R-E-N-D-E-L.
What's his purpose, can't you guess?
N-E-M-E-S-I-S.

These are the same lines that a very young Grendel had first attempted to sing as he playfully explored the new world outside his cave (see Scene 5). The reprisal of this song, now sung with astute professionalism, demonstrates that Grendel has fully evolved and is now perfectly happy to have become 'man's anti-man' as signified by his gleeful articulation of the word 'N-E-M-E-S-I-S'. After this interjection, the Shaper's Boy continues his song:

For Beowulf is hard as nails, and, as we know,
he never fails.
The moon is shining brightly on the white
snow-covered mountains that surround our hall.
They soon will show the blood-red traces of his
final paces as he leaves us all.

For Beowulf would have it so, and so it must be,
exactly, deadly so.
And so it must be, so it will be, Q.E.D., exactly, deadly so.

Unferth sits brooding while he listens to the Shaper's Boy. He is 'put out by this glorifying of the bumptious Beowulf'[34] and, unable to stand it anymore, he unobtrusively exits the hall. But the King, noticing that he has left, quietly instructs Beowulf to pursue him. In the darkness of the night, Beowulf moves silently towards Unferth and drives his sword into his back, leaving his lifeless body in a bloody heap.

Scene 67

Grendel walks up to the meadhall; he finds the lifeless body of Unferth (see Figure 2.25a). He is shocked and horrified as he picks up the corpse. His revulsion at what he sees is underscored by a dramatic animated camera move. At first Grendel is tempted to just walk away, but then he takes another hard look at the bright red blood which covers his hands (see Figure 2.25b). This is what ultimately pushes him over the edge; the evidence is too strong against the humans, and it convinces him that he must accept (at least to some degree), his appointed role of 'king-wrecker'.

For the next two minutes of the film there is absolutely no dialogue, just tense music and sound effects, as Grendel approaches the meadhall and engages in battle with Beowulf. This use of cinematic pantomime differs greatly from the novel, which becomes exceedingly dialogue heavy as Beowulf and Grendel engage, not only in a physical battle, but also in a battle of words.

Grendel storms up to the meadhall; the music rises into a dramatic crescendo as Grendel smashes down the door. This time, however, there is a new and terrifying group of warriors waiting for him. He is ambushed by a horrific foe, stronger than any other that he has encountered. Beowulf wraps himself in a vice-like grip around Grendel's arm. Stitt describes the scene in his book:

FIGURE 2.25 (a) Grendel discovers the body of Unferth, who has just been murdered by Beowulf at the behest of the King; (b) he then contemplates the bloody stain left on his hands (*Grendel Grendel Grendel*, Alexander Stitt, 1981).

Grendel flaps, roars, rolls and rages across the space of the hall, but cannot dislodge the irritating passenger. Panic sweeps through him; panic of a kind he hasn't experienced since he landed in a mess in that stupid tree a dozen years or more ago, when he encountered the King and these other humans for the first time. He catapults himself to the nearest window, eager to be out of their awful hall.[35]

At one point the 'half-human' Troll leaps into the battle, sinking his teeth into Grendel's leg, ultimately helping Beowulf to win. (This is paralleled in the

FIGURE 2.26 Beowulf rips off Grendel's arm (*Grendel Grendel Grendel*, Alexander Stitt, 1981).

original poem, where one of Beowulf's men also comes to his aid, helping to distract Grendel as he is dealt a fatal blow.)

Gardner goes to great lengths to conflate the Dragon together with Beowulf during this final scene, by describing Beowulf with increasingly dragon-like terminology:

> His hand still closed like a dragon's jaws on mine. Nowhere on middle-earth, I realize, have I encountered a grip like his. My whole arm's on fire, incredible, searing pain – it's as if his crushing fingers are charged like fangs with poison.[36] [...] The meadhall is alive, great cavernous belly, gold-adorned, bloodstained, howling back at me, lit by the flickering fire in the stranger's eyes. He has wings. Is it possible? And yet it's true: out of his shoulders come terrible fiery wings. I jerk my head, trying to drive out illusion.[37] [...] He laughs and lets out fire.[38]

In the novel, it is very much a psychological battle in which Grendel engages. Beowulf taunts him and whispers very unsettling, dragon-like things in his ears. This evocation of a Dragon distracts and hampers Grendel, and because the Dragon is ultimately a figment of Grendel's imagination, it is essentially Grendel who assists in defeating himself. In Stitt's film, the conflation of the dragon and Beowulf is much more discreet and is limited, visually, to the dragon-like red cape that Beowulf wears, yet sonically, the same voice actor, Arthur Dignam, performs the role of both characters.

The final defeat of Grendel occurs when Beowulf manages to rip off Grendel's arm at the shoulder, leaving him slowly to die (see Figure 2.26). Stitt incorporates clever staging to surprisingly and dramatically portray Grendel's demise – initially it appears that Grendel has somehow managed to escape, but then it is revealed that he has been dealt a deadly blow. This surprising series of events is described by Stitt:

> Grendel struggles through the window frame, gets himself mostly outside, hanging perilously in space, supported by his good right arm which is

still inside the window, pinned firmly inside by the desperate Beowulf. Then Grendel is free, falling through space, landing heavily on the snowy ground below. He climbs down the hillside before he falls again, aware that something is painfully, dreadfully wrong. Inside the hall, a grinning Beowulf holds high a grisly trophy of his victory: Grendel's arm, torn away like a lizard's tail from the fleeing monster. Hrothgar looks on, silently debating this outcome, and trying to assess his likely future status now that all overt threats have been removed. And outside in the snow, Grendel rests on his back.[39]

Initially, when Grendel is shown resting on the hillside outside the meadhall, one probably assumes that he has managed to escape from Beowulf's clutches and is relatively unscathed. Thus, it is quite a shock when the scene cuts back to show Beowulf, gloating and holding aloft Grendel's arm, dripping with blood. It constitutes a very effective sequence of visual storytelling. Additionally, as Beowulf continues triumphantly to clutch Grendel's disembodied arm, its clenched hand opens up releasing an apple, which rolls across the floor, stopping at the King's feet (see Figure 2.27). This decidedly understated action suggests that perhaps Grendel had no real intention of killing the King, and that he merely intended to throw an apple at his royal nose – thus humiliating him in the same manner that he had done to Unferth in an earlier sequence (see Scene 43). It is a narrative element that is exclusive to the film, and one that further expresses Grendel's non-monstrous inclination.

FIGURE 2.27 The King stares at an apple that has just fallen from Grendel's dismembered arm (being held aloft by Beowulf on left) – implying that Grendel had merely intended to pelt the King with apples (*Grendel Grendel Grendel*, Alexander Stitt, 1981).

Scene 68

A dying, one-armed, Grendel lies upon a moonlit hillside, crying mournfully (see Figure 2.28).

> Oh, What a silly accident. Mamma! Oh, if I hadn't just walked in like that. Who was that? Lucky for him I didn't know he was there. Unlucky for me, however. Well I wouldn't have just walked in like that, would I? Oh, Mamma! I'm dying, mama.

Dramatically, with his last monstrous breath, Grendel utters, 'Poor Grendel's had an accident'. Then, the music builds in a reprisal of the opening theme song:

> *Grendel, Grendel, Grendel.*
> *Your mother loves you, Grendel.*
> *Lying there, all twelve feet four*
> *Or more of you,*
> *Mother loves every hair, scale, tooth, nail,*
> *Fang and claw of you.*

Finally, the camera pans upwards showing the endless starlit sky and the film ends. Stitt intended this ending to be a highly emotional moment, hoping that the audience would 'shed a tear at the end'.[40] It is indeed to be an emotional conclusion; however, there is also an unintended abruptness to the film.

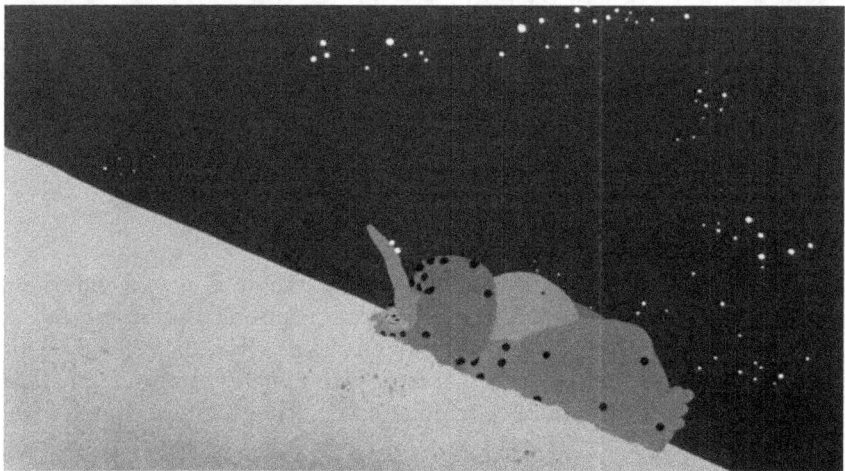

FIGURE 2.28 Grendel dies alone under the stars (*Grendel Grendel Grendel*, Alexander Stitt, 1981).

FIGURE 2.29 Frame grabs from the closing credits sequence (*Grendel Grendel Grendel*, Alexander Stitt, 1981).

Although Grendel's death was inevitable, it is very unconventional for the main character to die in the final seconds of an animated feature film.

Gardner's ending to the novel is suggestively, but only slightly different to the film. In the novel, rather than dying alone, Grendel finds himself surrounded by forest creatures, which are none to sorry to see him go. But more significantly, Grendel speaks four additional words (which the film omits). After lamenting, 'Poor Grendel's had an accident', he cries out, '*So may you all*'. Those four extra words profoundly change his sorrowful lament into a piercing curse. On one hand, this curse can be read as being directed towards the animals that surround him; however, it can also be interpreted as a curse that is directed at the reader. In placing this curse (albeit a playful one) upon the reader, Gardner cleverly extends the narrative beyond the final page. The reader cannot help but ponder just what it is that Grendel meant, and consider further the distinction (if any) between humans and monsters. The first part of the sentence, 'Poor Grendel's had an accident', is a dark, slightly droll, ironic understatement. But the added, 'So may you all', is a very unsettling indictment of human society that persists, and therefore goes a long way in compensating for the fact that the protagonist of the novel has just been killed off. Because the film does not include this final curse, the ending feels somewhat truncated.

End credits

Because Stitt opted to cut short Gardner's slightly more elongated ending, he obliged Grendel to die a more emphatic death. However, Stitt also chose to bring Grendel back (along with virtually every other character in the film) for one final sequence – an energetic dance routine which accompanies the final credit sequence (see Figure 2.29). In doing so, he delivers a more conventional cinematic ending of sorts. He also implies a meta-reference to the medium by reminding the viewer that this is, in fact, a cartoon – and cartoon characters can always bounce back (in Loony Tunes fashion) brimming with endless animated life.

Notes

1. Alexander Stitt, *Grendel Grendel Grendel – the Book of the Animated Feature Film* (Melbourne: Penguin Australia, 1981).
2. Lee Tulloch, 'Lee Tulloch Talks to Grendel and Friend, Grrumph!' in *Vogue Australia*, January 1981, p. 65.
3. Ibid.
4. Ibid.
5. J.R.R. Tolkien. 'The Monsters and the Critics', in *The Monsters and the Critics and Other Essays* (London: HarperCollins, 2006), p. 5.
6. This introduction sequence has been omitted from the recent (2013) digitally restored DVD and online streaming versions.
7. Bruce Smeaton, Interview by Dan Torre and Lienors Torre (November 2019).
8. John Gardner, *Grendel* (New York: Alfred A. Knopf, 1971), p. 6.
9. Seamus Heaney, *Beowulf* (London: Faber and Faber, 1999), lines 87–98.
10. Gardner, *Grendel*, p. 21.
11. Ibid., p. 23.
12. Ibid., p. 28.
13. Michael Crichton, *Eaters of the Dead – The Manuscript of Ibn Fadlan, Relating His Experiences with the Northmen in A.D. 922* (New York: Random House, 1993), p. 130.
14. Alexander Stitt, *A Film Study Guide – Grendel Grendel Grendel*, Melbourne: Al et al, 1981.
15. Gardner, *Grendel*, p. 41.
16. Terry-Thomas, the popular British actor (who displayed a signature gap-tooth smile) and star of such films as, *Those Magnificent Men in Their Flying Machines* (Ken Annakin, 1965), also provided the voice of Sir Hiss in Walt Disney's animated feature film, *Robin Hood* (Wolfgang Reitherman, 1973).
17. Gardner, *Grendel*, p. 52.
18. Kenneth L. Zeeman, 'Grappling with Grendel or What We Did When the Censors Came', *English Journal;* February 1997; 86, 2, p. 46
19. Gardner, *Grendel*, p. 55.
20. Ibid., p. 56.
21. Stitt, *Grendel Grendel Grendel – The Book*.
22. Crichton, *Eaters of the Dead*, p. 130.
23. Gardner, *Grendel*, p. 79.
24. Ibid., p. 85.
25. Ibid., p. 90.
26. Ibid., p. 92.
27. Stitt, *Grendel Grendel Grendel – The Book*.
28. Marie Nelson, 'John Gardner's Grendel: A Story Retold and Transformed in the Process', *Journal of the Fantastic in the Arts;* 2007, Vol. 18 Issue 3, p. 350.
29. Gardner, *Grendel*, p. 110.
30. John M. Hill, 'Beowulf and the Danish Succession: Gift Giving as an Occasion for Complex Gesture', *Medievalia et Humanistica* 11 (1982), pp. 177–97.
31. Thanks to Thomas Torre for first making this observation.
32. Gardner, *Grendel*, p. 154.

33 Ibid., p. 164.
34 Stitt, *Grendel Grendel Grendel – The Book*.
35 Ibid.
36 Gardner, *Grendel*, p. 168.
37 Ibid., p. 169.
38 Ibid., p. 171.
39 Stitt, *Grendel Grendel Grendel – The Book*.
40 Tulloch, 'Grrumph!', p. 65.

Chapter 3

THEMES OF *GRENDEL GRENDEL GRENDEL*

Building upon previous sections, this chapter further investigates several themes that permeate *Grendel Grendel Grendel*. These include the importance and fundamental role of monsters, the curse of Cain, the character of the Dragon (and the Dragon God), the recurring allusions to Lewis Carroll's *Alice in Wonderland*, and the complimentary roles of the Shaper and of the Sculptor. Some of these subjects are exemplified both in Gardner's novel and in the film, while others (such as the Sculptor, the Dragon God and references to *Alice in Wonderland*) are uniquely represented in Stitt's animated feature.

A monstrous introduction

The original *Beowulf* narrative might appear inconsequential without the monstrous characters of Grendel, Grendel's mother and the Dragon. Unquestionably, it is the *monsters,* which generate much of the original poem's narrative impetus; they support Beowulf's heroic status, and ultimately define his raison d'être. Gardner notably amplifies the significance of these monsters, by repositioning Grendel as the protagonist of his novel. Stitt in turn further advances the monsters' centrality by making Grendel not only the central character, but also making him into a very *likeable* character.

Grendel Grendel Grendel opens with producer Phillip Adams delivering a prefatorial address in which he seeks to identify the centrality of monsters in human cultural history.[1] This brief introduction describes how monsters originated, how they have evolved over the centuries, how they have served to augment human societies and, specifically, how Grendel is situated within this trajectory. Adams begins by speculating on the fundamental role of monsters:

> From the minotaur to the bogeyman; from the dragons of legend to the Creature from the Black Lagoon, monsters have haunted the human imagination, going bump in our night. It's almost as though we needed monsters, those metaphors for death, as aphrodisiacs for life; to unite us in our common struggle against the implacable fates.

Next, Adams provides a brief genealogy of monsters, suggesting how they might have evolved over the centuries:

It's strange to see how monsters change with the fashions. Carl Sagan speculates that the mythic dragon, common to so many cultures, may be a race-memory of the giant reptiles, the dinosaurs, Tyrannosaurus rex. Certainly, the monsters in Japan's post-war movies – the great Godzillas who are awakened from ancient slumbers by nuclear tests, whereupon they trample all over Tokyo – are clearly echoes of the nightmares of Hiroshima and Nagasaki. In Medieval times, the Holy Mother Church confronted a timid peasantry with the apparition of the Devil, while the skeleton with the scythe and hour-glass reminded man how human life was harvested in reoccurring plagues. And what better image of a parasitic aristocracy, than the blood-sucking Count Dracula?

Adams next considers how the evolutionary trajectory of monsters has been furthered by twentieth-century technology, changes in geopolitics and the proliferation of global warfare:

In modern times, as we begin to wonder just where medicine and science might be taking us, we saw the birth of Dr Frankenstein's monster, of Jekyll and Hyde. Technological anxieties gave us the relentless robot, while cold war fears filled our skies with flying saucers and intergalactic ghastlies that, impervious to our weapons, could only be destroyed by a combination of prayer, and the common cold.

Following this he introduces the viewer specifically to Grendel, the central monster of the animated feature. However, at this point, he also inadvertently gives away the ending of the film by confirming that Beowulf will ultimately triumph over Grendel by 'cutting off the monster's arm' (although anyone familiar with the *Beowulf* story would have been privy to this). Adams continues:

Now meet the most venerable monster in the English language, from the most enduring Anglo-Saxon myth. Grendel, that featured player in our nightmare since the fifth century. Grendel, whose story has been told and retold in every era. Grendel, ancient monster, child of a more monstrous mother, who would emerge from his cave to terrorise the little kingdom of good King Hrothgar, devouring his subjects and killing his bravest warriors, until his majesty called in the help of the mighty hero, Beowulf. Beowulf, who would fulfil a prophesy by cutting off the monster's arm and leaving him to die beneath the stars.

Adams subsequently builds the argument that we (particularly in our post-Vietnam era) have begun to question the concept of the unadulterated hero – and by extension, the very concept of the monster. Furthermore, he advocates strongly for our appreciation of the role that monsters have played in society:

Our version of Grendel is seen through twentieth century eyes when perhaps we are a little suspicious of the military hero and more inclined to see humanity in a monster. For Grendel, ancient Grendel, who has watched human society developing, growing more complex as it invented things, like politics, religion and art, is deserving of our sympathy and our thanks. For without our monsters, our misunderstood monsters, who are after all only doing their job, which is to stimulate our imaginations and encourage our social cohesion, we wouldn't be in the civilized mess we are today.

As images of the animated film's production process flash across the screen, Adams concludes: 'Ladies and Gentlemen, it is with pride that we introduce the lonely, loveable monster who has been living and dying for fifteen centuries with our very best interests at heart.'

Ultimately, it is a surprisingly poetic and erudite introduction to an animated feature film (particularly for that era). Adam's main proposition is that monsters are essential to human society, and as he rather ironically states, 'Monsters ... have our very best interests at heart.' However, one key point that is overlooked in the introduction, and one that Stitt makes very emphatically in the animated film, is that *humans* are actually the ones that can harbour the greatest levels of monstrosity.

Between monster and human

There are a number of characteristics which can fundamentally define a monster. These may include a monster's appearance (such as its claws, fangs or major disfigurement), or its potential to do harm (such as its propensity to maim or kill). Some have suggested that what makes a monster most fearsome is 'its *impact*'.[2] As Noel Carroll writes: 'Monsters are not only physically threatening; they are cognitively threatening.'[3] Arguably, it is a monster's unknown qualities which can produce the greatest psychological threat. In the original *Beowulf* poem, Grendel is scarcely described at the outset. It is only after one has read the whole of the poem that 'we have a moderately clear notion of Grendel's nature: what (roughly) he looked like'.[4] What makes Grendel's initial approach to the meadhall so frightening is that neither the reader nor Beowulf and his men have any idea how the monster looks.[5] Grendel, by not being defined, becomes an embodiment of fear. Contrastingly, some writers have suggested that the deficit with most cinematic adaptations of *Beowulf* is that they reveal too much of the monster (and too soon), leaving very little to the viewer's imagination. By contrast, Gardner immediately provides the reader a full description of Grendel (thus stripping him of his psychological menace) while giving only the sketchiest of details of Beowulf (and thus imbuing the 'hero' with the monstrous character trait of the unknown).

John Gardner's Grendel was by no means the first novel to feature a sympathetic monster. In fact, there has been a long lineage of monsters which have educed varying degrees of sympathy, ranging from Mary Shelley's *Frankenstein* (1818) to the devil character in C.S. Lewis' *Screwtape Letters* (1942). However, Gardner's 1971 novel marked a significant turning point because of his *comprehensive* depiction of the monster Grendel.

Of course, animated feature films have also revelled in depicting sympathetic monster characters; in the past several decades there have been a large number of these films, mainly aimed at children, which have featured friendly monsters. These films often provide comforting themes, encouraging the young viewers to overcome their childhood fears. One notable early mainstream feature was the animation/live-action hybrid film, *Pete's Dragon* (Don Chaffey, 1977), which was based on Seton Miller's 1957 short story, 'Pete's Dragon and the USA (Forever After)'. In this film, the dragon, Elliott, proves not only to be sympathetic, but also exceedingly kind and helpful to the human boy, Pete. Numerous other friendly monster-animated films have ensued, including *The BFG* (Brian Cosgrove, 1989), based on the Roald Dahl book; Disney's adaptation of the fairy tale *Beauty and the Beast* (Gary Trousdale, Kirk Wise, 1991); *The Iron Giant* (Brad Bird, 1999) which features a very sympathetic monstrous robot; *Monsters, Inc.* (Pete Docter and David Silverman, 2001); and the *Shrek* movies – *Shrek* (Andrew Adamson, Vicky Jenson, 2001), *Shrek 2* (Andrew Adamson, Kelly Asbury, Conrad Vernon, 2004) and *Shrek the Third* (Chris Miller, Raman Hui, 2007). What nearly all of these films have in common is that the central monster-character is befriended by a human character – who then helps to reveal the hidden humanity within the monster. Additionally, this human-friend then acts as a conduit, espousing the monster's benevolence to the rest of human society. In Disney's *Beauty and the Beast*, Belle acts as the conduit-character as she assists the Beast in expressing his humanity. The Beast's humanity is fully revealed, quite literally, when the evil curse is lifted and he is transformed once again into a human (as are his friendly companions: the talking teapot, cup and saucer, and candelabra). *Monsters, Inc.* also presents a very sympathetic view of monsters. In this film, the human child called 'Boo', helps the monsters to not only discover and express their humanity, but also their kindness and humour. Thus, Boo helps the monsters to invert the very conventions of monsterhood by transforming them from frightening creatures to hilarious monster-comedians in order to entertain the world's children. The animated feature, *Shrek*, uniquely parallels *Grendel Grendel Grendel* in that it features a large green monster, a fire-breathing dragon, and a self-serving and diminutive King (who behaves in monstrous ways). In this narrative, Princess Fiona ultimately reveals the kindness within Shrek, but in a stark contrast to most other monster narratives, she chooses to adopt a monster form rather than return to her human form. But what sets *Grendel Grendel Grendel* apart from these other animated films is that Grendel does *not* make friends with any of the humans, instead remaining stalwartly a 'friendless' monster. He also continues to do some very monstrous things, such as biting off Wiglaf's head. Yet these monstrous actions are presented in an ironic and darkly humorous manner, allowing that Grendel, in a sense, 'makes friends' with the audience. Even though Grendel is a monster, morally and ethically he seems far more genteel than many of the humans.

In the original poem, the character of Bewoulf exhibits some rather superhuman capabilities; for example, he is able to kill the monster Grendel with his bare hands; also to hold his breath underwater for perhaps hours on end. Because of this, it has been suggested that Beowulf might embody some degree of monstrousness.[6] In Stitt's film, Beowulf unquestionably expresses a great deal of sinister violence. The King calls upon Beowulf, not only to kill Grendel, but also to engage in some rather outrageous actions so as to ensure his grip on power. Knowing that Beowulf is on his way, the King ruthlessly kills the Shaper, and subsequently orders Beowulf to kill Unferth. Notably, one of Beowulf's human companion warriors is aptly named Troll, and his character design quite strikingly resembles a slighter version of the monster Grendel. Because of his similarities to Grendel, Troll literally illustrates the concept that humans can be like monsters, and unquestionably many of the humans in the film behave like them. Imbued with varying levels of hypocrisy, ignorance and brutality, they appear ready to attack and kill each other at the slightest provocation – which ultimately encourages the viewer to consider their own monstrous physiognomies.

The curse of Cain

The original *Beowulf* poem proclaims that Grendel (and other monstrous creatures that inhabit the world) are the cursed descendants of the biblical figure Cain, who out of jealousy killed his righteous brother Abel. The original poem states:

> Grendel was the name of this grim demon
> haunting the marches, marauding round the heath
> and the desolate fens; he had dwelt for a time
> in misery among the banished monsters,
> Cain's clan, whom the Creator had outlawed
> And condemned as outcasts. For the killing of Abel
> the Eternal Lord had exacted a price;
> Cain got no good from committing that murder
> because the Almighty made him anathema
> and out of the curse of his exile there sprang
> ogres and elves and evil phantoms
> and the giants too who strove with God
> time and again until He gave them their reward.[7]

The concept that the monster Grendel was actually a descendant of the brother-killer Cain further calls into question the demarcation between monsters and humans. As one writer has noted, 'For many critics of the poem, Grendel's descent from Cain encourages readers to consider the relationship between monsters and humanity.'[8] If it is to be believed that virtually all monsters are the descendants of Cain, then these monsters are, by extension, descendants of *humans*. Unferth, it is revealed, had also killed his own brother, thereby placing him (at least partially) in Cain's accursed group. In the original epic, when Unferth accuses Beowulf of exaggerating his heroic past, Beowulf immediately silences Unferth's denigrations by referencing his brother-killing past. Gardner also has a very complicated relationship with Cain. As mentioned earlier, when the author was just eleven years old, he killed his younger brother in a tragic farm machinery accident, and it was a tragedy that haunted him for the rest of his life. By elevating Grendel (a cursed descendant of the brother-killing Cain) to the protagonist of his novel, Gardner was able to challenge the Cain narrative. It would seem that if Grendel is a monster merely because he is a descendant of a brother-killing human, then certainly Unferth, Gardner himself, and virtually all of humanity would inherently encompass at least some degree of monstrosity.

Stitt also featured the Cain narrative prominently in his film. The topic first arises when the Shaper sings 'The Creation Song' which describes the creation of the world and also the creation of monsters like Grendel. The lyrics to the song are as follows:

God saw the darkness, and he made it right.
God halved the darkness into day and night.
God saw the garden, and he made it fresh.
God halved the garden into clay and flesh.

God saw his image, and he gave it life.
God halved his image into man and wife
Man, wife united to create two sons.
God halved his kingdom for the chosen ones.

God's love was Abel's to perpetuate.
Cain halved his feelings into love and hate.
God-fearing Abel loved his brother so.
Cain halved his brother with a bitter blow.

Cain bore the fury of both God and man.
God halved his children into loved and damned.
Now and forever, all the beasts of Cain
Live halved from grace, in foul, black pits of pain.

Upon hearing this song, Grendel is devastated by the idea that he is descended from such a horrible person. He cries out in despair, 'Halved us from grace? Us? Me? Am I one of the dark, damned half? A child of this awful brother? But, they are the ones who murder each other. Can I be more damned than they?' Grendel then attempts to beg for forgiveness, but the humans mistake his repentant approach as an act of aggression and subsequently attack him. In an earlier version of the script, Grendel had further beseeched the humans by saying, 'Forgive us! Forgive me! That we could all forgive great-great-grandfather Cain?' Grendel is clearly overwhelmed by guilt, but at the same time he realizes that all of humanity must bear this burden of guilt – but clearly the humans do not recognize their own culpability. As the humans attack Grendel, they further reinforce their own monstrousness.

The Dragon

The Dragon (in both the novel and the film) is, in fact, a dreamed-up character, and Grendel's interactions with the Dragon are located purely within the realm of his imagination. Gardner scholar, Howell, notes that Grendel's 'intensely realized fantasy or hallucination' of the Dragon is similar to 'Dorothy in The Wizard of Oz, who turns Kansas farmhands into the Cowardly Lion, the Strawman, and the Tinman'.[9] Because Grendel overhears and eavesdrops on many of the human's actions and conversations, these observations often inform the Dragon's actions and speech. The Dragon is ultimately Grendel's subconscious, attempting to make sense of his conscious perceptions.

But Stitt takes this concept much further and creates what is perhaps the greatest irony within the film – that the monster-fearing humans actually worship a monster-deity, the Great Dragon God. They pray exuberantly to their god, calling out: 'Great Dragon Spirit! Defend our people and kill our enemy, the terrible world-rim-walker, the foul night-stalker, the Great Boogy.' They also sacrifice wild animals and create countless monuments and statues depicting this Dragon God. It is from these observations that Grendel's subconscious generates his own version of this revered figure, dreaming up the Dragon character. Thus, in the film, Grendel's Dragon is ultimately *a cognitive manifestation of the human's God*.

The King, however, does not seem to take his religion quite so seriously and, rather than devoutly praying to the Great Dragon God to deliver his kingdom from the monster Grendel, he instead seeks assistance by more secular means. He approaches the great warrior, Beowulf for help. To the King, Beowulf will be not only the saviour of his kingdom, but also his own personal saviour (as Beowulf will also be employed to kill off his main political rival, Unferth). Grendel observes the King's shifting devotion from the Dragon God to Beowulf; consequently, Grendel appears cognitively to conflate the characters of the Dragon and Beowulf. In the novel, particularly during the final fight scene, he is so confused that he imagines great dragon wings emerging from Beowulf's shoulders. Stitt, on the other hand, chose more subtly and uniquely to contribute to this conflation by employing the same voice actor to perform both Beowulf and the Dragon (see Chapter 4), and tactfully embellishing Beowulf's character design with a dragon-red cape and spiked shoulders.

The Dragon is a very dynamic and complicated character. In the novel, the Dragon recites extensive philosophical ideas, quoting, for example, large sections from A. N. Whitehead's text, *Modes of Thought* (but doing so rather out of context), also delving into existentialist thought. He does so, in order, among other things, to convince Grendel that his fundamental role is to spur the humans to greatness. In Gardner's novel, the dragon asserts:

> You improve them, my boy! Can't you see that yourself? You stimulate them! You make them think and scheme. You drive them to poetry, science, religion, all that makes them what they are for as long as they last. You are, so to speak, the brute existent by which they learn to define themselves.[10]

Stitt chooses to hone this central point more humorously – as his Dragon enthusiastically explains to Grendel, 'You are here, you exist, simply to go bump in their night. You will drive them to poetry, science, religion in their efforts to explain you!' The Dragon asserts that, by acting as humanity's oppositional force, Grendel will positively affect the human species. Then through a raucous jingle, the Dragon attempts to explain the fundamentals of a theologically based dualism, singing:

> *For everyone who fails,*
> *Another will succeed,*
> *And every act of charity*
> *Supplants an act of greed.*
> *For every deity, the laity*
> *Is slaving at the yoke,*
> *And every hollow laugh demands a joke.*
>
> *For every answer, there's a question.*
> *To each exception, there's a rule.*
> *For every sound, a silence.*
> *For every sage, a fool.*
>
> *For everyone who's mean,*
> *Another one is nice.*
> *For everyone who's virtuous,*
> *Another's full of vice.*

For every synonym, an antonym
Is waiting round the bend,
And every bright beginning has an end.

However, Grendel is not quite convinced by the Dragon's rather simplistic, black-and-white assessment of the world. Certainly, one of Stitt's main points in the film is that the world is not as unequivocal as some may assert – there is monstrousness in the humans, and humanity in the monsters. This lack of dualistic clarity, or at least Grendel's uncertainty, is humorously articulated in their final verbal exchange. As the Dragon begins to fade away, he utters the incomplete line, 'And for everyone who's right, another one is …' Grendel, attempts to complete the Dragon's sentence by saying, '… left?' Of course, within this context, it can be assumed that the Dragon had intended to say, 'And for everyone who's right, another one is … *wrong.*' Although one might initially laugh at Grendel's misinterpreting of the word 'right' to signify direction, it does effectively illustrate that such apparently simple disjunctions can sometimes embody overlapping or tangential concerns.

The Dragon character serves as meta-reference to the dragon in the original *Beowulf* poem. As the novel and the movie focus only on the first third of the original *Beowulf* poem, the inclusion of an imagined dragon character effectively references the dragon at the end of the poem (which is killed by Beowulf, but also inflicts him with a mortal wound). In the animated film the Dragon reveals to Grendel, 'Did you know, Grendel, that my death is inevitable? A certain man will kill me absurdly. A terrible pity. Loss of a remarkable form of life. Conservationists will howl!' In this way, the narrative is able to engage with all three monsters (Grendel, Grendel's Mum and the Dragon) which effectively structure the original poem.

When the Dragon utters the line, 'A certain man will kill me absurdly', he is of course providing an inside joke for those that are familiar with the full *Beowulf* narrative. But moments later, the Dragon claims that 'conservationists will howl' as a result of his untimely death (and presumably the extinction of his entire species at the behest of humans). Here, Gardner (and Stitt) is also humorously paying tribute to the burgeoning conservationist movement of the era – a movement that had been spearheaded by the writings of Rachel Carson, particularly in her highly influential book, *Silent Spring* (1962), in which she pointedly asks, how can humanity 'wage relentless war on life without destroying itself, and without losing the right to be called civilized'.[11] The Dragon, by referencing this real-world destruction of the environment, further underscores, with tongue in cheek bravado, the uncivilized and monstrous nature of humanity.

Stitt also uses the Dragon scenes to develop a meta-referencing of the inherent qualities of the animated form – the Dragon is the most cartoonish and entertaining element in the film. This is by no means surprising, given that the filmmakers had one of the more comedic sections in the novel to work from. Howell describes Gardner's dragon chapter:

> Though Gardner risks boring his readers, as well as Grendel, with the dragon's highly erudite and allusive monologue, the incongruity of a dragon lecturing a monster makes the chapter highly amusing and entertaining. Gardner's cartoon portrait of the dragon is richly imagined and humorous. Egocentric, miserly, nihilistic, and comically irascible, the dragon speaks of a meaningless and entropic universe, and his responses to Grendel's boredom are part of the humor.[12]

The exaggerated philosophical musing of Gardner's dragon does instinctively evoke notions of the animated cartoon, of which Gardner himself noted:

> I seem incapable of writing a story in which people do not babble philosophically, not really because they're saying things I want to get said but because earnest babbling is one of the ways I habitually give vitality to my short-legged, overweight, twitching cartoon creations.[13]

Although Gardner confessed to have had a great love of animation – as a writer, this adoration tended to be manifested in the exaggeration of the literary form. Stitt did retain some semblance of the Dragon's 'earnest babbling', but he also translated much of this literary amplification into exaggerated *movement* – creating a sort of animated analogue to the Dragon's over-stated and decontextualized philosophical rhetoric.

As the Dragon sequence is essentially a dream sequence, the animators enjoyed a great deal of freedom in bringing it to fruition. Thus, the scenes are replete with metamorphosis and impossible graphical actions. Animation director, Frank Hellard, who animated the Dragon scenes, noted that 'with animation, you can make the character do things that are outlandishly unreal. For example, the Dragon is talking to Grendel at one stage; and he goes into his block.'[14] That is, the Dragon transforms from his regular character shape into a large red square (or sometimes a red circle). The Dragon engages in this metamorphic action as a defensive strategy – a reaction to when Grendel queries something that the Dragon finds uncomfortable, or difficult to answer. Equally playful movements emerge when Grendel chastises the Dragon saying, 'Oh that's silly', and the Dragon responds, 'Silly? Silly, silly, silly!', spinning his head right round as he says it. Of this Frank Hellard notes:

> It's very hard to get an actor to do that! But you can do things with the animated character, you can stretch the character's reactions so much, and take acting beyond humanity. As long as there's a link [to reality] you can see the kind of thing you mean a character to be doing. But it's exaggerated so much, that it's completely impossible. That's one of the exciting things to work with in animation, this stretching, acting beyond possibilities.[15]

The Dragon engages in many other impossible actions, drawing enduring graphic lines in mid-air, twisting and flattening his entire form so that he

FIGURE 3.1 The Dragon multiplying himself in order to add emphasis to his lyrical performance (*Grendel Grendel Grendel*, Alexander Stitt, 1981).

appears to exist on a two-dimensional plane, even turning himself invisible. Additionally, the Dragon metamorphoses, radically changes scale and even replicates himself into multiple dragon-clones. For example, when the Dragon sings the repeating line, 'For every entertainer, for every entertainer, for every entertainer', he replicates himself, so that each newly minted dragon is also able to sing each repetition of the phrase. This newly formed dragon trio continues to sing in sequence the words, 'is a bore, is a bore, is a bore', which is followed by the repetitive, 'encore, encore, encore!' (see Figure 3.1). Finally, the dragon once again coalesces into a single dragon form, uttering one last 'Encore!' Later when the dragon sings the words, 'demands a joke', he immediately produces a cream pie out of thin air and hurls it at Grendel's face – to which Grendel retorts, 'ha, ha', with a deep degree of sarcasm. Although the Dragon assumes the role of mentor, often he appears to be only partially interested in Grendel's well-being, and much more concerned with the meta-narrative of the animated graphics – and perhaps of simply *being an animated dragon*.

Grendel in Wonderland

Stitt appears to have been uniquely inspired by the nonsensical writings of Lewis Carroll, weaving numerous references into his film. There are several parallels that can be made between the film *Grendel Grendel Grendel*, and the writings of Carroll, in particular the *Alice* stories: *Alice in Wonderland* and *Alice through the Looking Glass* (and by extension, Walt Disney's adaptation of *Alice in Wonderland* [Clyde Geronimi, Wilfred Jackson, Hamilton Luske, 1951]).

Both Stitt's film and Carroll's stories involve 'monsters' entering into strange worlds, wherein they try to make sense of their surroundings. In the case of Grendel, the monster leaves his mother's cave and swims through the lake of fire snakes emerging into the land of humans; similarly, Alice journeys down the rabbit hole and emerges into Wonderland (and later through the mirror into Looking-glass Land).

Although one might not readily equate Alice with Grendel, the child is frequently referred to as a monster by the residents of Wonderland. For example, in her meeting with the Lion and the Unicorn in *Alice through the Looking Glass*, Carroll writes:

> The Lion looked at Alice wearily. 'Are you animal – or vegetable – or mineral?' he said, yawning at every other word.
> 'It's a fabulous monster!' the Unicorn cried out, before Alice could reply.
> 'Then hand round the plum-cake, Monster', the Lion said, lying down and putting his chin on his paws.[16]

Monstrosity ultimately depends upon one's point of view; for the inhabitants of Wonderland, Alice represents a creature previously unknown and is generally regarded with fear or suspicion. Contrastingly, from Alice's point of view (and the reader's), many of the creatures in these worlds are clearly monsters – the dragon-like Jabberwocky, being just one example. As Jack Zipes notes, Alice is 'a grim tale about a ten-year-old girl who basically tries to make sense out of the absurdity of life, in particular, of life in the Victorian world'.[17] One could also easily describe Grendel in this manner, as he also tries to make sense of the 'absurdity of life': in this case, the post-Vietnam war era. By blurring the innocence of Alice with the monstrosity of Grendel, Stitt succeeds in further obfuscating the conventional human-monster divide.

In the film, Grendel engages in numerous conversational exchanges which unmistakably correlate to the tone of the nonsensical writings of Carroll, particularly in Grendel's interaction with the Dragon. For example, Grendel is continually berated by the Dragon's claim of omniscience: 'I know everything!' he insists repeatedly. Similarly, in Carroll's *Looking Glass* the character Humpty Dumpty also repeatedly insists to Alice that he knows everything: 'Did you think I didn't know the answer to *that*?'[18] Another parallel can be found when Humpty Dumpty queries Alice:

> So here's a question for you. How old did you say you were?
> Alice made a short calculation, and said 'Seven years and six months'.
> 'Wrong!' Humpty Dumpty exclaimed triumphantly. 'You never said a word like it!'
> 'I thought you meant "How old are you?"' Alice explained.
> 'If I'd meant that, I'd have said it', said Humpty Dumpty.[19]

Similarly, Grendel also asks a question of the Dragon who, like Humpty Dumpty, insists on responding to the literal linguistic meaning of his query rather than replying to the spirit and contextual meaning of Grendel's question:

> GRENDEL: Did you say that I will kill the king?
> DRAGON: Did I say that? Did I say that? Let's see what year is this?
> GRENDEL: Just tell me, will I kill him!
> DRAGON: Temper! That's not what you asked me. You asked if I had *said*. It's so difficult to remember what I had said or am about to say, you see I wouldn't like to make a mistake would I?

Another similarity to Carroll's writing can be found between the author's celebrated logic puzzles and a nonsensical riddle that the Dragon expresses to Grendel. In Lewis Carroll's book, *Symbolic Logic, Part I*, the following logic problem is presented:

> Every eagle can fly;
> Some pigs cannot fly.
> Some pigs are not eagles.[20]

When Grendel asks, 'What am I doing here?' the Dragon replies, somewhat diffidently, in Carroll's logic problem form:

> All pigs eat cheese;
> The king is a pig;
> Do pigs eat kings? – or something.

After leaving the Dragon for the last time, Grendel fumes to himself, 'Riddles. Stupid old goat. All you want is a simple answer to a simple question and all you get is abuse and riddles [...] I think dragons are very much overrated'. Similarly, after Alice leaves Humpty Dumpty having been equally flummoxed with riddles and nonsensical speak, she murmurs quietly to herself, 'of all the unsatisfactory people I ever met'.[21]

Another passage in *Through the Looking Glass* that seemingly would have piqued Stitt's interest was Carroll's nonsensical caricature of Anglo-Saxons (the very cultural group that created *Beowulf*):

> 'But he's coming very slowly – and what curious attitudes he goes into!' (For the Messenger kept skipping up and down, and wriggling like an eel, as he came along, with his great hands spread out like fans on each side.)
> 'Not at all', said the King. 'He's an Anglo-Saxon Messenger – and those are Anglo-Saxon attitudes. He only does them when he's happy.'[22]

But perhaps the most overt reference to *Alice* can be found in the sequence in which Grendel sings his soliloquy. As Grendel sings this heartfelt (but rather nonsensical) song, a chorus of singing oysters join in. Set along a rocky seashore, the scene clearly references the 'Walrus and the Carpenter' sequence in *Through the Looking Glass* (as well as Disney's animated feature, *Alice in Wonderland*). In this sequence, the characters Tweedledum and Tweedledee recite the poem of 'The Walrus and the Carpenter' to Alice:

> *Four other Oysters followed them,*
> *And yet another four;*
> *And thick and fast they came at last,*
> *And more, and more, and more—*
> *All hopping through the frothy waves,*
> *And scrambling to the shore.*
>
> *The Walrus and the Carpenter*
> *Walked on a mile or so,*
> *And then they rested on a rock*
> *Conveniently low:*
> *And all the little Oysters stood*
> *And waited in a row.*[23]

Carroll's text was illustrated by John Tenniel, several of whose images feature groupings of oyster characters, replete with little feet and hands (see Figure 3.2a), and it is clear that both Disney and Stitt utilized Tenniel's design as the basis for the oyster character designs in their respective films (see Figure 3.2b). As Grendel sings his soliloquy, a chorus of these oysters join in, singing several of the lines to the song. At one point, Grendel reclines upon the sand, looking somewhat walrus-like, and a whole row of oysters rush up to him (with visible legs, arms and eyes). After exchanging a few lines in song, the oysters pick up Grendel and carry him along the shore, before placing him down upon the sand. Later, Grendel, reaches down and picks up one of the singing oysters and eats it (referencing how, in Carroll's text, the Walrus had greedily consumed all of the oysters).

Several additional parallels can be found between Stitt's film and the Disney film version. For example, in the opening sequence Alice pensively looks down into a pond, contemplating her reflection, which she then disturbs by dropping her hand into the water. As a result, her animated reflection ripples apart in a colourful and dramatic manner. Grendel also engages in a similar action at the start of his film when, upon seeing his reflection in the water, he angrily throws a rock at it, disrupting it in the same way. Also, King Hrothgar, with his small stature and general ineffectualness, is quite reminiscent of the King of Hearts in the Disney feature. Finally, in the Disney film, the Mad Hatter unexpectedly takes a bite out of his saucer as he partakes in a tea party with Alice. In a similar manner, one of Beowulf's warriors takes a bite of his goblet when they sit down to dine at Hrothgar's table in his newly built meadhall.

FIGURE 3.2 (a) Dancing and singing oysters engage with Grendel (*Grendel Grendel Grendel*, Alexander Stitt, 1981); a sequence that is reminiscent of (b) John Tenniel's illustration in Lewis Carroll's *Through the Looking Glass* (1872).

Grendel in Pepperland

Another animated feature film that undoubtedly draws inspiration from Carroll's classic is The Beatles *Yellow Submarine* (George Dunning, 1968). *Yellow Submarine* is also replete with references to Carroll's story, albeit from a slightly more psychedelic perspective. In this film, the four band members (Ringo, Paul, George and John) enter into a fantastic realm known as *Pepperland*, which is, of course, an allusion to Alice's *Wonderland*. In a similar manner to how Alice enters into Wonderland through a rabbit hole, the Beatles enter into Pepperland through a submarine porthole. Soon after entering the land, John Lennon (like Alice) is transformed after drinking a potion, and all four band members shrink down in size and further transform as they travel through time. At one point, the character of John Lennon blows smoke-like letters out of his mouth, asking, 'Who?', which is very similar to the manner in which the caterpillar in Disney's *Alice in Wonderland* puffs out smoke-typography demanding that Alice answer the question, 'Who are you?'

However, in addition to the shared references to *Alice in Wonderland* there are a number of other similarities that can be articulated between *Grendel Grendel Grendel* and *Yellow Submarine*. To begin with, both films are branded as animated musicals – a genre of feature animation that was much less common in that era than it is today. Also, rather uniquely for that time, both animated films were aimed primarily at mature audiences, and both films were also made by small independent studios on a shoe-string budget. Significantly, there was also some crossover that occurred between production staff of the *Yellow Submarine* and *Grendel Grendel Grendel*. Animator Anne Jolliffe, who had previously worked as an animator for many years with Alexander Stitt, travelled to England to work as an animator on *Yellow Submarine*, before returning to Melbourne to work on *Grendel Grendel Grendel*. Similarly, Maggie (Margaret) Geddes, who also had a long history of working with Stitt, was employed as Trace and Paint Supervisor both on *Yellow Submarine* and on *Grendel Grendel Grendel*. Australian, Dick Sawers, who had worked for many years with Stitt as a designer, also later worked as a designer on *Yellow Submarine*.[24]

Given this crossover of production talent and the immense popularity of *Yellow Submarine* it is natural to draw some aesthetic comparisons between the two films. For example, both films feature bold and colourful graphics and some of the background elements, namely the rocks and trees, share visual similarities (though, these comparisons are more noticeable in some of the early designs and pre-production work for *Grendel Grendel Grendel* than they are in the final film). However, upon closer analysis the visual styles between the two films are quite distinct. Stitt's designs are simple, bold and unified; while the graphics of *Yellow Submarine*, although bold, are much less unified and much more complicated – invoking a pop art sensibility with shimmering psychedelic imagery. What these two films unquestionably *do* have in common is that neither looks at all like the typical Disney animated features of the era. Arguably, it is this starkly un-Disney aesthetic and narrative content that most ardently binds Grendel to Pepperland.

Prior to the production of *Yellow Submarine*, the Beatles' persona had remained somewhat cartoon-like (being best known for their upbeat pop-tunes and somewhat blithe live-action films). This identity was most explicitly demonstrated in their animated television series, *The Beatles* (1965–7), which projected an exceedingly simple aesthetic and narrative. But by the late 1960s the

Beatles songs (and public persona) had begun to achieve a much higher level of sophistication, and correspondingly, the animated design in *Yellow Submarine* went some way in reflecting this shift. In parallel, Gardner's character Grendel emerged from a relatively sophisticated work of literature, but Gardner himself would occasionally refer to Grendel (long before he was made into an animated film) as a 'cartoon character'.[25] As both *Yellow Submarine* and *Grendel Grendel Grendel* are essentially animated musical comedies, both quite instinctively shed many of the complexities of their source material – but at the same time, both animated features also manage to add new and intriguing facets to their original sources.

Of Shapers and Sculptors

Minstrels (or 'scops') played an important role in Anglo-Saxon culture. Gardner coined the term 'Shaper' to describe the main minstrel figure in his novel. The term 'Shaper' also describes one of the character's key roles, which is actively to 'shape' people's perception of reality. The Shaper clearly succeeds in his position as he composes and performs an array of poignant and emotionally compelling songs. After singing a song about the (highly embellished) heroics of the King and his men, the audience in the meadhall is dumbfounded as it grapples to understand the Shaper's fictitious retelling of history. King Hrothgar asks, 'Did we do all that?' to which Dung nods in wonderment and replies, 'We must have!' Even Grendel is completely awestruck by the performance, and although he had witnessed the actual events described in the song and knows what really

FIGURE 3.3 The Sculptor at work (*Grendel Grendel Grendel*, Alexander Stitt, 1981).

transpired, he wholeheartedly accepts the Shaper's version. The Shaper presents a significant dilemma for Grendel; on one hand, he realizes that the Shaper is a peddler of lies; but at the same time, he cannot help but believe in and be moved by the Shaper's artistry and messages. Stitt considered the Shaper to be 'an analogy of the story itself, representing as he does a character like the one who would have first performed the Beowulf poem'.[26] And it was primarily because of this that Stitt chose to transform his film into a musical.

Stitt created a new character for his film, which he called the 'Sculptor' (see Figure 3.3), to serve as a kind of visual analogue to the role of the Shaper. The Sculptor is also able to shape people's minds, not through song, but through imagery carved in stone. Similarly, both the humans and Grendel seem to have a difficult time telling the difference between the Sculptor's images and reality. The Sculptor creates numerous images of the human's deity, the Great Dragon God. Although the human worshipers undoubtedly understand the distinction between a stone carving and their actual deity, they do nonetheless directly worship and sacrifice animals *toward* these stone images. As a result of seeing these statues and the human's devout reverence to the dragon form, Grendel imagines his own version of this deity and visits him in his dreams. Later, when Grendel is not in the midst of a vision and wishes to speak with the Dragon, he simply borrows one of the Sculptor's stone carvings and carries on a conversation with it. In one scene Grendel asks the carving, 'You did say I'd kill the King, didn't you?' And after a momentary pause, Grendel replies, 'Yeah, that's what it seemed like you said' (see Figure 3.4).

When Grendel encounters stone images of *himself*, he attempts to conform to these as if they are prophetic dictums. At one point, he encounters two

FIGURE 3.4 Grendel speaks to the Dragon through a human-made effigy of the Dragon God (*Grendel Grendel Grendel*, Alexander Stitt, 1981).

sculptors in the midst of carving an image of Grendel, in which he is depicted holding aloft two terrified humans. Grendel, taking the visual cue from this carving, grabs the two men and holds them aloft as decreed by the image. He also makes a humorous show of seeking to properly mimic the pose as he repeatedly studies the image, while adjusting his hold of the two terrified men (see Figure 3.5). Later, while singing his 'Soliloquy' by the seashore, he pauses next to a great sculpture of himself, momentarily emulating its dramatic pose. But the proliferation of so many very unflattering images of himself does occasionally take its toll on his mental health. At one point, after walking past many of these images, his anger noticeably increases and he storms angrily towards the meadhall, smashing down its great wooden doors.

FIGURE 3.5 Grendel attempts to mimic the Sculptor's engravings; also, note the use of 'mock-runes' (*Grendel Grendel Grendel*, Alexander Stitt, 1981).

In both the novel and the film there is an underlying sense that Grendel is seeking to emulate the Shaper. As he grows and establishes his identity, he also becomes better able to express himself through poetry and song. John Gardner, in an interview, describes this evolution, saying, 'When the first Shaper dies, a kid [the Shaper's Boy] is chosen to succeed him, but the real successor is Grendel.'[27] In the film, Grendel also is shown to progress in his singing abilities. When he sings his first duet with the Dragon, he does so quite clumsily, but later, when he sings his own Soliloquy, he has become a much more accomplished vocalist. His growth as a singer is most clearly shown through his increasing ability to sing his own theme song. As a young Grendel at the commencement of the film he can barely mumble the words, but by the end of the film he is able to sing his song with great confidence, clarity and melodic prowess, belting out: 'Who's the beast who looks so swell, G-R-E-N-D-E-L! What's his purpose can't you guess, N-E-M-E-S-I-S!'

In addition to acquiring the talents of the Shaper, Grendel also gains a semblance of the *Sculptor's* abilities by being able to 'sculpt' and concretize spoken words into visualized text formations. When a mature Grendel sings his theme song, he not only sings it well, but simultaneously conjures up elaborate typography (see Figure 3.6a). In doing so, he joins the ranks of the other monster characters of the film.

Grendel's Mum and the Dragon are also able to transform their spoken words into visible text. This is an incredible talent, for it demonstrates that their words can literally have a concrete and animating effect upon their world. For example, when Grendel's mother sings the opening title song, she is able to actualize many of her heartfelt words into animated graphics (see Figure 3.6b). Her loving lyrics are literally shaped into visible typography. Perhaps the most proficient in this capacity is the Dragon who, when he speaks, is able effortlessly to draw and conjure words in the air. For example, when he proclaims, 'I know everything you see. The beginning the present, the end – everything,' dozens of mathematical equations and scientific notations appear in the air. Later when he says, 'For everything subtracted there is something else to add,' he literally draws visible 'minus' and 'plus' signs in the air. Most entertainingly is when he ruminates, 'Games, my boy, games, games. No total vision, no total system. Merely vague schemes with a vague family resemblance!' large physical letters which spell out the word, 'GAMES', appear on the screen. The text is monumental in scale; however, after speaking the word into existence he soon notices that the letter 'E' has appeared backwards. So, he walks over to it and picks up the letter but, as he is somewhat distracted, he merely flips it over, instead of turning it to face in the correct direction (see Figure 3.6c).

In addition to sculpting pictorial images and forms, the Sculptor is also involved in writing messages in 'runes'. Runes were a form of writing used by the Anglo-Saxons (and other cultures) and were believed to have been adapted by modifying early Greek or Roman characters so that they could easily be carved across the irregular surfaces and contours of stones. In his student study guide for

FIGURE 3.6 (a) As Grendel sings out the letters G-R-E-N-D-E-L and N-E-M-E-S-I-S, they appear as 'concretized speech' above his dancing form; (b) examples of 'concretized speech' from Grendel's Mum during the opening title song; (c) the Dragon, after conjuring into existence the word 'GAMES', adjusts the backwards facing letter 'E' (*Grendel Grendel Grendel*, Alexander Stitt, 1981).

the film, Stitt writes, 'Watch out for many messages that appear throughout the film in mock-runes: English without the vowels.'[28] In fact, Stitt did spend a good deal of time researching runes (as well as related Celtic Oghams) for the film and had originally planned to decorate the various stone monuments that populate the film's backgrounds with more historically 'authentic' rune writing. Instead, he conceived the humorous idea of 'mock-runes' – a system which dictated that all words be written in capitals letters (in English), but with the vowels removed. Thus, 'God bless King Hrothgar' would translate to, 'GD BLSS KNG HRTHGR'. Additionally, to make them more decipherable, a plus-sign (+) would denote a missing vowel at the start or ending of a word. In these cases, for example, 'GR+T DRGN G+D PR+TCT HRTHGR FR+M GRNDL+ THE GR+T B+GY' would translate to, 'Great Dragon God protect Hrothgar from Grendel the great bogey'. The result was an archaic-inspired typographical design, but one that could be entertainingly deciphered by the observant viewer (see Figure 3.5).

Notes

1. This introduction sequence has been omitted from the recent (2013) digitally restored DVD and online streaming versions.
2. Asa Simon Mittman, 'Introduction, the Impact of Monsters and Monster Studies', in *The Ashgate Research Companion to Monsters and the Monstrous,* ed. Asa Simon Mittman and Peter J. Dendle (Farnham: Ashgate, 2012), p. 7.
3. Noel Carroll, quoted in Mittman, 'Introduction', p.8.
4. Michael Lapidge, 'Beowulf and the Psychology of Terror', in *Beowulf – A Prose Translation, Backgrounds and Contexts Criticism* (second edition), trans. E. Talbot Donaldson, ed. Nicholas Howe (New York: W.W. Norton & Company, 2002), p. 135.
5. Ibid., 143.
6. Alan S. Ambrisco, 'Trolling for Outcasts in Sturla Gunnarsson's *Beowulf and Grendel*', *The Journal of Popular Culture* 46, no. 2 (2013), p. 249.
7. Heaney, Seamus, *Beowulf* (London: Faber and Faber, 1999), Lines 102–14.
8. Ambrisco, 'Trolling for Outcasts', p. 248.
9. John M. Howell, *Understanding John Gardner* (Columbia, SC: University of South Carolina Press, 1993), p. 69.
10. John Gardner, *Grendel* (New York: Alfred A. Knopf, 1971), p. 72.
11. Rachel Carson, *Silent Spring* (Boston, MA: Houghton Mifflin, 1962), p. 13.
12. Howell, *Understanding John Gardner*, p. 71.
13. John Gardner, *On Writers and Writing* (Berkeley: Counterpoint, 1996), p. 248.
14. Frank Hellard, Interviewed by Dan Torre and Lienors Torre (3 September 2004).
15. Ibid.
16. Lewis Carroll, *Through the Looking Glass and What Alice Found There* (London: Macmillan and Co., 1872), p. 153.
17. Jack Zipes, *The Enchanted Screen – The Unknown History of Fairy-Tale Films* (New York: Routledge, 2011), p. 294.
18. Carroll, *Through the Looking Glass*, p. 116.
19. Ibid., p. 120.
20. Lewis Carroll, *Symbolic Logic, Part 1, Elementary* (London: Macmillan and Co., 1896), p. 40.
21. Carroll, *Through the Looking Glass*, p. 136.
22. Ibid., p. 140.
23. Ibid., p. 75.
24. Two other notable Australian animators worked on *Yellow Submarine*, including Cam Ford and Diana Ford (as Diane Jackson).
25. For example: Gardner, *On Writers and Writing*, p. 248.
26. Alexander Stitt, *A Film Study Guide – Grendel Grendel Grendel*, Melbourne: Al et al, 1981.
27. Joe David Bellamy and Pat Ensworth, 'John Gardner', in *The New Fiction: Interviews with Innovative American Writers*, ed. Joe David Bellamy (Urbana: University of Illinois Press, 1974), p. 180.
28. Stitt, *A Film Study Guide*.

Chapter 4

MAKING *GRENDEL GRENDEL GRENDEL*

Grendel Grendel Grendel was 'Al et al' studio's first animated feature film.[1] Although, the studio had previously produced a number of animated short films and hundreds of animated commercials (as well as a wide range of illustration and graphic design work for print), it was a somewhat herculean task for this small studio to transition to a feature film production. It required a great deal of strategic planning and innovation from its creators. This chapter commences with a pre-history of the Al et al studio, describing the backgrounds of a number of the film's key artists and animators and the emergence of the independent animation studio, in Melbourne, that would ultimately produce *Grendel Grendel Grendel*. Subsequently, the entire pre-production and production process is detailed, from initial concept through to completed animated film.

As with most animated feature productions of the era, the making of *Grendel Grendel Grendel* involved numerous and lengthy pre-production and production phases. One of the first steps in the pre-production process involved securing the film rights to John Gardner's novel, *Grendel*. Next, Alexander Stitt wrote the script and drew the storyboards for the entire film (which went through several revisions). He also designed the characters and the general stylization of the film. Around the same time, Stitt also wrote the lyrics to the songs and began collaborating with Bruce Smeaton to compose the music for the film. Subsequently, the recording sessions were held for both the voice actors and musicians; and many of the film's sound effects were also created and recorded at this time. Next, the production phase of the animated film commenced with Stitt and animation director Frank Hellard creating the layouts for each scene and Stitt creating virtually all of the film's backgrounds. The film was animated in the traditional manner, drawing each frame of action on paper. After each scene was animated, the pencil drawings were transferred onto cels, and each cel was meticulously painted. Next, each cel was photographed (one at a time) on top of its corresponding background image. Finally, each filmed scene was edited together, along with the completed soundtrack, to create the final animated feature film. However, along the way, a number of very innovative and non-conventional approaches were employed in the production of *Grendel Grendel Grendel*.

Pre-Grendel – The early years

The pre-history of *Grendel Grendel Grendel* can be traced back to the 1950s in Melbourne, Australia, and involved numerous creative individuals as well as the emergence and development of a few different animation studios.

The film's director, Alexander Stitt, got his start in animation while studying advertising design at RMIT University in Melbourne. Stitt had always been enamoured with animation, including Disney, but, in particular, the Fleischer Studios' *Superman* cartoons of the early 1940s for their strong sense of design. Later, and most significantly, he embraced the work emerging from the UPA studio and was particularly impressed with *Gerald McBoing Boing* (Robert Cannon, 1950). Stitt also recalls that it was after watching UPA's *A Unicorn in the Garden* (Bill Hurtz, 1953) that 'I knew this was what I wanted to do, to make films – make that film, in fact!'[2] As there were no official animation courses at the time, Stitt began experimenting with animation on his own. He acquired an old Bell and Howell camera, constructed a home-made camera stand, and found that 'if you pressed the release button just enough, it would take one frame of film' instead of continuous motion. In this way, he made his first rudimentary animated films.[3] After graduating from university, Stitt landed a job at Castle Jackson Advertising, becoming a third member of the agency's art department, and was given design work for clients right from the start. He also made it known that he could make animated commercials – 'which I'd never actually done, but I had the feeling I would be able to!' – and during the next two years produced several of these which went to air.[4]

In 1957, a new animation studio was formed in Melbourne. This was a significant event in the burgeoning era of animation and television broadcasting in Australia. Norm Spencer, a producer at Melbourne's Channel Nine television, visited America on the station's behalf and met with John Wilson, an English/American entrepreneur and animation director. John Wilson had worked for several years at UPA, and subsequently set up his own studio, Fine Arts Productions, in California. In addition to running his own studio, he began working as a consultant, advising and assisting television stations on how to establish their own in-house animation studios. Before long, he had successfully established animation studios in America, Spain, Portugal and Mexico. Norm Spencer, impressed with Wilson and his achievements, suggested to Channel Nine that they invite him to visit Melbourne.[5] A few months later, Wilson came to Australia bringing with him a core group of industry professionals. Pat Matthews, an experienced Disney and UPA animator, headed the American training team; his wife Connie Matthews took charge of backgrounds; cameraman Jean Balty set up a camera department; while Phyllis Hay led the ink and paint department.

Channel Nine then began recruiting, mostly newspaper cartoonists, to join its new animation studio, which, for lack of a better name, was called John Wilson Productions.[6] The initial team of trainee animators were Frank Hellard who had been an illustrator for the *Herald* newspaper; Gus McLaren had drawn a daily front-page cartoon for *The Argus* newspaper; Anne Jolliffe had regularly drawn comic strips for *The Age* newspaper; Wally Driscoll who drew a comic strip for *The Globe* newspaper; Ralph Peverill who was an illustrator and had worked on numerous publications; and Bruce Weatherhead who was a designer. Alexander Stitt was also employed, recalling, 'I became – I suppose I was the Art Director of the Unit. I actually had a reel – after all, I'd made five animated commercials!'[7] A number of other artists were hired, including Dick Sawers who became the chief background artist, and approximately a dozen ink and paint staff, including Maggie Geddes.

As was common at the time, most animators and designers were male. So Anne Jolliffe, who had applied to be an animator at the studio, was instead put in charge of inking and painting, even though she had had some prior animation experience making educational films for the CSIRO film department (Commonwealth Scientific and Industrial Research Organization). Seeing that this was unjustified, some of the other newly hired animators convinced the management to let her take an animation test – which she passed. Later Jolliffe found out that, not only was she the only one of the new recruits with previous animation experience (other than Stitt), but that she was also the only one who was forced to take a 'test' to become one. 'I realised then', said Jolliffe, 'that even though women do animate, they have to work about six times harder than men, and have to battle all the way through.'[8]

With all the staff in place, Pat Matthews began to lead them through his intensive three-month animation training course. The parent company, Channel Nine, became nervous about the high-cost of running the training programme. So in order to oblige the studio to become profitable, it forged ahead to secure numerous contracts to produce dozens of animated commercials. This forced the trainees to begin working on productions almost immediately, and to learn on the job. With so much work in the pipeline, it also gave the new animators the chance to take part in the production discussions and to write stories and produce storyboards. In between jobs, the formal animation training continued. Frank Hellard recalls:

> Pat Matthews would stress all the time that what was important in animation was what he called the 'little business'. He screened a film called *The Showman* that had a character applying for a job on the stage, smoking a cigar. He would lick his lips before he put the cigar in his mouth: and this made all the difference. You couldn't imagine that such a tiny thing could make so much difference. And the 'little businesses', as he called them, were what changes animation from being a mechanical device into an exciting art form.[9]

Matthews also screened reels of recent American animated commercials and short animated films from UPA, which 'everyone fell in love with'.[10] The animators were also encouraged to see the French mime artist, Marcel Marceau, who coincidently was set to perform two shows in Melbourne; John Wilson took the whole group of animators to both performances. Hellard quickly realized that Marceau was 'using exactly the same things that animators do – it was animation absolutely'.[11] After about nine months, Wilson, Mathews and the rest of the training crew returned to America. In 1958, Channel Nine rebranded the now fully functioning animation studio as Fanfare Films.

The influence of the UPA animation style (limited animation with a strong sense of design) remained with the studio. Fanfare Films went on to produce hundreds of animated television advertisements, and significantly, produced what is regarded as the first Australian animated television series, *The Adventures of Freddo the Frog*. The series was directed and principally animated by Gus McLaren (who had by then become the animation director of the studio) with backgrounds created by Dick Sawers, and broadcasted in 1962.

But due to falling profits, Fanfare films began laying off its artists, effectively halving its staff in 1963. By 1964, the studio had closed its doors completely. Most of the animators continued in the animation industry – although not necessarily in Melbourne. Anne Jolliffe went to London where she began working on the animated Beatles television series (at the same time that Artransa studios in Sydney were also producing episodes of the Beatles series), and then on the Beatles' feature film, *Yellow Submarine* (George Dunning, 1968). Following this, Jolliffe worked as an animator on Bob Godfrey's Academy Award winning animated short film, *Great* (1976), before returning to Australia. Dick Sawers also moved to London to work on *Yellow Submarine* and other productions. Gus McLaren became a freelance animator, subsequently working with Zoran Janjic on *Arthur! And the Square Knights of the Round Table* at Air Programs International (API) animation studios in Sydney, Australia, also on numerous other productions for other studios, including Hanna-Barbera Australia. Ralph Peverill moved to the remote town of Alice Springs, where he continued with a steady amount of freelance animation work.

Alexander Stitt and Bruce Weatherhead soon teamed up to form their own studio, calling it simply, Weatherhead & Stitt. They purchased Fanfare Films' extensive collection of animation equipment, hired Frank Hellard as their animation director, and soon had their own fully functioning animation production house. Producing a wide variety of animated advertisements and short films, Weatherhead & Stitt studios flourished for several years. In 1971, wanting to expand and try out other ventures, they launched an ambitious toy company that became known as The Jigsaw Factory and created impressively designed, educational books, toys and games. In addition to toys, art classes for kids, and many other ventures, the studio continued to produce animated films. Unfortunately, after a few years the Jigsaw venture proved to be too broad in its scope and ultimately unsuccessful. In 1973, the entire company closed its doors.

In 1974, Alexander Stitt formed a new studio, and called it 'Al et al' (the 'Al' for Alexander Stitt, and 'et al', Latin for 'and others'). Stitt drove the visual style of the studio, while animation director Frank Hellard, by now an extremely talented animator (and still greatly influenced by the UPA approach), drove the animation style. Stitt soon went about recruiting a number of the original staff that he had worked with at Fanfare films. Many of the original animators joined his new studio, including Gus McLaren, Ralph Peverill and Anne Joliffe. Maggie Geddes (who had also just returned to Australia after working as ink and paint supervisor on *Yellow Submarine*, and as an animator on several other productions) took on the role of production and ink and paint supervisor at Al et al. David Dalgarno resumed his role as an artist, and Fanfare Film's original company secretary, Janet Arup, also joined the new studio. A few new staff members also joined the team at this time, including the animator David Atkinson.

The Al et al studio, while concentrating on animated television commercials, also made several short animated films, one being the fifteen-minute *One Designer, Two Designer* (Stitt, 1978), which was commissioned by the Industrial Design Council of Australia. Written by Stitt, it was a humorous, although educational, look at the concept of design, and what it means to be a designer. It screened in cinemas as the opening short film for the live-action Australian feature film, *The Chant of Jimmy Blacksmith* (Fred Schepisi, 1978).

For a number of years, Stitt had been working closely with film producer, and advertising executive, Phillip Adams, who through his advertising agency, Monahan Dayman Adams (MDA) provided Stitt's studio with a steady stream of animation work and advertising campaigns. A number of these animated campaigns were used to support charitable organizations or to promote particular causes. In 1974, Adams was approached by the Victorian State Government (specifically by a parliamentarian who had previously been a professional football player) to devise a campaign directed towards fitness and health. The original intention was to try to get people to 'exercise energetically', but it occurred to Adams that a different approach might be better; he suggested that

> rather than asking a few people to do a lot – it might be better to ask a lot of people to do a little. And I said we should come up with a campaign that would encourage people to start with tiny steps, including the simple step of walking; to simply get off the couch and stop watching television.[12]

He immediately thought of an animated film campaign that would avoid dealing with specifics (such as age) so that anyone could relate to the characters. He devised the title *Life. Be in It* and asked Stitt to design sample storyboards to be put to the minister at a meeting the following day. Stitt literally worked through the night, and produced four, sixty-second storyboard options. One featured 'Norm', the anti-fitness, *Life. Be in It* character; another, that Stitt imagined would be considered totally outrageous and unacceptable for commercial television, recommended to viewers that they turn off the television set and go for a walk instead. Presented to the client the next day, all four concepts were accepted. The studio went on to make dozens of *Life. Be in It* animated commercials and soon it became one of the most recognized and long-lived ad campaigns in Australian advertising history.

A monstrous idea

Both Adams and Stitt 'had a great belief that animation should be seen as a more serious medium than it was'[13] and began making plans to produce a more substantial animated work. Adams suggested to Stitt, that if he was interested in doing an animated feature, then he would raise the funds for it. Stitt at the time had just become absolutely enamoured with John Gardner's novel, *Grendel*. He suggested to Adams that this could 'make an interesting animated film', Adams replied, 'Yeah, O.K. Do a storyboard. I'll put it in the briefcase and show it to everybody with all the rest'.[14]

Consequently, in early 1977, Stitt began work on a first draft of the storyboard – a process in which, working part time, would take approximately six months to complete. He decided to title the film, *Grendel Grendel Grendel* – as a means, of not only differentiating the film from the book (clarifying that it was an *adaptation*), but also to further emphasize the importance of the central character, Grendel. (And, as animation director Frank Hellard quipped – it was also 'three times as good'.)[15] This first version of the storyboard was drawn on the small pre-printed storyboard sheets that the studio normally used for television commercials, and rendered with marker pens in full colour (see Figure 4.1). Armed with this early draft of the storyboard, Adams was able to secure funding, but the production budget would need to be limited to a miniscule $600,000. Half of this would come from the Victorian Film Corporation (the State Government funding body); the rest from private investors. It was also agreed that Stitt and Adams would share the role of producer for the film.

Next, they set about securing the rights to the novel, contacting John Gardner's literary agent in America, Georges Borchardt. However, much to Stitt and Adam's surprise, they learnt that the novel had already been optioned to another animation director.[16] Stitt was dumbfounded, wondering, 'Who'd be silly enough to want to make a film out of it?'[17] It turned out that the other person who was 'silly enough' was the American independent animation director, Michael Sporn – who, like Stitt, had been thoroughly moved by the book. Sporn had contacted John Gardner directly and, although he had no resources at the time to make the animated film, was permitted to option the novel. Michael Sporn had then shopped the project around to a number of production companies, including United Artists and Cinema V, but despite Gardner's strong name recognition, they had all declined. By the time that Adams and Stitt had contacted the Georges Borchardt agency, Sporn's option on *Grendel* had nearly lapsed. Sporn recalls:

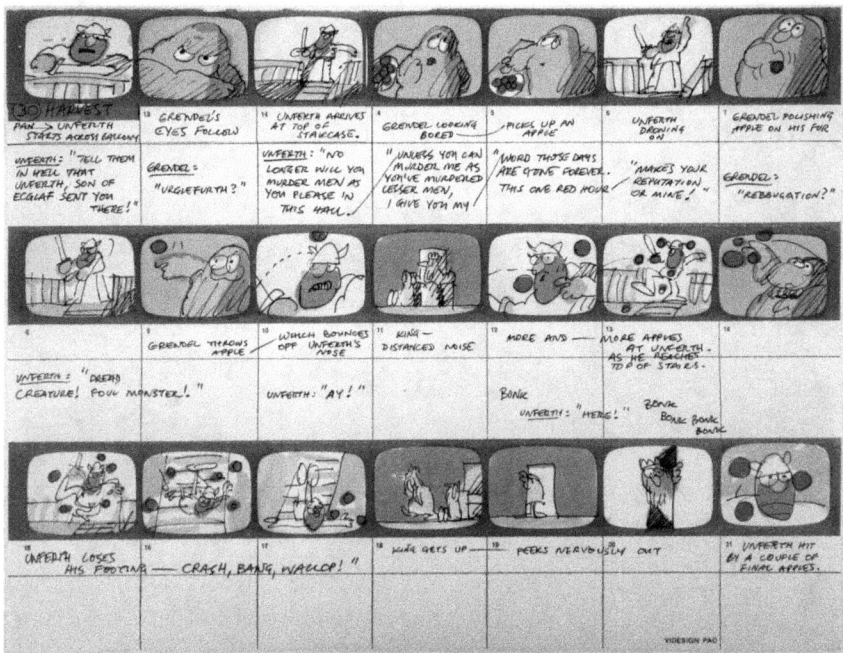

FIGURE 4.1 A page from the first version of the storyboard for *Grendel Grendel Grendel* (copyright Estate of Alexander Stitt, used with permission; courtesy Bruce Smeaton/National Library of Australia).

My last ditch effort before [Gardner] sold it was to call Roger Corman. Corman took my call (the magic of John Gardner's name) and tried to think how we could raise, at least, the $25,000 to secure the rights. He asked me to give him a week. At the end of the week, Corman decided to let it go, and I had to surrender.[18]

After Sporn's option expired, Stitt and Adams entered into negotiations with Gardner's agent, making it clear that their animated film would constitute a very liberal interpretation of the novel. A contract was finally signed in March of 1978, giving Adams and Stitt the exclusive film rights for a period of twenty years.

During this time Stitt had continued his pre-production work on the film. But until the rights were secured, he had kept the project fairly low-key, initially only confiding in a very few people (such as his animation director, Frank Hellard), as he worked away at the storyboards. But studio animator, David Atkinson, soon noticed that something momentous was in the works, recalling:

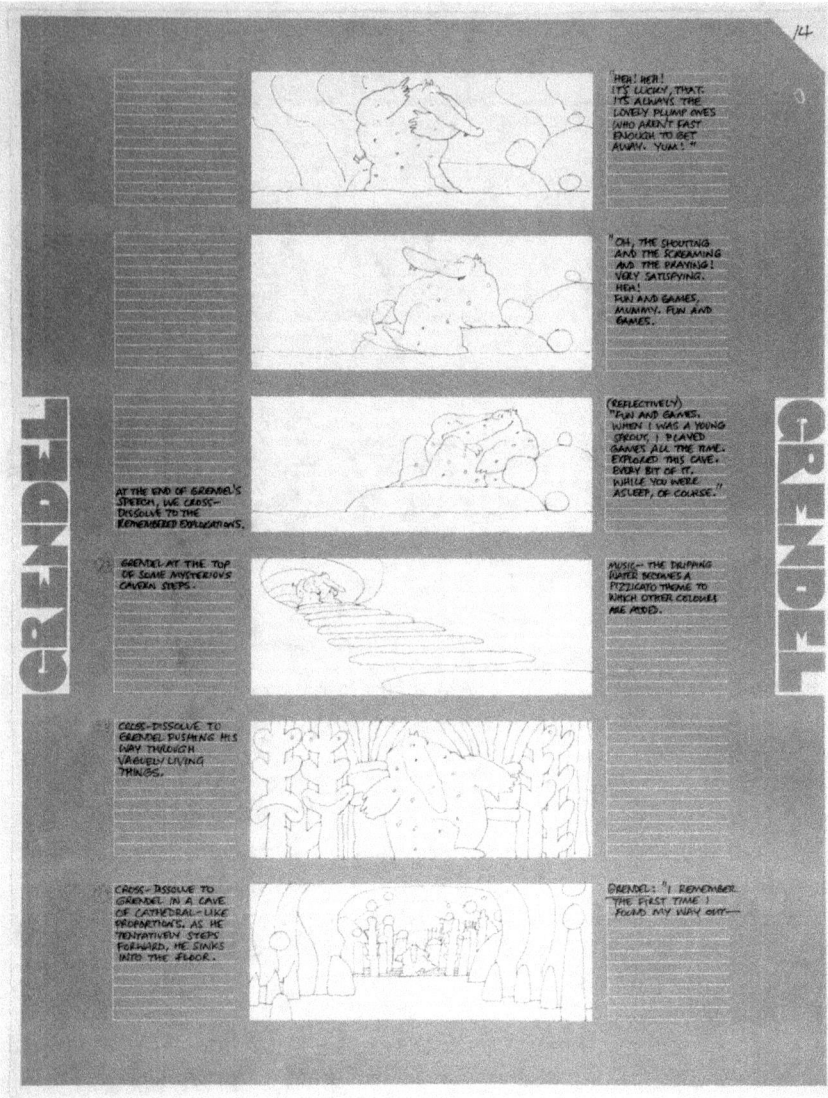

FIGURE 4.2 A page from the second version of the storyboard for *Grendel Grendel Grendel* (copyright Estate of Alexander Stitt, used with permission; courtesy RMIT Design Archives).

Alex was just fiddling around in the background – and then we started to see little story boards appear around the studio. Sometimes I would work back late and Alex had gone home and I'd go up to Alex's desk and poke around seeing if I could learn something and there's these wonderful storyboards.

You know within a few strokes Alex could say so much in terms of his composition and his shapes and I was enchanted by these things because they were really splendid little pieces of communication, the size of a matchbox. So, it was pretty obvious that something was going to happen, and that we were building up to something.[19]

Once the film rights were secured, the pre-production process accelerated significantly. Atkinson was then asked to do extensive research and help with the visual development work, producing, 'pages and pages of sketches',[20] while Stitt continued to work on the character designs and the overall look of the film. Stitt also began working on the second version of the storyboard, on large custom printed 'Grendel' storyboard sheets (see Figure 4.2). It was during this draft that the narrative, character actions and dialogue were further developed. This revised second version comprised 200 pages and featured approximately 1,200 story panels.

Bruce Smeaton

Because music would play a significant role in *Grendel Grendel Grendel*, composer Bruce Smeaton was quickly brought on to create the film's soundtrack. Smeaton, who had worked with Stitt previously, was by this time a highly regarded and nationally recognized musician and composer.

Bruce Smeaton had first become interested in music composition through listening to jazz music. A pivotal moment occurred when, as a young boy, he happened to walk past the local pub when a traditional jazz band burst forth. He was astounded by what he heard and soon began to collect jazz records (which at that time were recorded at 78 rpm), and would attempt to learn how to play them. Smeaton recalls:

There was an old upright piano next door and my older brother had a wind-up gramophone. I'd listen to various jazz recordings and try to play along by slowing the speed down until I could pick up the lines and the harmonies. I would gradually speed the music up by shifting the speed lever which meant I had to learn to play the same piece in a different key.[21]

This proved to be exceptionally effective 'ear training'. As his interest in music grew, he took up piano lessons, then the alto saxophone and numerous other instruments. He began experimenting with writing his own music compositions. Eventually Smeaton began to play semi-professionally, 'picking up work in pit-orchestras and town hall dances'. He continued to write his own music, becoming extremely prolific, and soon began to have some success with his compositions. In fact, within just a few years, nearly 150 pieces of his original music compositions had been performed on the Australian, ABC radio. 'The ABC were', he quipped, 'only too willing to have free music.'[22]

Eventually, however, Smeaton realized that 'the only way that I could exchange my music for money was to do [advertising] jingles'.[23] At this time, the late 1960s, the commercial radio and television sectors were burgeoning in Australia, so he began contacting advertising agencies across the city, literally knocking on doors. It was a strategy that proved to be immensely successful; within a span of less than ten years, Smeaton had composed an incredible 2,500 radio and television commercials. In doing so, Smeaton inevitably crossed paths with both Phillip Adams and Alexander Stitt.

> I did a lot of important and good commercials with Al [Stitt]. He was really good at briefing. He never made the mistake of telling me how the music should go, he always told me what he wanted the music to do. That is a very important distinction. Al would give me the elbow room, whereas others wouldn't let you move. They also didn't want you to express yourself. But Al did.[24]

By this time, Smeaton had also begun doing feature film scoring, composing the soundtrack to such successful features as: *The Cars That Ate Paris* (Peter Weir, 1974) and *Picnic at Hanging Rock* (Weir, 1975). So, when Stitt contacted Smeaton, he was quite willing to take on another feature film project (and particularly an animated one, since he had a great love of the medium). Furthermore, Smeaton had also become familiar with John Gardner's novels, having just finished reading, *The Sunlight Dialogues* (Gardner, 1972), and was immediately sold on the project. In preparation, he set about re-reading Gardner's *Grendel*, as well as revisiting his old paperback version of *Beowulf*, because he 'wanted to understand the difference of viewpoints' between the two texts.[25]

Sounding out Grendel

The plan was to have the majority of the film's soundtrack (music, dialogue and many of the sound effects) locked into place before the animation production commenced. Stitt gave Smeaton a copy of the storyboards and discussed with him in depth about 'the progress of the story, and what the music should achieve'.[26] At this point in the pre-production there were not too many other visuals to work from, but Smeaton was given a few additional drawings and painted pre-production cels from which to glean some inspiration.

While Smeaton began work on the film score, Stitt began recruiting the various voice actors for the film. The central character, Grendel, would be the most important voice role to fill. Peter Ustinov was quickly chosen because Stitt 'imagined Grendel as a haughty prince among monsters, and a tragic figure of operatic size. Who better than Peter (later Sir Peter) Ustinov to perform the voice part?'[27] Peter Ustinov, of course, was a well-known British actor, playwright, screenwriter and film director who had won many awards, including an Academy Award for Best Supporting Actor for *Spartacus* (Stanley Kubrick, 1960). But he was also no stranger to animation having performed several animated roles previously, ranging back to the 1950s when he lent his voice to the French animated feature, *The Curious Adventures of Mr. Wonderbird* (Paul Grimault, 1952) as the voice of the Wonderbird. Ustinov had also starred in the animated feature, *The Mouse and His Child* (Charles Swenson, Fred Wolf, 1977), playing the character known as 'Manny the Rat'. But Ustinov's animated film performance that had perhaps left the biggest impact on Stitt was his role as Sir John in Walt Disney's *Robin Hood* (Wolfgang Reitherman, 1973).

Stitt and Adams contacted Ustinov, sending him a copy of the storyboard. Stitt recalls that

> we had no idea how the budget could get us to London to record him if by any chance he agreed, but Ustinov replied, saying he liked the project, and as it happened, he would be touring Australia in the next couple of months. We couldn't believe our luck.[28]

Once Peter Ustinov had committed to the project, Stitt went about casting the rest of the character roles. The next big role that he needed to fill was that of the Dragon. He wanted a high-profile comedic voice for the role, so he provisionally lined up Australian actor and comedian Barry Humphries. However, Humphries was unable to do the film which left Stitt scrambling to find a replacement. In the meantime, he had recruited accomplished Australian actor Arthur Dignam to play the role of Beowulf. Dignam possessed a very wide vocal and character range (particularly in comedy) and Stitt realized that he would also be perfect to take on the role of the Dragon. As a rather serendipitous result of this development, Stitt was now able to actualize a central component of Gardner's novel – that the characters of Beowulf and the Dragon become inextricably linked in Grendel's consciousness. Gardner goes to great lengths to conflate the two characters together – to the point where, in the final battle scene, Grendel is virtually unable to distinguish between the two. What better way to pay reference to this literary blending than to have the same voice actor perform both roles?

As Stitt continued to fine tune the narrative of his film, he also continued to add in more songs, and before long he realized, to his surprise, that 'the film had turned into a musical'. Although Stitt had always intended for there to be a lot of music in the film, it was when he began to flesh out the minstrel character known as 'The Shaper', that he realized that this character was a metaphor, really, for the original declamatory style of Beowulf, and the plot dictated that he should have a couple of big numbers. After including those, it seemed a pity not to let the other principal characters have a sing, too. We finished up with seven songs.[29]

After writing the words to each song, Stitt would simply mail the handwritten lyrics to Smeaton for music composition. This long-distance form of collaboration posed more than a few challenges for Smeaton, one being, the challenge of adapting Stitt's sometimes 'difficult' lyrics 'into some sort of musical structure'.[30] The other was being unable to discover the vocal range and skills of each singer prior to the recording sessions. As this was often unknown to him, he would have to fabricate a number of contingency plans.

> Ustinov is a good example. I had no idea of the range of his voice and could not contact him. I decided to break some new ground by recording the vocals to what I called 'dummy' tracks. Possibly a better description would be 'original, simplified temp tracks in various keys' to return with a successful vocal so I could then set about orchestrating the song and expand the harmonic palette to better give Al what he wanted. The song is coloured and shaped by the interaction with the orchestra. The disadvantage is that the singer does not get an emotional 'belt' from the simplified piano accompaniment.[31]

Ultimately, the plan was to record the singers' vocals to discrete piano tracks, which Smeaton would later replace with a finalized orchestral composition.

The first dialogue and vocal recording session

As a result of Ustinov's busy schedule (he was touring a one-man show across Australia), Ustinov's recording session was scheduled to take place over the span of a single morning; thus it would be an enormous challenge to record the entirety of Grendel's dialogue, as well as Ustinov having to learn and sing two songs he had never seen before. They would need to keep precisely to schedule, particularly since they were scheduled to record Arthur Dignam performing both the voice of the Dragon and of Beowulf during the afternoon session.

Ustinov arrived in Sydney the day before the scheduled recording session, and producer Phillip Adams hired a limousine and driver, and picked him up from the airport. The driver took the scenic route around the harbours of Sydney, before dropping the celebrity off at his hotel. Adams recalls that

> Ustinov got out of the car and went into his hotel, and the driver turned around to me and said, 'I've got some of his LPs!' I said, 'what do you mean? Who do you think you've been driving?' The driver said, 'Burl Ives'. And

I said, 'No, no, no – he's Peter Ustinov'. So, I told Peter the story the next day and his response was quite rueful. He said, 'After you dropped me off, I walked up the hill towards Kings Cross and a group of giggling women came up and said, "we know who you are!"' And [Ustinov] thought modestly to himself, 'you should I'm an Oscar winning actor, writer, director, of immense fame and celebrity'. And they said, 'we saw you on the Mike Walsh show.' They had no idea who he was, but they had this vague idea that they'd seen him on television.[32]

The next morning, a slightly humbled Ustinov arrived at the recording studio, noticeably jet-lagged. Hoping to revive himself, he asked if he could have some juice or perhaps a piece of fruit. The limo driver rushed off to procure his order, and he soon came back with 'a whole box full of cantaloupes, bunches of grapes, apricots and peaches'. Ustinov, was rather taken aback when the box was presented to him, saying, 'Good lord, I'm not a hippopotamus, am I?'[33] But

FIGURE 4.3 (left to right) Alexander Stitt, Peter Ustinov and Phillip Adams at the first recording session in Sydney, 1978 (photo by Mary Smeaton, used with permission).

there was little time to waste, so Stitt began briefing Ustinov (grapes in hand) on the essential character qualities of Grendel and how he would like Ustinov to perform his lines. The recording session commenced shortly after this, and over the next three hours Ustinov performed the entirety of his lines – often they would only have time for one or two takes for each section of dialogue. Smeaton recalls that despite the gruelling schedule, 'Peter could adapt his voice to anything he was a genius, a fantastic mimic.'[34]

After completing his marathon dialogue recording session, it was time for Smeaton to direct Ustinov in the singing portion of his role (see Figure 4.4). Smeaton recalls that prior to the recording session he didn't really know the range of Ustinov's voice, so he had arrived in Sydney 'in a high state of nervousness and with multiple arrangements' for the songs that Ustinov was to sing. Fortunately, he was also able to recruit a highly talented pianist 'who could transpose my music on sight. And once I heard what [Ustinov] was doing, I could on the spot write another little bit into the piano part in pencil'.[35] As a result, Peter Ustinov was able to perform his songs to the re-doctored piano track. The main song that Ustinov performed was titled 'Grendel's Soliloquy' which is a heartfelt, melancholy piece, interspersed with nonsensical humour that expresses Grendel's general feelings of isolation. Ustinov performed the song with a convincing, yet playful, voice. However, some months later, Stitt decided to alter the song, replacing several of the lines that had originally been sung by Ustinov with a chorus of animated oyster-characters. The altered lines were then recorded in Melbourne, and sung by a chorus of two female singers and one male falsetto singer. These lines were changed in order to add greater depth to the song, but also to synchronize with the newly introduced herd of singing oysters – which were a last-minute addition to the storyboards, providing a clear reference to Lewis Carroll's book *Through the Looking Glass and What Alice Found There* (and also, by extension, to Walt Disney's animated feature, *Alice in Wonderland* [1951]) (see Chapter 3).

Next, Ustinov sang a few discrete lines which would be used during a flashback scene of when Grendel was a young monster-boy. In that scene, the young Grendel totters very awkwardly through the forest and, half-sings and half-mumbles, 'Who's the beast who looks so swell, G-R-E-N-D-E-L. What's his purpose can't you guess, N-E-M-E-S-I-S.' Stitt then asked Ustinov to sing these lines again, but with great confidence and gusto. These re-recorded lines are sung by an adult Grendel towards the very end of the film (see Figure 3.6a). Stitt intended that these contrasting performances would illustrate Grendel's development and ultimate discovery of his identity and placement in the world. This parallels the original novel in which Gardner describes Grendel's development from someone who can barely compose the simplest rhyming couplet, to a mature Grendel whose vocal talents nearly rival those of the Shaper.

Ustinov's final singing piece was a duet to be sung with the Dragon character (played by Arthur Dignam). Although it was a duet, each performer actually sang their part of the song separately. Ustinov recorded his lines first; Arthur Dignam recorded his a few hours later. The two tracks were then combined. Despite the rushed session (as well as Ustinov's jet-lag, mistaken identity and overabundance of fruit), the actor managed to give a convincing performance. Undoubtedly, most felt that if there had been time for additional retakes, some of his lines (particularly those performed towards the end of the recording session) would have come across more robustly.

Arthur Dignam

Arthur Dignam had starred in a number of live-action films and television series. As he was based in Sydney, his recording session was scheduled to take place directly after Ustinov completed his recording; he would therefore need to record the entirety of his lines (in both the roles of the Dragon and of Beowulf) – as well as sing a song – in just a few hours.

Dignam adroitly performed his two different character roles with surprising variance. In the role of Beowulf, Dignam sounds simultaneously condescending, menacing and artificially polite. Stitt noted that 'Arthur Dignam performed Beowulf with a chilling, George Sanders-ish edge.'[36] Interestingly, the real-life George Sanders had, some ten years earlier, performed the voice of the villainous tiger character, Shere Khan, in Disney's animated feature, *The Jungle Book* (Wolfgang Reitherman, 1967). It is this characterization which clearly helped to shape Dignam's inflection in his performance of Beowulf. In stark contrast to the Beowulf character, Dignam performed the Dragon character in a highly comedic fashion. Animator David Atkinson, who was also present at the recording session, noted that, 'when Arthur Dignam stepped in, you could feel a lightness – a joyous talent behind the voice of the Dragon.'[37] This comedic playfulness was, in turn, punctuated by a great deal of playful animation in the final film.

Keith Michell

The next scheduled dialogue and vocal recording session took place in Adelaide, South Australia (over 700 km away from the Al et al studios in Melbourne), and featured the performances of Australian actor Keith Michell. Although the actor resided in England at the time, he would be in Adelaide for a few days and had agreed to provide the voice for the Shaper while he was in town. Once again, the session was limited to just a few hours' duration; Michell first recorded his lines of dialogue, and subsequently performed his three songs. Stitt was particularly pleased with Michell's performance and noted that, 'Keith's awesome, commanding voice was just what we needed for the Shaper,

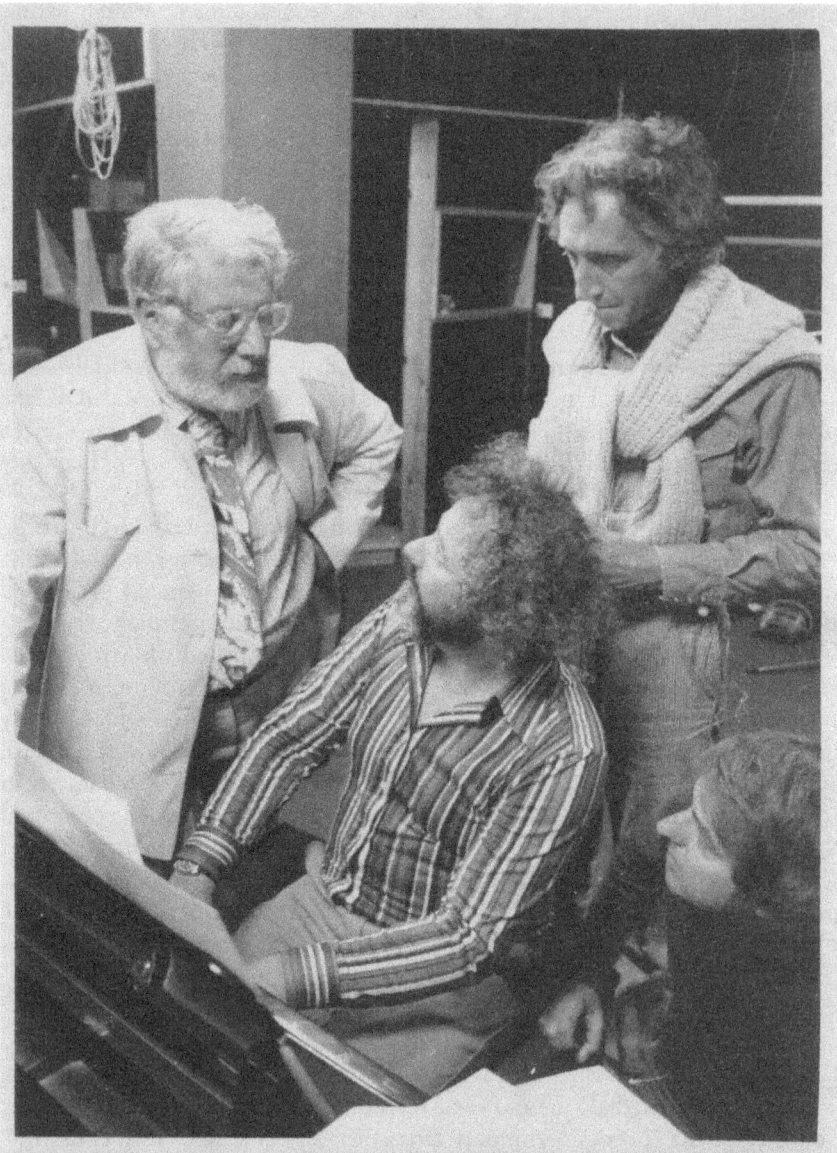

FIGURE 4.4 (left to right) Peter Ustinov, Bruce Smeaton and Arthur Dignam rehearse before recording session (Albert's Studio, Sydney, September 1978) (photo by Mary Smeaton, used with permission).

a blind minstrel with a gift of prophecy, whose songs recounted the history of the times.'[38]

As he did with the other singers, Smeaton had composed multiple and original temp piano tracks for Michell to sing to (which would later be replaced with a full orchestral backing). Michell's first song was titled 'The Revenge of Wiglaf'. In the film, the powerful delivery of this song serves to not only secure the Shaper's employment as the king's minstrel (by flattering the king and rallying his people around him), but it also has an utterly profound effect on Grendel. Indeed, Grendel is so moved by the song that as he walks away from the meadhall, he can be heard happily whistling the tune of the song (the whistling, however, was performed by the session pianist, Peter Jones). The next song that Michell performed was called 'The Creation Song'. This song signified an important turning point in the film, as it not only highlighted the evolving religious beliefs of Hrothgar's kingdom (specifically the shift from paganism to Christianity, which is also hinted at in the original *Beowulf* poem), but it also clarified Grendel's place within human society. The humans had come to view Grendel not only as a monster, but also as a descendant of Cain, and therefore he was categorically excluded from their society. Michell performed this song with the power and grandeur needed to instigate the shattering of Grendel's world view, as he eavesdropped upon the meadhall. The Shaper's third and final song, 'We Know a Lovely Monster', is a comedic, irony-infused patter song. However, it also has a profound effect on several of the characters. For example, it so enrages Unferth that he swings his battle-ax at the King's taunting children. Additionally, the use of irony and subtlety of speech serve to confuse the King, and also mislead Grendel into believing that perhaps the humans do like him after all. Ultimately, Michell's light-hearted and up-tempo delivery adroitly belies the song's prophetic nature.

Julie McKenna

Julie McKenna sang two different songs, and in doing so, performed the singing voice of two different characters: The Shaper's Boy and Grendel's Mum. The first piece that she performed was the opening title song, 'Grendel Grendel Grendel', which functions as a love song from Grendel's Mum to her son. However, paradoxically, Grendel's Mum is unable to actually speak in the film (nor in Gardner's novel) beyond her animal-like grunts and growls. Thus, this song effectively projects the feelings and emotional bonds that normally exist between any mother and child. The title song is somewhat reminiscent of a ballad in a Broadway musical; or perhaps even the opening theme song of a James Bond movie – such as the one sung by Shirley Bassey in *Diamonds Are Forever* (Guy Hamilton, 1971); or the Nancy Sinatra song in *You Only Live Twice* (Lewis Gilbert, 1967). On one hand, the song is intended to evoke feelings of empathy for Grendel; at the same time, Stitt wanted the song to create a sense of unease, instructing Smeaton to imbue the song with a 'mixture of innocence and fear'.[39]

Smeaton had worked with McKenna for a number of years prior on various radio and television commercials, so he was familiar with her vocal range. But during an initial rehearsal, Smeaton found that the combination of Stitt's complex lyrics, and his own equally complex music (made all the more challenging through his effort to convey a sense of unease), proved to be a very tall order for the singer. Then, Smeaton had an inspiration: he would write 'a fake piano part, composed of very simple chords, so that Julie could pitch to it'.[40] The strategy paid off and when McKenna's voice was subsequently mixed with Smeaton's atonal and chromatic full music score it achieved precisely the effect that Stitt was looking for.

The second song (and second character) that Julie McKenna performed was 'The Moon Is Rising', as sung by the Shaper's Boy in the final acts of the film. Originally, the highly acclaimed British jazz singer Cleo Laine (whom Stitt had met while she toured Australia) was tipped to be the voice of the Shaper's Boy. However, after she was unavailable to do it, Stitt lined up local jazz musician and actor, Smacka Fitzgibbon to take on the role. Unfortunately, he also could not perform as he became seriously ill just prior to the scheduled recording session. Finally, Stitt employed Julie McKenna to take on this additional role.

Prior to this moment in the film, the Shaper's Boy appears to be completely mute. Thus, it is a surprise when he does burst into song, and a further surprise when he sings in the rich female voice of McKenna. 'The Moon is Rising' is intended to foretell the coming battle between Beowulf and Grendel. Its opening lyrics are:

The moon is rising on his final evening in the
world he shares with you and me.
The monster, the Great Boogy, doesn't know that
he is walking to eternity.

As with the opening theme song, this too was intended to convey a sense of disquiet and apprehension. Smeaton facilitated this effect by extending the harmonies and sprinkling the melody with 'odd notes'. Of all the songs in the film, this is probably the one with the most complex lyrics – giving Smeaton the technical challenge of 'accommodating the words in the song'.[41]

It is a very interesting coincidence that Julie McKenna found herself singing in the role of these two, effectively mute, characters. In Stitt's film, the Shaper's Boy relies solely on gestures to communicate with others; and it is only after the Shaper has died, that he finally 'finds his voice' and is able to sing a song. Contrastingly, in Gardner's novel, the Shaper's Boy is able to speak, making Stitt's recasting of the Boy as a mute a curious choice. His rather discordant pairing of a blind Shaper and a mute assistant suggests an inverted evocation of the 'blind leading the blind' analogy, which ultimately serves to question the veracity of the Shaper's intentions. Similarly, Grendel's

Mum has (presumably over the centuries) lost her ability to speak and relies on grunts and growls to communicate with her son. Gardner took a large literary step forwards by giving Grendel a voice in his novel. Stitt, arguably, took an even further literary step by also giving the character of Grendel's Mum a voice.

Final recording sessions

The final voice recording sessions happened over several days in Melbourne, using local actors. These included Ed Rosser who performed the voice of King Hrothgar; Ric Stone as Unferth; Bobby Bright as Dung; Ernie Bourne as Wiglaf; Barry Hill as the Foreign King; Alison Bird as Wealtheow; Rho Schepisi played the King's son; while Colin McEwan played the King's second son, as well as the Old Priest; Peter Aanensen performed the character of One-eyed Arthur; and Jack Brown performed the role of his companion, Basil. Most of these actors had previously done voice work for Alexander Stitt on animated commercials, or had been sourced through his wife, Paddy Stitt (who worked at the MDA advertising agency). Furthermore, many of these actors had done extensive voice work for the medium of radio.

Animation director, Frank Hellard attended most of the voice recording sessions, bringing an animator's perspective to the proceedings. Hellard would often advocate the casting of a seasoned radio actor over a film or television actor, noting that film actors 'think mostly of their outside', but in contrast a skilled voice or radio actor will better understand how to convey character entirely through voice, 'because they're *thinking* of the image, but they're not giving you an image'.[42] Once a strong vocal performance had been captured, Hellard believed that it required an equally strong set of listening skills to effectively interpret the recorded performance.

> An animator hears the soundtrack more than anyone else; he hears it hundreds of times, literally. He can play it over and over again and do little sketches right through the piece of work until he knows when the character would move his head – would he move his head as he finishes that sentence: or would he stop and think and, as he starts again, move his head? It becomes quite clear to an animator after listening to the soundtrack enough and doing the sketches, to know exactly what the character does between pauses, between sentences.[43]

From this perspective, the tasks of the animators become much easier if they are able to work to strong and vocally expressive recordings.

In the course of the film, and as Hrothgar's kingdom grows, there are numerous religious ceremonies that take place. Stitt thought that it would be

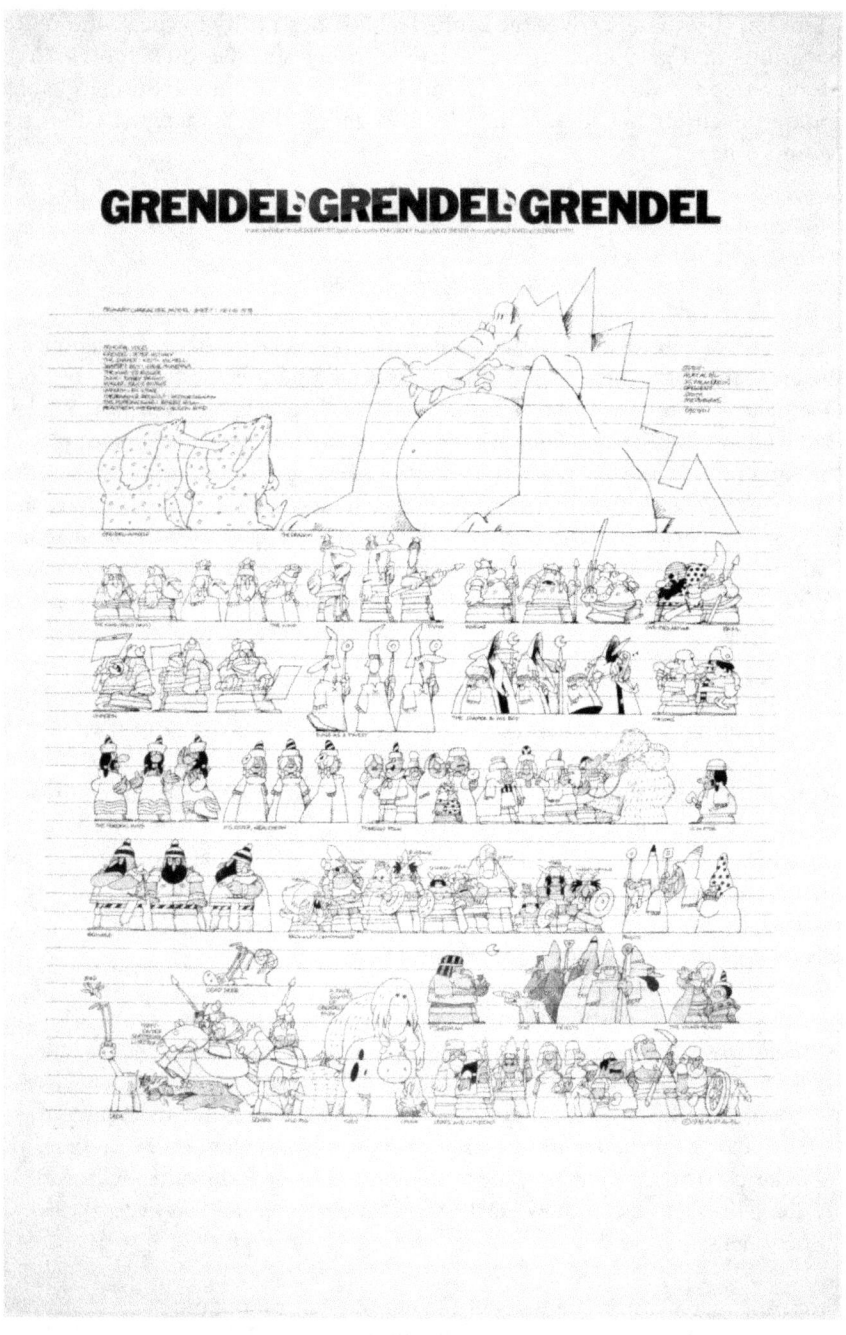

FIGURE 4.5 Character model sheet from *Grendel Grendel Grendel* (copyright Estate of Alexander Stitt, used with permission; courtesy RMIT Design Archives).

important to have the attendant priests sing while conducting these rituals and so Smeaton arranged for several singers, two tenors and two baritones, to attend one of the final recording sessions. Smeaton recalls that Stitt had intended to write particular lyrics for these priestly songs, but the recording day arrived and the lyrics had not yet been written; so after some discussion they went ahead and simply recorded the singers, reverently singing a few simple phrases in pig-latin. The final pig-latin sequence consisted of the following phrases: 'Igpay atinlay, Onor-hay, Ayth-fay, Ower-pay, Alor-vay' and 'Reat-gay, Oogie-bay, Im-ray, Alker-way'. When translated, it becomes 'Pig-Latin, honour, faith, power, valour' and 'Great Boogy, rim-walker'.

Once all of the dialogue and the song vocals were recorded (against discrete piano tracks), Smeaton set about finalizing the orchestral score for the film and the replacement music for the songs. The music was written with a full orchestration in mind: strings, piano, woodwinds, percussion, as well as a few other less conventional instruments (such as the waterphone, prepared piano, a small pottery ocarina and Japanese shakuhachi). Much of Smeaton's music is technically complex; it is multi-layered and references a great many genres and aural aesthetics. Ultimately, they would need a large studio facility with a host of skilled musicians to actualize the musical score. However, all that was available at the time (that fit within budget) was the very modest sized, A&M recording studio in West Melbourne. In order to accommodate all of the instruments, musicians and recording equipment, Smeaton had to carefully measure the facility, calculate the precise space needed for each instrument and then place them accordingly into a scaled diagram. Needless to say, it proved to be a very tight fit. A number of musical sound effects were also recorded at this time. In one sequence of the film, King Hrothgar's sons wreak havoc with the Shaper's musical instruments – to express this, Smeaton brought in one of his old guitars to the recording session and smashed it to bits in front of the microphone. In other sequences, Grendel swims through a lake of fire snakes to and from his underground cavern – for this, Smeaton recorded a waterphone to create a mysterious other-world effect. In the end, they managed to work their way through the recordings and ended up with the nearly fifty minutes of original music. And, now that the soundtrack was complete, animation could finally begin.

Animating Grendel

Al et al studio had been at their location in South Melbourne for several years, occupying the ground floor of a modern building (see Figure 4.6). But with the looming production of a feature film, they soon commandeered the upstairs level as well. As the upper floor was air-conditioned (something that was still relatively uncommon in 1970s Melbourne) it proved to be the perfect temperature controlled facility to set up a full-sized ink and paint department.

FIGURE 4.6 Al et al studio where *Grendel Grendel Grendel* was produced, Melbourne, Australia (photo by Mary Smeaton, used with permission).

The clean, modernish exterior of the building hid the mass of orderly untidiness inside. Virtually every square inch of the interior was littered with mounds of production materials. As the production ramped up, and as the staff became more familiar with the monstrous (yet lovable) nature of the film's lead character, Grendel was soon venerated to mythical status. One tongue in cheek article remarked, 'The production staff at Al et al are so convinced of Grendel's existence that they were horrified the day they all arrived at work and found the upstairs door kicked in.'[44] It turned out, according to police, to have been a burglar looking for valuables; however, 'Al et al staff aren't so sure', quipped the writer.[45] Nevertheless, the production team now had someone to blame for the messy state of the studio.

> There's little doubt that Grendel resides in Al et al's rabbit-warren of a building in wrong-side-of-the-tracks South Melbourne: stickers on doors and graffiti on walls warn you of Grendel's imminent presence: wherever you look there's a shamble of paper, boards and paint pots that announce Grendel's rather destructive nature.[46]

Grendel was unquestionably a very small production. The entire animation department consisted of Frank Hellard (who doubled as the 'Animation Director'), Anne Jolliffe, Gus McLaren, Ralph Peverill and David Atkinson.

FIGURE 4.7 (left) Animation director Frank Hellard and (right) animator David Atkinson at work on *Grendel Grendel Grendel* (photo by Mary Smeaton, used with permission).

Only Frank Hellard and David Atkinson worked exclusively at the studio (see Figure 4.7), while Anne Jolliffe split her time between the Al et al studio and her own newly formed studio, Jollification Animation. Gus McLaren worked at his home studio in Warrandyte (approximately 50 km from the studio), and would only drop by the studio every couple weeks to pick up or drop off work. Ralph Peverill worked very remotely (over 2,000 km away) in the town of Alice Springs in the Northern Territory, and the studio would 'post him a parcel of punched animation paper, along with track readings, layouts and the rest, and he would send back the drawings'.[47] Although Hellard was the animation director, he actually spent most of his time animating rather than closely directing the other animators. Unquestionably, it was Frank Hellard, who produced the greatest quantity of animation for the film. The paint department was run by Maggie Geddes (whose official credit on the film was 'Production Supervisor'). The paint department consisted of Marilyn Davies, Suzan Harris, Sharon Johnson, Fiona Mackay, Christine Neely, Denis Pryor and Sally Anne Rozario. Additionally, studio manager and artist David Dalgarno also took on the role of painter, as did the studio receptionist, Janet Arup. The main cameraman for the film was John Pollard, shooting on the studio's in-house rostrum camera. Later, towards the end of the production, Dennis Tupicoff was also brought in to assist with the camera work, photographing several of the scenes. Alex Stitt served, unofficially, as the production's third cameraman; shooting two of the more complicated scenes which involved frequent pans, multi-passes and dissolves between still graphic images. It was a process that Stitt excelled at, 'for Alex, the camera was not just some passive recording device, but a creative tool in its own right', recalls animator, David Atkinson.[48]

But having a very small budget to work with, they had to devise a very strict and economical production schedule.

> The maths were very simple. We decided to make one minute a week. Therefore, to make ninety minutes, and with a bit of messing around, it was going to be a two-year production project. We assigned four major animators, each responsible for fifteen seconds of work a week. And we set a budget of about six hundred cels per minute because we couldn't afford to be buying the cels, let alone tracing and painting and doing everything else. So, it was utterly pragmatic in that sense.[49]

In order to help pay the bills and to keep up their standing in the commercial business, Al et al continued to produce about one animated television commercial per month. But this was a fraction of their normal output – which gave other local animators, such as Dennis Tupicoff, a chance to 'pick up some extra commercial animation work'.[50] The studio also continued to produce a

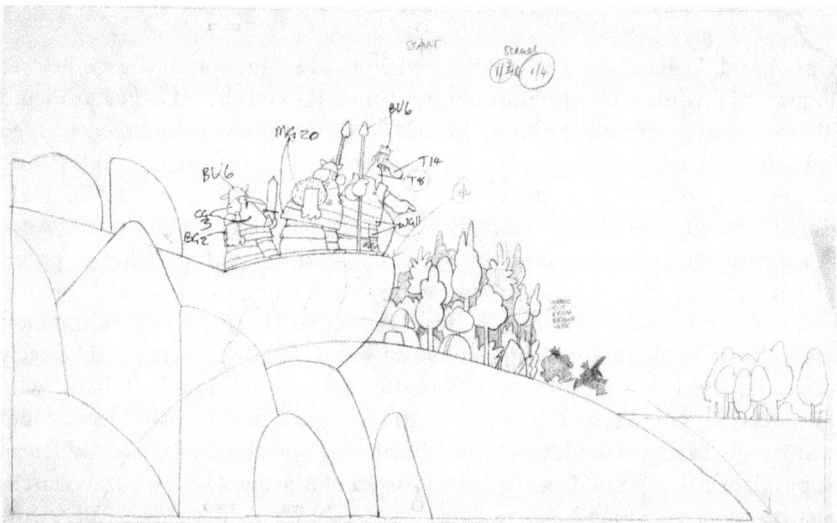

FIGURE 4.8 Layout drawing for *Grendel Grendel Grendel* describing composition and indicating paint colours and placement of cel overlay (so that background characters can appear to emerge from forest); notation states, 'Yobbos out from behind here' (copyright Estate of Alexander Stitt, used with permission; courtesy RMIT Design Archives).

steady stream of graphics work for print media as well. And about halfway through the production, they were also compelled to take on a major 'Made in Australia' ad campaign, which put further stress on the studio.[51]

For each sequence, the animator would be given storyboards, layouts (see Figure 4.8), exposure sheets and a cassette tape of the soundtrack. Because of the limitations of the production, there were no assistant animators; thus each animator would produce all of their own key drawings and in-betweens and even, in some cases, clean-up their final drawings. Furthermore, as time and budget were so limited, there were no opportunities for pencil testing or reviewing the animation drawing (other than through the simple hand-flipping method). Thus, what the animator handed back would, almost without exception, then go straight to the ink and paint department.

While the animators and the ink and painters were hard at work, Stitt was busy painting the backgrounds. He was striving for a cohesive image, one in which backgrounds and the animated characters would be treated in a similar manner.

> I've always had a hatred for animated things where you know the bits that are going to move in the scene, all these little bits that are signalling to you 'Hey, I've got a black outline around me, so I'm going somewhere,' and you know that that house painted on the background is never going to go anywhere![52]

Stitt initially designed the film so that everything would have a black line around it, both the characters and the backgrounds (see Figure 4.9). But about two months into the production, Stitt came to the realization that the overall design of the film was not strong enough. Up until that point Stitt had viewed the completed animation sequences on a small editing screen, but when they finally screened the first several minutes of completed animation in a theatre setting, Stitt found 'the results were disappointingly flat and visually undramatic'.[53] He knew that he had to change the design

> I decided the solution was to eliminate the outlines and add a feeling of light and shade to the forms of the characters. The animation work was fine, but it was a decision that meant scrapping many of the completed cels. It also meant devising a new tracing system to eliminate the line work.[54]

Stitt went back and reworked the backgrounds, creating them anew without any line work at all. Next he met with Maggie Geddes, and a few of the others from the paint department, and explained the new approach.

> We would handle the animation material by taking the animator's pencil drawing, turning it over on the trace and painter's light box, laying the cell on top of that. And the painter would then paint the flat colour on to the back of the cell in the usual way; but instead of painting up to the black line or any

sort of line that had been drawn on the cell previously for them to paint up to, they were painting through to the animator's pencil line.[55]

It meant that the painters now had to be extremely precise with their brushwork. Previously, the 1 mm width of black line would create, to a certain extent, a very thin matte, which would help to obscure the slight imperfections of the edge of the under-layer of paint. Equally important, the animator's drawings would need to be more precise, 'it had to be a very clean pencil line, so the painters could paint right up to it'.[56] Not only would their approach to painting all future cels need to be changed, but they would also need to repaint all of the cels that they had already completed. However, in a very few instances, the painters were

FIGURE 4.9 Early test cels showing the original design style of the film (with inked, black outlines on both the characters and the background elements) (copyright Estate of Alexander Stitt, used with permission; courtesy RMIT Design Archives).

able to obscure the black ink line by over-painting on the front of the cel, but in most cases, it meant that they would have to start from scratch.

Furthermore, the colour treatment of the characters needed to change, because without the delineating black lines, the flat expanses of a single colour would often render a figure undiscernible. So Stitt ordered in a whole range of additional cel-paint colours, those which were on either side of his previously established colour scheme. 'So that when, for example, the Dragon's arm moved over his body – the arm colour would change to a different tone of red or orange.'[57] Atkinson adds, 'Of course you also had to figure out which order to apply the colours. So, if there is going to be an arm across the body you do the arm first and then the body colour goes straight over everything and makes its own matte.'[58] Usually, the portion of the character that was in the foreground would be slightly lighter in colour, and the part that was in the background darker. This turned out to be quite a challenge for the paint department; Geddes had to carefully supervise the painters, ensuring that they would apply the paint in the correct order and change the colour tones at the right instance, which 'kept us all on our toes.'[59]

Choosing to throw away the line entirely constituted a very bold move. Many other studios had previously tried to find innovative ways to integrate the line work of their animated films. For example, in Disney's big-budget *Sleeping Beauty* (Clyde Geronimi, 1959), the characters were inked in a corresponding colour of ink – thus if the dress of a character was to be painted red, that part of the cel would be outlined in a red-tinted ink. This, of course, proved to be a very expensive undertaking. Contrastingly, in the production *One Hundred and One Dalmations* (Wolfgang Reitherman, Hamilton Luske, Clyde Geronimi, 1961), they opted to use xerography to copy the line from the animator's drawings onto the cel and, in order to make these cohesive with the backgrounds, they applied a similar photo-copied black line-treatment to the background paintings. To further compensate for the lack of line-work, Stitt also began to apply heavy

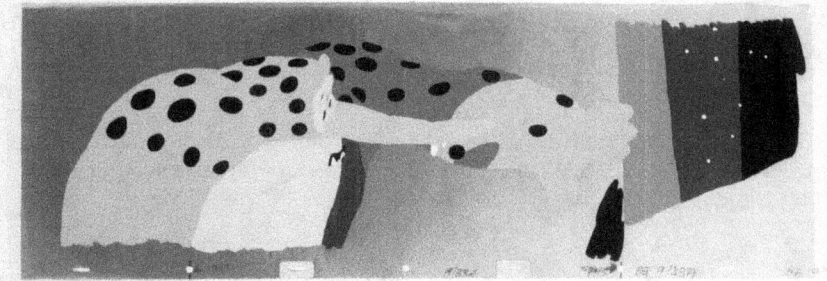

FIGURE 4.10 A production cel set up (used in a camera pan sequence) displays the finalized, line-free, look of the film (copyright Estate of Alexander Stitt, used with permission; courtesy RMIT Design Archives).

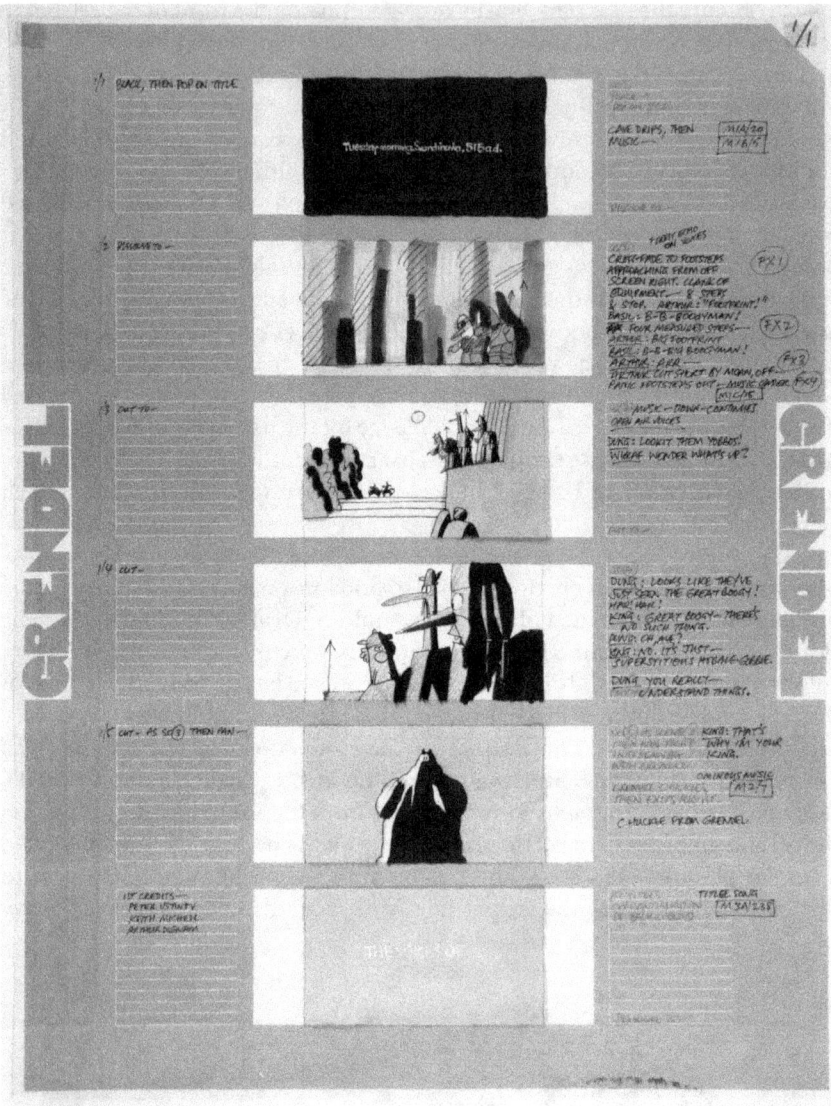

FIGURE 4.11 A page from the third (and final) version of the storyboard for *Grendel Grendel Grendel* (copyright Estate of Alexander Stitt, used with permission; courtesy RMIT Design Archives).

shadows on the characters, painting two-thirds of it in a particular colour, and the remaining third a colour about four shades darker. 'It gave a hard-shadow line on parts of the characters – which I was also using on the backgrounds. Suddenly the whole thing had this strong, integrated quality.'[60] Additionally, as a consequence of changing the film's style, Stitt felt compelled to redo the entire storyboard one last time, producing what would be the third and final version. This final version he created more detailed drawings significantly revised the layout of each scene and rendered it in full colour to reflect the updated colour styling of the film (see Figure 4.11).

One afternoon, Frank Hellard dropped in as a guest lecturer to the animation department at Swinburne University to update the animation students on the film's progress. Dennis Tupicoff, who was one of these students, recalls how Hellard was extremely excited as he burst into the classroom and exclaimed, 'You know what Alex has done? It's genius! He's decided to not use any lines on *Grendel Grendel Grendel*, and it works really well.' Hellard then, to the student's delight, gave a demonstration of the new painting process. Hellard also went on to explain that, because the film now lacked the detail defining line-work of traditional animated films, the animators would have to pay very close attention to ensuring that the characters were drawn in clear and readable poses – with consistently strong silhouettes.[61]

Although the new line-free design facilitated a very strong and unified sense of design, the loss of detail in the characters was indeed one of the downsides to this new approach. While the characters were actually moving, their forms were easily read. But in still frames and held-cels – unless they were depicted in a pose with a strong silhouette – their readability might suffer. The fact is a simple pen line can actually convey a great deal of important information. Even though Stitt was very keen to completely eliminate all inked lines, some compromises had to be made. For example, the mouths and eyes of most characters still required inked outlines in order for the lip-synch and facial expressions to remain discernible. In other cases, the loss of facial detail was deemed acceptable. One of the characters in the film, known simply as 'The Foreign King', was intended to parody Terry-Thomas, the well-known British actor. Terry-Thomas, in addition to speaking in an exaggerated British accent, had a large gap between his two front teeth. In the original character design of 'The Foreign King', this tooth gap was delineated by a simple black ink-line. However, with the new design, this line was eliminated, leaving the character with a solid bar of perfect, gapless white teeth. Thus, the process also eliminated an identifiable visual link between the animated character and the real-world actor, Terry-Thomas (although the *vocal* link did remain through the impersonation talents of voice actor Barry Hill).

Because of the change in the film's design, the ink and paint department soon became simply the *paint department*. The radical shift in design ultimately required the reworking or repainting of thousands of cels. As a result, within a few months, the studio precipitately ran out of several colours of paint, including the primary 'Grendel-green' that they had been using for painting Grendel. They quickly put in another order of 'Cel-Vinyl' paint to Cartoon Colour, of Culver City, California. But, because of the lengthy delays with shipping to Australia, the paint did not arrive for several weeks.

Production could not wait, so for a period of time the studio had to resort to using a slightly different tone of green. Although to most, this went unnoticed.

The upper floor of the studio was devoted entirely to the paint department, where the seven full-time painters would, working over light-boxes, paint-trace the pencil drawings on to cels. At any point in the production, there would be many hundreds of cels laid out on rows and rows of drying racks. Soon, the upper floor became as crowded as the ground floor of the studio. To further add to the crowded atmosphere, production supervisor, Maggie Geddes would normally bring her nine-month-old son, Toby, to work with her, placing him in a cot in one corner of the studio. As the weeks progressed he was becoming more mobile, and one afternoon, while everyone was hard at work, he walked over to a row of drying racks and began pulling dozens of the still damp cels onto the floor. At that very moment, Stitt walked in. 'He didn't say a word', recalls Geddes, 'but I just knew by the look on Alex's face, that that was it – Toby was going to childcare!'[62] As the workload increased, a light box was set up at the reception desk, and the studio's receptionist, Janet Arup, would be busily painting cels while answering the phones and performing her other duties. Similarly, artist and studio manager, David Dalgarno, also began painting cels whenever there was a spare light box available.

Grendel by design

Alexander Stitt meticulously designed each scene, but he tended to be much freer in regards to his actual direction of the animation. He would carefully plan out the structure and look of each scene, but then he would leave it up to the others to fill in the details with their own creative approaches. 'And I think this was Alex's brilliance – he was able to just put it in the hands of the animators.'[63] He welcomed the surprises that each animator would bring to a scene. 'I imagine Alex's heart would have been broken occasionally looking at stuff, and there were other times where he would have been absolutely delighted.'[64] But regardless of whether he was disappointed or delighted, more often than not, the sequence would have to go directly into the film as it was.

The character model sheets were very basic – simply depicting relative sizes and in some cases (but certainly not all), basic character turn arounds would be shown (see Figure 4.5). It was up to the animators to work out how the characters would move – and this was a challenge to some, as many were fairly stocky characters with very wide, short legs. Atkinson recalls that the animators were generally dismayed by the prospect of having to animate the film's very short, stumpy characters, exclaiming 'well we don't even know how to get clearance for their feet to swing through to make them walk'. Alex's reply was simply, 'You'll figure it out, don't worry'. And in the end, they did, but often with rather different approaches. Some would have the characters simply shuffle along, while animator Gus McLaren would 'make their legs grow so they could get their feet swinging underneath them and when they hit their spot they'd sort of shrink again'.[65]

Similarly, although Hellard was the animation director of the feature, for the most part he tended to respect the abilities and decisions of the other animators. Of course, his own style of animation unquestionably set the tone for the film. He was still very much influenced by the UPA style and the idea of limited animation, and considered it to be a far superior way of working.

> The UPA people treated that business of cutting the number of drawings down; and they were very experienced animators, lived years and years through millions of complicated inbetweens; and they knew exactly how many drawings they'd need, and how few they could get away with. They used that and made it look funny – and that's a real triumph! That's without losing anything. Cutting the animation right down. Limited animation gets a very bad name because it's usually done by a producer who wants to make an animated series for so much an episode.[66]

Although Hellard rarely demanded that an animator redo a sequence, he would often assert his directorial powers to insist on the simplifying of a scene. But, as deadlines were most pressing, rather than having the animator redo any drawings, he would simply remove what he felt were the most extraneous drawings. Frank Hellard also believed strongly in working *within* the limitations of the medium of animation.

> Working in a medium that has limits is what makes for interest in working with it. Like carving things in wood: if you carve things in wood as you would carve things in plaster, you make a mess of it. So, you depend on the limitations to make it artistic. That's what art is. It's working within strict limitations. If you break those limitations, if you go against them, you're going to make a mess of it. But if you work with the limitations, even if you stretch them, you'll get something interesting. And if it's an original idea, people will feel that this is special; this has really got something new about it. And once you get past the possible into the impossible, it's limitless where you can go. And that's what animation does more than anything: it goes into impossible territory. That's where it's fun![67]

Hellard, without a doubt, produced more animation than any of the other animators. He was incredibly focused and other animators would marvel at the fact that 'he could come to work in the morning and immediately pick up from exactly where he had left off the night before'.[68] Hellard described his animation process:

> Once I was into a job, I was deep into it, and I don't think I ever had trouble finding it again. I would do thumbnail drawings right through the whole thing, of what each character does: how they react to each other. I'd have all those drawings – just very rough drawings – but I would look at those often enough to know what that character is going to do, and know what he's feeling, and know what he's going to do next. He never goes over there, without going over *there* first – that sort of thing. So, if I was in the middle, actually doing the animation, the real key drawings, I could look at my sketches and know what I was aiming at. And the inbetweens – that's at the end of the week when I'd finished and I'd come back late from lunch and do the in-betweens.[69]

Many years later, Hellard did lament his somewhat hands off approach to animation directing on *Grendel Grendel Grendel*, noting that there was a good deal of inconsistency in the treatment of the characters – both in movement and in form.

> You see, with a feature film you have to get into drawing the character, but the problem is that you can't do the whole film yourself; other people will be drawing the same character, and they have to draw it in precisely the same proportions. But they won't draw the character looking exactly the same. They certainly won't draw the character *acting* the same. Even the look of the lip-sync won't be the same. Some animators animate with floppy mouths; other animators hard, machine-like mouths; and all the inbetween ones. Characters move quite differently with different animators. [...] *Grendel* was an example: if you look through '*Grendel*' you can see the animators change – there, there and there! It's quite clear, to an animator, to see the difference; whether the public knows – or cares – I don't know.[70]

The film was limited to just under, 60,000 cels, which is a very small number for a feature length film (see Figures 4.10 and 4.12). However, due to Stitt's strong sense of design, and Hellard's clever use of animation timing and strategies, the end result appears far less limited than it might have been. There are many sequences which, due to the staging and layering, give the effect of fuller animation, but actually required a much fewer number of drawings. Additionally, there are interspersed moments where they pull out all the stops and incorporate, for example, dramatic animated camera moves – in which the camera (seemingly) rotates around the characters. To facilitate these unconventional sequences, the animators would sometimes build small dimensional models to aid with animating in perspective. One example, which was used twice in the film, was a dramatic animated camera move in which Grendel is seen standing among some stone monuments and looking up towards King Hrothgar's meadhall just before he confronts the humans. 'We made a cardboard model of all the shapes and we took photographic references as we turned that around', recalls Atkinson.[71]

Making Grendel Grendel Grendel 153

FIGURE 4.12 Production cel depicting a silhouetted Grendel (in his signature retreating walk cycle), carrying dead bodies past a towering pedestal, which proudly displays a sculpture of King Hrothgar's head from *Grendel Grendel Grendel* (copyright Estate of Alexander Stitt, used with permission; courtesy RMIT Design Archives).

For the most part, the production went very smoothly; despite the fact that it was the studio's first feature film, that it had an extremely low budget and that the director had made the very risky decision to change the entire look of the film mid-production. The results, though not perfect, and in some ways, fairly uneven, do showcase an incredibly well-designed aesthetic. *Grendel Grendel Grendel* would prove to be very much an auteur film. Alexander Stitt wrote the screenplay, wrote the lyrics to the songs, drew all the storyboards, designed all the characters, colour styled the film, produced many of the layouts and created all of the backgrounds. Of course, animation director Frank Hellard, the other animators and production staff, and composer Bruce Smeaton all contributed enormously to the production – but it still reads very much as, *a film by Alexander Stitt*.

Notes

1 The studio would go on to produce a second feature, *Abra Cadabra* (Alexander Stitt, 1983), which is based loosely on *The Pied Piper of Hamlin* and is regarded as the world's first 3D-format animated feature film.
2 Alexander Stitt, interview with Dan Torre and Lienors Torre (17 April 2005).
3 Ibid.
4 Ibid.

5   Frank Hellard, interview with Dan Torre and Lienors Torre (3 September 2004).
6   Ibid.
7   Stitt, Interview, Torre and Torre.
8   Anne Jolliffe, interview with Dan Torre and Lienors Torre (15 January 2005).
9   Hellard, Interview, Torre and Torre.
10 Stitt, Interview, Torre and Torre.
11 Hellard, Interview, Torre and Torre.
12 Phillip Adams, interview with Dan Torre and Lienors Torre (November 2019).
13 Ibid.
14 Stitt, Interview, Torre and Torre.
15 Hellard, Interview, Torre and Torre.
16 Adams, Interview, Torre and Torre.
17 Lee Tulloch, 'Lee Tulloch Talks to Grendel and Friend, Grrumph!' in *Vogue Australia* (January 1981), pp. 64–5.
18 Michael Sporn, 'Grendel', 30 June 2006, www.michaelspornanimation.com (accessed 11 December 2018).
19 David Atkinson, interview with Dan Torre and Lienors Torre (2019).
20 Ibid.
21 Bruce Smeaton, interview with Dan Torre and Lienors Torre (2019).
22 Ibid.
23 Ibid.
24 Ibid.
25 Ibid.
26 Ibid.
27 Alexander Stitt and Paddy Stitt, *Stitt Autobiographics – 50 Years of the Graphic Design Work of Alexander Stitt* (Melbourne: Hardie Grant Books, 2011), p. 177.
28 Ibid.
29 Alexander Stitt, 'An Animated Progress Report on *Grendel Grendel Grendel*', *Cinema Papers*, 21 May–June 1979, pp. 339–40
30 Smeaton, Interview, Torre and Torre.
31 Ibid.
32 Adams, Interview, Torre and Torre.
33 Smeaton, Interview, Torre and Torre.
34 Ibid.
35 Ibid.
36 Stitt, 'Animated Progress Report', pp. 339–40.
37 Atkinson, Interview, Torre and Torre.
38 Stitt, *Stitt Autobiographics*, pp. 177–8.
39 Smeaton, Interview, Torre and Torre.
40 Ibid.
41 Ibid.
42 Hellard, Interview, Torre and Torre.
43 Ibid.
44 Tulloch, 'Grrumph!' in *Vogue Australia*, pp. 64–5.
45 Ibid.
46 Ibid.
47 Stitt, *Stitt Autobiographics*, p. 196.
48 Atkinson, Interview, Torre and Torre.

49 Stitt, Interview, Torre and Torre.
50 Dennis Tupicoff, interview with Dan Torre and Lienors Torre (2019). Tupicoff would later become an established independent animator, creating such highly acclaimed animated short films as: *His Mother's Voice* (1996), *Into the Dark* (2001), *Chainsaw* (2007) and *A Photo of Me* (2017).
51 Stitt, Interview, Torre and Torre.
52 Ibid.
53 Stitt, *Stitt Autobiographics*, pp. 177–8.
54 Ibid.
55 Stitt, Interview, Torre and Torre.
56 Maggie Geddes, interview with Dan Torre and Lienors Torre (2019).
57 Ibid.
58 Atkinson, Interview, Torre and Torre.
59 Geddes, Interview, Torre and Torre.
60 Stitt, Interview, Torre and Torre.
61 Tupicoff, Interview, Torre and Torre.
62 Geddes, Interview, Torre and Torre.
63 Atkinson Interview, Torre and Torre.
64 Ibid.
65 Ibid.
66 Hellard, Interview, Torre and Torre.
67 Ibid.
68 Atkinson, Interview, Torre and Torre.
69 Hellard, Interview, Torre and Torre.
70 Ibid.
71 Atkinson, Interview, Torre and Torre.

Chapter 5

AESTHETICS OF *GRENDEL GRENDEL GRENDEL*

Grendel Grendel Grendel is a distinctive and meticulously designed film. As noted in the previous chapter, one of the most striking visual aspects of the film is its line-free design. The use of inked or photocopied black outlines around characters had become one of the hallmarks of cel animation, but Stitt's approach was virtually unprecedented in a feature length work. By opting not to use line work, Stitt not only created a distinctive visual style, but also achieved a strong unified design. The characters, backgrounds and even the components of effects animation, such as falling snow or running water, all showcase an unparalleled degree of visual homogeneity. This stylistic choice also had a strong influence on the use of colour, the design of the backgrounds, the layout and composition of each scene – even upon how the characters moved. One reviewer described the film's unusual aesthetics as being,

> a visual puzzle, as it tends to build images out of huge blocks of colours and shapes. In a sense, it is comparable to some modern painting styles which are better apprehended sensually, by allowing the images to flow past the eye rather than searching for sense within them.[1]

However, as a result of these design choices, much of the film's imagery had become bereft of the original detail that the animators had drawn on paper. If one compares some of the original animation drawings to the finished cel images, it becomes clear how much of the dimensional and decorative detail was lost (see Figure 5.1). By taking this approach, Stitt not only removed a good deal of detail within the characters and the background forms, but also many of the depth cues that had previously existed within the scene composition. Alternative approaches were needed in order to infuse the newly hyper-flattened imagery with indicators of dimensionality and graphic believability.

Stitt also employed a radical use of colour throughout the film. Upon the film's release, another reviewer noted:

> The colors are bright pastels, happily and rhythmically hopping through the spectrum, so that at one moment a Viking has a green and mauve face

and the next a grey and beige one. The result is a series of flowing patterns, elegantly angular and colourfully harmonious.[2]

As with most animated films, each of the characters was designed with a particular colour scheme – Grendel is green, Beowulf wears a blue uniform adorned with a large red cape. But from scene to scene a character's tones and

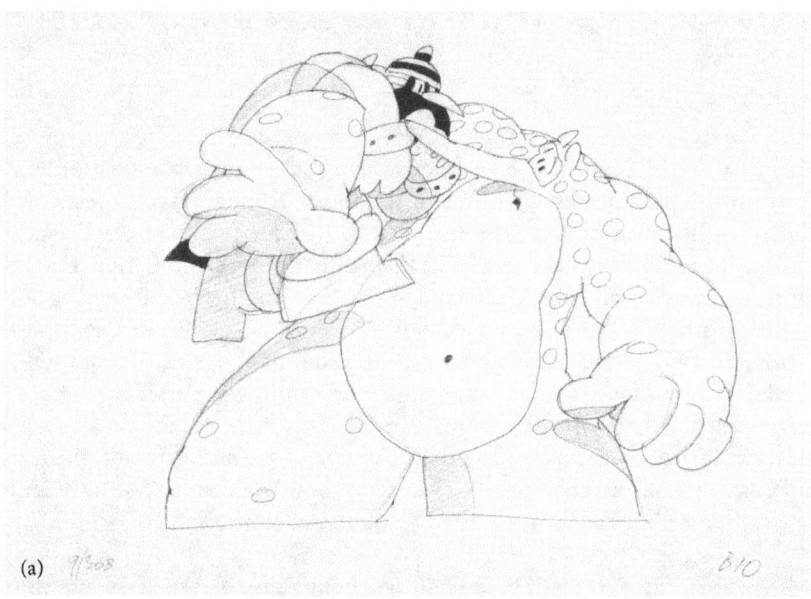

FIGURE 5.1 These two images show the difference in character detail between (a) production drawing (copyright Estate of Alexander Stitt, used with permission; courtesy RMIT Design Archives) and (b) corresponding frame grab from the film (*Grendel Grendel Grendel*, Alexander Stitt, 1981).

hues will readily change, usually dependent upon the shifting design of the backgrounds and the ambience of the narrative. Although the film is cohesive in its general design, it is clear that each individual scene would be independently designed and crafted if required.

Variations of colour were often employed to give the flat-coloured, lineless imagery a sense of depth. For example, Grendel's form is usually coloured in three or four shades of green in order to articulate the placement of his arms and legs – to signify which appendage is in front of the other. Additionally, highlights, shadows and dramatic lighting are also frequently used on the characters and background elements. This contrasts dynamically with the starkness of the flat planes of colour, and the even starker use of black silhouettes, providing a greater sense of depth.

Although the characters are devoid of outlines and internal line work, many forms (both characters and backgrounds elements) feature some sort of patterned design – such as spots or repeating hatch-marks. This patterning helps not only to provide texture and visual interest to the otherwise vast expanses of flat colour, but also additional means of unifying the scene's constituent elements. For example, Grendel's spots might be reiterated upon a tree or a rock in the background, or a striped pattern might exist on both a rock in the foreground and a tree in the mid-ground. These repeated patterns create a simultaneously unified image and an unconventional suggestion of depth as the eye is encouraged to navigate the surrounding landscape, and to suggest how the characters might conceivably move through the imagery.

The film's backgrounds frequently change dramatically from scene to scene. In some instances, a background will comprise just a single thin strip of colour to denote a ground plane, and a contrasting colour to denote the sky. Sometimes these were constructed by paint on cel – but in several cases were achieved simply by placing a solid sheet of coloured paper as a backdrop. In other cases, the backgrounds will exhibit a great amount of detail.

In some scenes, the landscape is constructed of absurdly shaped hills, rocks and planes. Occasionally the visual theme of 'Vikings' is instilled into the geological landscapes; for example, some of the rock and cliff structures become reminiscent of giant horned Viking helmets (see Figure 5.2). Such playful designs often took precedence over concerns as to how the animated characters might actually move through these spaces. In a few instances these backgrounds posed a great challenge to the animators, who were obliged to make a character leap, scramble and climb over the unconventional landscape forms, simply in order to move the character across the scene from point A to point B.

The forested landscapes tend to be the most opulent of the film's backgrounds, frequently adorned with striking colours and patterns, and with particular attention devoted to the depiction of plant life. Additionally, many of these plant forms appear to be imbued with personified characteristics. One of the things

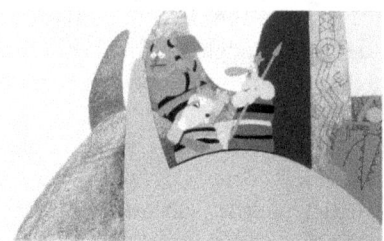 

FIGURE 5.2 Unusual rock formations, reminiscent of Viking helmets, populate the film's landscape (*Grendel Grendel Grendel*, Alexander Stitt, 1981).

that Dean Swinford points out in his analysis of Gardner's work is that, while the character of Grendel can be described as being a part of the 'supernatural' realm in the original *Beowulf* poem, he is clearly part of the 'natural' world in the novel.³ Stitt also sought to show that Grendel was very much a part of the natural landscape, often using patterns to emphasize this connection. Thus, a spotted Grendel might sit upon a spotted rock and, as he crouches down, become almost indistinguishable from the rock form.

Grendel also embodies subtle plant-like characteristics. In particular, his colour scheme reflects the leafy green colour of the landscape's trees and bushes, while his spotted patterning frequently also adorns plant life. In one of the film's earlier scenes, a young Grendel falls off a cliff and becomes tightly wedged in the branches of a large tree from which he is unable to escape (see Figure 2.6). The following day he is discovered by a small group of humans (King Hrothgar, Dung and Wiglaf). Because Grendel effectively blends in with the tree and is so tightly fused to it, these men become greatly puzzled – unsure whether he belongs to the animal or to the plant kingdom. After much discussion, they ultimately surmise that he must be a part of the tree, noting that he is probably 'some sort of beast-like fungus' or perhaps some sort of 'tree-spirit'. Such a categorization effectively situates Grendel somewhere between plant life and animal life. Not surprisingly, many cultures of the Anglo-Saxon era did in fact believe in the existence of such hybrid creatures, some of which were later classified under the blanketing term of *zoophyte*. Once the humans agree that Grendel is indeed of a zoophytic nature, the King quickly makes a further royal assumption that Grendel must be of the carnivorous variety, and offers the giant carnivorous-plant-creature a pig to eat.⁴

In the film, Grendel's cave is also full of animated plant forms, which appear to have large rudimentary mouths and eyes (see Figure 5.3). Although this is a unique addition to the film, it does seem to echo Gardner's repeated personification of plant life in his novel. For example, Gardner describes how Grendel traverses the landscape, noticing how 'the tender grasses peek up, innocent yellow, through the ground: the children of the dead'. Later he equates a field of wildflowers with the water snakes that inhabit the lake surrounding his mother's cave, noting, 'Here where the startling tiny jaws of crocuses snap at

FIGURE 5.3 Personified plants in Grendel's cave; note that Grendel is also sitting on a spotted rock which seems to mimic his general form and patterned design (*Grendel Grendel Grendel*, Alexander Stitt, 1981).

the late-winter sun like the heads of baby water snakes'. Still later, a disgruntled and agitated Grendel takes out his aggression on a grouping of trees: 'I reel, smash trees', he announces. Later he refers to them as 'Disfigured son of lunatics' and, after his temper has settled down, apologizes directly to the trees (albeit insincerely): '"No offense", I say, with a terrible, sycophantic smile, and tip an imaginary hat.'[5] Although Grendel is very much an outcast who does not seem to fit in with either the natural world or the human world, he does seem to identify more with the natural worlds of flora and fauna.

Shadows and silhouettes

Shadows serve as prominent visual elements in the film. Character ground shadows are used frequently, usually depicted with the simple application of opaque black paint. Occasionally these ground shadows will emulate the basic shape of the characters, but more frequently are depicted simply as long thin lines, which extend either screen left or screen right from the character. This distinctive treatment allows for a greater sense of depth, particularly when the ground plane is represented as a narrow band of colour at the base of the screen image.

In order to provide a greater sense of volume to the otherwise super-flat characters, internal shading or character shadows, were also used (see Figure 5.4). Stitt recalls:

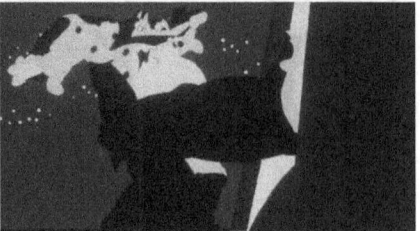

FIGURE 5.4 Periodic use of dramatic lighting, which both underscores mood and provides dimensionality to the otherwise flatly rendered forms (*Grendel Grendel Grendel*, Alexander Stitt, 1981).

> I was creating heavy shadows on the characters. On any shape, you could paint two thirds of it in a colour, and the remaining third a colour down about four shades. It gave a hard-shadow line on parts of the characters – which I was also using on the backgrounds.[6]

In cases in which the lighting is intended to be quite stark, the character shadows may be represented in pure black. Occasionally these black body shadows will then fully envelop the characters, transforming them from a coloured character with an edging of black shading, into a fully black-silhouetted form. One such example occurs when, standing before an open window, the Shaper and Unferth discuss a plot to overthrow the King. As the two characters begin their conversation, their forms are articulated in colour, with just a narrow band of black shadow around one edge of their forms. Then, as they lean in to speak in more hushed and conspiratorial tones, their character shadows totally envelope their forms, effectively transforming them into pure black silhouettes. For a time, they remain in this silhouetted state, accentuating the darkening and sinister mood of the scene. But upon hearing the King call out, they suddenly burst out of this blanketing of pure black; looking very startled, they are once again rendered in full vibrant colours (see Figure 5.5).

Silhouetted characters, which appear frequently throughout the film, are utilized for a variety of reasons. Sometimes they are used simply to conform

FIGURE 5.5 Unconventional shifting from (a) black silhouetted forms to (b) coloured forms – in order to emphasize the dark shift in mood; in this case when the Shaper and Unferth plot to overthrow the King (*Grendel Grendel Grendel*, Alexander Stitt, 1981).

to the intended design and lighting of a scene – for example, if the character is depicted in the distance and is starkly backlit by the setting sun. At other times silhouettes are used to express particular moods, to accentuate narrative tensions, create visual correlations, or in order to intentionally obscure detail in an image.

Although Grendel's Mum enjoys a prominent place in the narrative, there is only one brief scene in which she is visualized, even then she is depicted merely as a black silhouette. But there are no logical reasons for her to be depicted in this manner; all of the other elements within the conventionally lit scene are rendered in bright colourations. However, because she is meant almost exclusively to be an off-screen character, her silhouetted treatment allows her to be *physically* present in this important scene, yet *not fully visible*.

In a further unconventional design choice, as Grendel's mother chases away King Hrothgar, her silhouetted form projects its shadowiness outwards and onto the King's brightly coloured form, transforming him into a silhouetted character. The King then runs away through the brightly lit landscape, remaining as a black, silhouetted form – suggesting, in a very graphical way, that he has become overwhelmed by fear. Grendel's Mum proceeds to rescue Grendel, gently lifting him down from the tree (see Figure 2.6b). During this action she remains as a silhouette, yet (unlike the King) Grendel maintains his bright green colouring. Clearly, he does not fear his mother's presence, most probably finding great comfort in it.

Black silhouettes, ubiquitous throughout the film's backgrounds, are also used in surprising ways. In the opening scene, the background is essentially broken into two-colour schemes. Both the foreground imagery and the background imagery are rendered in what is predominately a yellow-green tone, while the mid-ground imagery is depicted as a solid black silhouette. The luminance of the yellow-green foreground is replicated in the distance with a luminous sky, and green mountains slightly muted to show distance, but is also remarkably similar in tone to the foreground. The result is essentially a sandwiching of a black silhouette between two nearly identical brightly coloured planes. Moments later, in a further unconventional approach, two silhouetted characters emerge from the central, silhouetted part of the forest and run across the brightly coloured landscape, remaining as black silhouettes. Although such scenes do not adhere to standard rules of colour perspective, they do manage to convey a surprising sense of depth, and suggest ample layout space in which the animated actions occur.

Black-spaces and black-mattes

The use of black-spaces (and black-mattes) also constitutes an important design component in the film. These large expanses of blackness are frequently utilized, either to create ambiguous spaces in which the characters can exist, or to create

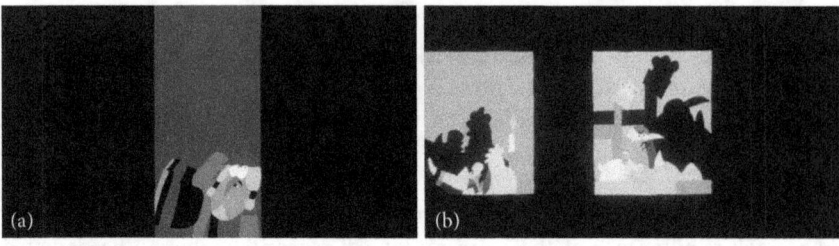

FIGURE 5.6 Frequent and unconventional use of black-screen space; (a) King Hrothgar trapped in Unferth's bear pit (b) a frightened King, seen through an open window, during Grendel's night-time attack on the meadhall (*Grendel Grendel Grendel*, Alexander Stitt, 1981).

exaggerated solid formations through which the characters are unable to permeate. For example, when King Hrothgar falls down into Unferth's bear trap pit, the scene is depicted as a cut-away shot, the surrounding earth represented in pure blackness (see Figure 5.6a). Since this black space encompasses most of the screen image, creating a cinematic black frame, it suggests that the King is trapped in an inescapable prison.

At night, the walls of the King's meadhall are also depicted in pure black, rendering them invisible except for the illuminated windows that adorn their façade. The result is an array of rectangle shapes through which the hall's interior is visible, floating upon an expansive black void (see Figure 5.6b). In this manner, the scenes take on the appearance of a comic strip, each of the panels representing a different scenic view of the building's interior spaces. In order to simulate a camera pan across the side of the building, the rectangle shapes of the windows are made simply to slide across the black screen in a free-flowing manner.

One of the more innovative uses of negative black-space occurs within the Dragon's lair, featuring backgrounds of solid black. As these scenes are intended to represent a dreamscape, their ambiguous black non-space seems quite appropriate. The blackness simultaneously creates a kind of backdrop, but also an endless void into which characters can recede and emerge. At times the black-space seems to have a shifting physical presence, which is occasionally used to obscure the characters from view. For example, when the Dragon produces (seemingly from nowhere) a large scroll – one side is composed of white parchment adorned with text, while the reverse side is represented as pure black. This rectangle shape of blackness blends in seamlessly with the black background. Thus, when the Dragon holds it up in front of him, it completely obscures a portion of the Dragon's form. At the same time, due to its identical appearance to the background, it also appears *to cut a hole* right through the Dragon, apparently allowing the viewer to see the black space behind him (see Figure 5.7). Later, after Grendel has mysteriously disappeared into the black

FIGURE 5.7 A black matte (actually the reverse side of a scroll) effectively cutting a visual hole into the Dragon (*Grendel Grendel Grendel*, Alexander Stitt, 1981).

void, the Dragon reveals him again by opening what appears to be an invisible (yet opaque) door of blackness.

When sections of blackness are animated in this way, they can be regarded as an animated matte or a 'traveling matte'. This technique is used frequently in the film, particularly as a way to transition creatively from one scene to another. This use of animated mattes is highly reminiscent of those created by Pablo Ferro, in which he dynamically used the black space of the cinema screen selectively to frame imagery, and to wipe creatively from one scene to another. Ferro's approach was used extensively in Norman Jewison's live-action film, *The Thomas Crown Affair* (1968). Perhaps drawing inspiration from these live-action films, *Grendel Grendel Grendel* also adopts this approach, but, being a purely animated film, it succeeds in significantly extending this effect.

One recurring use of animated mattes in *Grendel Grendel Grendel* involves the effect of an opening door. Usually such scenes commence in pure blackness; a brightly lit figure will then enter into the void through the opening of a previously unseen door. A semblance of this visual trope is first introduced in the film's opening live-action sequence. This commences with a black screen (which was filmed inside a darkened studio); dramatically, a door opens displaying a brightly backlit doorway and the silhouetted figure of Phillip Adams (the film's producer), who enters through the doorway into the darkened studio space (see Figure 5.8a). A similar type of action is later repeated, several times, in animated form. For example, during a montage sequence in which King Hrothgar's soldiers are engaged in battle, a soldier bursts through a previously unseen door into a black-screen space, suggesting that he has just entered into the interior of a darkened hut (see Figure 5.8b). He then throws in a fiery red

FIGURE 5.8 Three sequences (read from left to right) which utilize animated black-screen elements: (a) the film's live-action introductory sequence featuring Phillip Adams entering a darkened soundstage (b) King Hrothgar's men attack neighbouring villages and burst into a darkened home and (c) Beowulf and his men arrive at the meadhall (*Grendel Grendel Grendel*, Alexander Stitt, 1981).

torch and retreats out through the doorway. Another very dramatic use of this device marks the arrival of Beowulf and his men at the King's meadhall. In this sequence the black of the screen is cinematically wiped away from the centre of the screen, simulating (in a very iconic manner) the opening of the double doors of the meadhall (see Figure 5.8c).

Additional sophisticated uses of animated-matte wipes are also used; for example, in one sequence, a black-haired figure walks across the screen, his long black hair subsequently filling the screen – effectively wiping it black, and transitioning to the next scene. Another sequence depicts a series of transitions between a number of ongoing battles taking place in a forest, the trees of which are represented as simple vertical black strips. Positioned behind these black strips, the soldiers furiously fight each other. Quite unexpectedly, the black tree trunks swell outwards, expanding like the shuttering of a Venetian blind, culminating in a solid black screen. After a beat, these 'shutter-tree trunks' reopen to reveal a different battle scene in another part of the forest.

Designed animation

Because of the film's line-free design and its heavy reliance on large blocks of flat colour, some have made cursory comparisons to animated films that use the technique of paper cut-outs. At the time of the film's release one reviewer noted,

'Stitt's cartoon creatures are sharply two-dimensional. They and their sparsely decorated surroundings have the clarity of pictures made with paper cut-outs.'[7] Such comparisons appear valid when examining still images from the film. But in terms of movement, the characters and forms unmistakably move like the hand-drawn animated figures that they are. Not only are the characters drawn and re-drawn in a frame-by-frame process, but beneath their extremely flat cel-painted rendering, they have clearly been constructed with a great deal of dimensional and volumetric detail (see Figure 5.1a). Thus, despite the fact that the characters are largely bereft of visual detail (and thus, to some, cut-out like), these characters do express subtleties of dimensional movement.

Although much of the film expresses a rather limited style of animation, there are occasional moments in which impressive rotational movement is used, giving a strong suggestion of three-dimensionality. These perspective-shifting, animated camera moves feature both rotating characters and revolving environments. Such animated effects are normally very challenging to achieve in drawn animation, as they involve the redrawing of each of the scene's elements in a frame-by-frame, perspective shifting, manner.

In sequences in which the animation is more limited – such as lengthy held-cels and minimal planar moves – the film can appear rather stiff. But in scenes where there are more dynamic movements, the film appears to express a greater degree of animated movement than perhaps actually exists. These moments of full animation contrast greatly with, not only the more limited animation scenes but, more importantly, with what most viewers would expect from such flatly rendered characters. It does seem that, in general, when a simply defined character expresses a greater complexity of movement, it succeeds in appearing more fully animated; contrastingly, when a form is complex in its detail, and expresses comparatively simple movement, it can appear under-animated and stiff.[8] Thus a limited animation approach worked well for the production since the filmmakers succeeded in creating sequences that often appear more animated than had the characters been rendered more dimensionally and ornately decorated. Animation director, Frank Hellard, proved to be extremely effective both at creating uniquely designed sequences of animated movement and in transforming the character's lack of detail into an asset.

In many sequences the characters prove to be virtually indiscernible when viewed as a still image. For example, there are several scenes in which Grendel is depicted at night, but visible only as an array of yellow spots against the black sky. As a still image, it is virtually unreadable – but as an overall moving sequence, it reads clearly as an approaching or retreating Grendel. (Intriguingly, these sequences parallel the contemporary aesthetics of visualized motion capture data – which also, as a still image, merely look like random arrays of dots, but with the application of motion-captured movement data, become very recognizable as human forms.)

As part of the production's limited animation strategy, the animators would often reuse or recycle particular animated actions across multiple scenes. In particular, Grendel's walk cycle was repeatedly retraced from an original sequence of drawings. In this way, not only did the production conserve cost, it also effectively established a series of iconic actions. In the film, Grendel expresses three signature walk cycles: an ambling shuffle, a determined stride and a distinctive retreat in which he saunters off into the distance. In most cases, new cels were created each time, but traced from the original sequences of drawings. This would allow for character images to be painted in different colour schemes that could reflect the colour, tone and mood of a specific scene.

One particularly striking use of a re-contextualized walk cycle appears near the start of the film, when Grendel strides angrily towards the meadhall. At first he is shown striding screen-right during the daytime, and is rendered in his normal Grendel-green. But in order to signify the passage of time, the lighting and scenery shift into a night-time colour scheme, and Grendel's colour design also shifts into a purple and black duotone. As he finally approaches the meadhall, he is transformed into a pure black-silhouetted form; as he draws nearer still, the artificial light emitting from the building partially illuminates him, imbuing his black form with a stark yellow highlight. Such a reuse of drawings enabled the creation of a very consistent stride (which would have been very difficult to achieve with straight ahead animation). In this case, by re-using the same animated cycle, but by gradually shifting the figure's colour scheme and the scene's background design, it indicates that Grendel has, presumably, been striding towards the meadhall over a period of several hours and over a great distance. Furthermore, by maintaining a nearly identical stride, Grendel effectively emotes a very determined and unwavering sense of resolve. In other scenes, Grendel is shown to amble across the landscape in a rather melancholy manner. This shuffling walk becomes another of his very iconic movements, coming to signify his persistent feelings of desolation.[9]

However, Grendel's most iconic walk, and one that is recycled seven times throughout the film, is his distinctive retreat in which he saunters off into the distance. Although Grendel's retreat involves the same repeated action each time, there are many different ways and contexts in which it is executed. A few iterations of his retreat take place in bright daylight, when he is depicted in his standard Grendel-green, but as he nears the horizon, he gradually transforms into a black-silhouetted form. In other instances, Grendel is depicted retreating away from the meadhall at night, where he appears initially illuminated by the bright lights of the meadhall and, as he retreats, is subsequently transformed into a silhouette. On two occasions he is depicted simply as an array of spots, painted as yellow dots upon a black form. Towards the end of the film, during Grendel's final visit to the Dragon – the Dragon performs a mimicry of Grendel's retreat, walking a short distance off into the blackness of his cave. At this point in the film, Grendel's retreating walk is well established, and his movements are clearly recognizable in the Dragon's animated movements. But because this scene is intended to take place in Grendel's imaginative dreamscape, in a sense it also represents Grendel's own cognitively generated animation. Grendel is essentially animating the Dragon in his dream. Consequently, it makes logical sense that the Dragon's form would embody some of Grendel's own frequently executed movements.[10]

Conclusion

The film's line-free aesthetic facilitated a number of unconventional and innovative graphic choices. Although the characters are reduced and represented as very simplified forms, their placement, layering and juxtaposition tend to accrue and therefore create a greater degree of complexity. In this way, *Grendel Grendel Grendel* is visually much more complex than it seems initially. This cumulative effect is analogous to the film's narrative and philosophical concepts, both of which are arguably more complex than they first appear. Alexander Stitt had a very distinctive approach to design. Each scene was carefully designed with regards to colour, form and composition. Equally so, animation director Frank Hellard took a distinctive approach to directing the animation. As noted in the previous chapter, Hellard truly believed in the innate possibilities of limited animation – and, although this approach readily coincided with the film's austere budgetary constraints, it is also an ethos that he devoutly followed.

As described in Chapter 3, there are a number of contrasting themes that are explored in the film, such as the divide between monsters and humans and, importantly, the overlapping nature of these disjunctions. Thus, there is evidence of humanity to be found in monsters, and monstrousness to be found in humans. Similarly, on a visual level, the aesthetics of *Grendel Grendel Grendel* also signify unexpected overlapping complexities, such as the interrelating concerns of the normally dichotomous nature of super-flat forms and fully dimensional movement; of vibrantly coloured forms and of black silhouettes; and of positive and negative spaces. Taken as a whole, the film showcases a distinctive and carefully designed use of form and of animated movement, which underscore the carefully designed themes of the narrative.

Notes

1 Lee Burton, 'Feature Films – Grendel, Grendel, Grendel', *Metro Magazine*, no. 56 (1981), pp. 64–5.
2 Neil Jillett, 'Cheers, Cheers, Cheers for Grendel', *The Age* (19 June 1981).
3 Dean Swinford, '"Some Beastlike Fungus": The Natural and Animal in John Gardner's Grendel', *Lit: Literature Interpretation Theory* 22, no. 4 (2011), p. 328.
4 For more discussions on zoophytes and personified plant life, see Dan Torre, *Carnivorous Plants* (London: Reaktion Books, 2019); and Dan Torre, *Cactus* (London: Reaktion Books, 2017).
5 John Gardner, *Grendel* (New York: Alfred A. Knopf, 1971), p. 7.

6   Alex Stitt, Interview by Dan Torre and Lienors Torre (17 April 2005).
7   Jillett, 'Cheers'.
8   For more on the correlation between detail of form and detail of movement, see Dan Torre, *Animation – Process, Cognition, and Actuality* (New York: Bloomsbury, 2017).
9   For more on the topic of cycles and recycled animation, see Torre, *Animation*.
10 For more on the topic of cognitive animation, see Torre, *Animation*.

Chapter 6

GRENDEL'LL GET YOU

Once the production of *Grendel Grendel Grendel* was complete (see Chapter 4), the producers faced the equally difficult task of promotion, convincing audiences actually to go to see the animated feature. 'Grendel'll get you!' became the celebrated marketing catchphrase for the film. The contraction of the words 'Grendel' and 'will', which resulted in the intentionally awkward sequence of three 'Ls', echoed the unconventional tripartite of 'Grendels' in the film's title. The catchphrase also conveyed the kind of typographical and design-based humour in which Stitt delighted (see Figure 6.1).

To coincide with the film's release, a series of newspaper advertisements were produced that featured cartoon-styled drawings of the film's characters conversing through speech balloons (see Figure 6.2). Below are descriptions of a sampling of these, each one expressing a slightly different interpretation of the catchphrase's meaning:

1. One Eyed-Arthur says to Basil, 'Julie McKenna singing that first song GOT ME, Basil!' and Basil replies, 'Those Fire-Snakes GOT ME Arfur'.
2. Wiglaf speaking to Dung, 'Those people with the funny names GOT ME, Wiglaf'. 'What funny names, Dung?' replies Wiglaf.
3. King Hrothgar proclaims, 'Grendel won't GET ME … I'm the King' and his son replies, 'You tell 'em, Dad!'
4. The Shaper says, 'All of those wonderful songs GOT ME!' The Shaper's Boy replies, 'That's because you sing three of them!'
5. Wiglaf says, 'Grendel GOT Rex Reed. He said it was "Stimulating, intelligent and Entertaining". He didn't mention about Grendel biting heads off, though. That GOT ME!'
6. Dung says to Wiglaf, 'Grendel GOT Screen International. Peter Noble said it was "Enchanting"' and Wiglaf replies, 'That's more than we can say for you, Dung.'[1]

Thousands of pin-on badges, posters and bumper stickers were also produced, each bearing the 'Grendel'll get you!' catchphrase (see Figures 6.1, 6.4 and 6.5). These stickers soon began appearing on cars, signposts and telephone poles around Australia's urban centres, effectively spreading the film's campaign.

FIGURE 6.1 Promotional bumper sticker featuring the catchphrase, 'Grendel'll get you!' (copyright Estate of Alexander Stitt, used with permission; courtesy Paddy Stitt).

FIGURE 6.2 Promotional newspaper advertisements for *Grendel Grendel Grendel* (copyright Estate of Alexander Stitt, used with permission; courtesy RMIT Design Archives).

Additionally, several film-related products appeared. A *Grendel Grendel Grendel* wall-calendar was created in 1981, featuring images of Grendel and the Dragon. Throughout the calendar, the Dragon and Grendel use speech balloons to recite song lyrics from the film. The Dragon begins (in the month of January) by declaring to Grendel, 'Are you ready, Grendel dear boy? I'm about to sing a song that will last right through 1981!'[2] Scotties-brand facial tissues produced tissue boxes featuring brightly printed characters from the film (see Figure 6.3). Decorated in Stitt's distinctive hand-lettering, the packaging warned, 'Block your ears when Grendel blows – his giant, outsize monster nose!'[3] A movie tie-in book, which included 'some two hundred scenes from the film and a text specially adapted from the screenplay', was produced. This publication claimed to be both 'a complete and self-contained entertainment, as well as a comprehensive record of the film'. Additionally, John Gardner's novel, *Grendel*, was re-published by Penguin Australia featuring a new cover designed by Stitt, and the subheading: 'The book that inspired the Australian animated film.'[4] (Later, in 2004, the film's musical score was released on CD through 1M1 Records.)

The film was intended to open in Australia over the 1980 Christmas season. But its release was delayed for several months, and it premiered instead at the Cannes film festival in May 1981 where it enjoyed four screenings (16, 19, 22 and 25 May). These were attended by the director and his wife, Paddy Stitt, who recalled her mounting anxiety during that first screening:

FIGURE 6.3 Promotional, animated film tie-in, tissue box for *Grendel Grendel Grendel* (courtesy Bruce Smeaton).

Sitting beside Alex watching the film at the Cannes Film Festival I found myself in high alert bordering on panic. [...] the familiar images on the screen looked vivid but alien. The voices and music I knew so well sounded melodramatic. The animation looked slow. [...] There weren't enough people in the cinema. The door kept swinging open and shut. One came in, two went out. How could they possibly understand the film without giving it more time?[5]

But it soon became apparent that 'swinging cinema doors do not necessarily spell rejection',[6] and the film ultimately received favourable critical reviews. Although the producers did not succeed in securing the large international deals they had anticipated, it did lead to some modest sales; these including one to the newly launched American cable television network, Nickelodeon. It had limited distribution in Europe and was eventually distributed by Satori in North America (but also in a very limited release).

The film's Australian premiere took place on 15 June 1981 in Melbourne. The invitation to the exclusive event read:

> The Victorian Film Corporation, TVW Enterprises and Hoyts Theatres have the pleasure in inviting you to attend the Australian Premiere of *Grendel Grendel Grendel* to be held on Monday 15 June, 8.00 p.m. at Hoyts Midcity Complex, 200 Bourke Street. The Director, Alex Stitt has returned from Cannes and the film has already received overseas acclaim. Alexander Walker, London Evening Standard: 'The most interesting animated film for adults that I have seen.' *Grendel Grendel Grendel* is a very rich and complex film full of imagery explaining much of man's social conscience. The voices of Keith Michell and Peter Ustinov, supported by Arthur Dignam and Julie McKenna and a highly skilled team, succeed in bringing Grendel and his populous world to life.[7]

The premiere was a festive affair. An impressive life-size (twelve-foot, four-inch tall) statue of Grendel stood in the cinema's lobby. Producer Phillip Adams launched the film. Animator David Atkinson recalled that the atmosphere was 'very electrifying', with the audience responding well.[8]

But after the premier, the film generally did poorly at the Australian box office, lasting just a few weeks at most venues. No box-office numbers are available but, according to Stitt, the film did recoup costs and eventually turned a very modest profit (which given its very small budget did not necessitate significant receipts). It was distributed in the United States by Satori without a MPAA rating, which inevitably relegated it to a limited number of art-house cinemas with mainly adult audiences. The copy in one of its American print advertisements states: 'Move over Dracula, Frankenstein, King Kong ... here comes *Grendel Grendel Grendel*. He'll break your heart ... (and maybe your bones!).' The advertisement, however, erroneously claimed

FIGURE 6.4 Promotional poster for *Grendel Grendel Grendel* (copyright Estate of Alexander Stitt, used with permission; courtesy RMIT Design Archives).

that the film was 'based on a novel by Alexander Stitt' (instead of by John Gardner').⁹ As Gardner was a very well-known American literary figure at the time, this was probably an unfortunate oversight. In 1982, the film slowly made its way into further markets, including Australia's neighbour, New Zealand.

Critical reviews

Grendel Grendel Grendel was released during a challenging era when the feature animation market was reserved primarily for children and largely dominated by the Disney studios. This left very little room for non-Disney or non-children's animated features. At the time, the highest profile alternative was 'adult' animated features, such as the X-rated *Fritz the Cat* (Ralph Bakshi, 1972). Many therefore considered animation to be either strictly for children or strictly for adults, which further complicated the film's promotion. Of course, there *were* a handful of other films produced at this time, such as *Yellow Submarine* (George Dunning, 1968), *Fantastic Planet* (Rene Laloux, 1973), *Allegro Non Troppo* (Bruno Bozzetto, 1976), *Wizards* (Ralph Bakshi, 1977), *Watership Down* (Martin Rosen, 1978), *The Lord of the Rings* (Ralph Bakshi, 1978) and, of course, *Grendel Grendel Grendel* (Alexander Stitt, 1981). Other than the fact that they were all *animated* features and dealt with slightly more mature themes, they were in fact very distinct films.

Watership Down, based on the novel by Richard Adams, was one of the more successful of these films. Although ostensibly about the livelihood and struggles of wild rabbits, it served as an allegory for human society. In this manner, the film brutally examines issues of violence, power and control, as well as the courage and creativity of the 'human' spirit. Because of its graphic violence, the film was rated PG – which at the time would have indicated that it was not intended for small children. However, this did not seem to register with some audiences. On this matter, animation director Frank Hellard noted:

> *Watership Down* is a really horrifying film for young kids. It was advertised as 'not a children's film'. Yet it would be packed with mothers and their babies going along to it. You cannot convince people that it is not for kids, especially when it is about animated bunny rabbits. It must be a kid's film![10]

Unquestionably, *Watership Down* is a mature and serious film, punctuated with only the slightest moments of comic relief (emanating primarily from the antics of the bird character, Kehaar). By contrast, *Grendel Grendel Grendel* is arguably more complex with regard to its social criticism and philosophical thought than most of these other animated productions. However, the film also contains a great deal of irreverent humour, making its categorization less than straightforward.

While many critics strongly praised *Grendel Grendel Grendel*, at the same time they were unsure how to categorize the film. Stitt went to great pains to clarify that the film was not a kid's film, (although it would still be suitable for older children), and that it certainly was not to be aligned with *Fritz the Cat*. He asserted that his film was 'an animated feature for grown-ups', clarifying 'I always use the word "grown-ups" because if you say "adult" then that suggests something else entirely'.[11] In another article, Stitt was referenced as saying that his film was 'suitable for grown-ups to dispel the idea that animation was merely kids' stuff'.[12] Finally, one reviewer, hoping to clarify things by channelling the ex-American president, Richard Nixon, declared: 'In the favourite phrase of an ogre of our own time, let me make one thing perfectly clear: this is *not* just a cartoon for kids, though they should enjoy it.'[13] Although officially rated 'G' in Australia, the film did contain some mild profanity, nudity and several sequences of cartoon-violence and blood; and despite their being presented in a very stylized manner, these are elements that many would not have expected to find expressed in a 'cartoon'. Of course, any mildly controversial material that might be unearthed in *Grendel Grendel Grendel* pales in comparison to much of the language and graphic imagery described in Gardner's novel. One reviewer noted at the time of the film's release:

> *Grendel Grendel Grendel* is a clever, intelligent film incorporating a subtle plea for understanding and tolerance, although it may have trouble finding an audience. Except for the sporadic attempts by Ralph Bakshi, the animated feature film has largely been relegated by the public to the restricted field of children's entertainment. [...] It is to be hoped that *Grendel Grendel Grendel* goes some way towards breaking down such considerations by generating an understanding of the animated film as a legitimate form of adult entertainment. Certainly, Stitt's film deserves serious consideration as an important landmark in the Australian film industry and as a development of that form of animation pioneered by UPA in the US in the 1950s, a tradition breaking away from the strongly naturalistic style which had dominated commercial animation up to that point.[14]

While children seemed to delight in the colourful visuals, and comedic actions, they tended to lose interest in some of the dialogue-heavy scenes. Unfortunately, adults also failed to see it in droves. Nevertheless, the film did garner some incredibly strong praise. The American *Cinefantastique* film magazine claimed it was 'one of the most thoughtful and delightful animated films in many years'.[15] A New Zealand newspaper went so far as to assert that it was 'easily the best animated movie ever'.[16] More recently renowned animator, Bill Plympton, has also highly commended the film, declaring 'Brilliant art. Brilliant story. Brilliant film.'[17]

In a curious contradiction to the general marketing approach of the film, that *Grendel Grendel Grendel* was intended for grown-ups, Stitt created a student's study guide to accompany it. He sent this guide out to primary and secondary schools across Australia. The study guide commenced with an open letter to school teachers:

> Dear Educator,
>
> After wallowing in a commercial world for more years than would seem reasonable, making animated commercials to sell all kinds of things on television, I took a couple of years off to spend a great deal of other people's money making an animated feature film.
>
> And having made it, and spent the money, it's essential to sell it. So this study guide, like many others you've no doubt received, is a thinly disguised effort to drum up trade for the movie.
>
> However, as the copious notes that follow will attest, I regard it as a film very worthy of study, in many different ways.
>
> The notes are thin on specific suggestions, especially of the 'draw a picture of a dragon' sort. I'm sure plenty of these will readily suggest themselves. And in any case, I wouldn't recommend the film, as an entertainment at least, to kids under say, eight to ten years of age. (There's no top cut-off, though. In fact we're billing it as a film for grown-ups, to overcome the 'cartoon' image discussed elsewhere.)
>
> Since it's an animated film, it speaks in a popular idiom – especially popular with kids. But what it speaks about has taken me some thousands of words – without giving too much away.
>
> I hope you'll support it. I hope you like it. And I hope it's rewarding for you and yours.
>
> Sincerely,
> Alexander Stitt.[18]

It is a slim, eight-page booklet, but it manages to cover a profound range of topics. The guide explains the origins of the film's narrative, from the original *Beowulf* poem to John Gardner's novel. It discusses the fundamental nature of storytelling, including songs, stories, as well as myths and legends. 'Special Concepts' covered in the guide include monsters, heroes and entertainers; and it further discusses the history of animation and details briefly how the animated feature was made. Decades later, Stitt acknowledged that

> in retrospect, it looks more like it was directed at scholars preparing doctoral theses than at teachers taking little kids on an excursion to the movies. Clearly I had become absorbed by the detail – obsessed, even – and wanted everyone to share the experience.[19]

As a result of this study guide, a number of teachers did, in fact, take their 'little kids on an excursion to the movies'. Some of these teachers, along with their students, then wrote to the director. Although much of the correspondence

FIGURE 6.5 Promotional badge featuring the catchphrase 'Grendel'll get you!' (copyright Estate of Alexander Stitt, used with permission; courtesy RMIT Design Archives).

was positive, there were also some rather harsh assessments. One group of Melbourne primary school teachers chastised the director regarding his use of adult language in the film, noting 'the words that lingered the most in the children's minds were "bloody hell" and "piss off"'. The teachers also noted that the film was overly long for young viewers, rather humorously suggesting that the film could have been compacted into simply, *'Grendel Grendel!'* Attached to their cover letter were numerous commentaries from the children who viewed the film, such as 'I think you shouldn't of used so many rude words like "piss off," "bloody hell" and all that junk'; and 'You could have cut out a few of the rude words and replaced them with other words.' By contrast, there was one student who seemed to respond positively to the colourful language, saying, 'I liked some places like when they used swear words; here are some of them: piss off, bloody hell and shut up'. Some of the students objected to the animated nudity (see Figure 2.19): 'That bit with the lady in a nude was quite disgusting'; another noted that 'The lady in the nude was disgraceful'. A few students complained that the story was difficult to follow. But most did respond well to the visuals of the film, with only one student reviewer advising that the characters should have been made 'skinnier'![20] Despite these humorous, and somewhat unfiltered, youth reviews, the vast majority of critical reviews for *Grendel Grendel Grendel* were very positive. But, of course, positive reviews do not necessarily equate to positive box office.

Reviving Grendel

In recent years, *Grendel Grendel Grendel* has grown in popularity as new audiences are exposed to the film through its periodic screenings, as well as its recent availability on DVD and online. This recent revival is due in large part to the efforts of Malcolm Turner and Helen Gibbins, the organizers of the Melbourne International Animation Festival (MIAF), who met with Alexander Stitt in 2013 to discuss the idea of digitally restoring *Grendel Grendel Grendel* and of making it more widely available. It so happened that Stitt had retained a previously unscreened 35 mm print of the film, and it was agreed that this could be used for the restoration process. After numerous enquiries, the team managed to secure a deal with a local digital conversion company to process the film at a substantially reduced rate. To raise the necessary funds, Gibbins spearheaded a successful crowd-funding campaign in which the public seemed only too happy to support this important restoration project. In the meantime, however, the local company, that was scheduled to process the film, had gone through substantial restructuring and was no longer able to complete the restoration. Faced with this substantial hurdle, the team were beginning to lose hope that *Grendel Grendel Grendel* would ever be restored. Fortunately, a few days later, and seemingly out of the blue, Turner received a phone call from neighbouring New Zealand: it was film director Peter Jackson's, post-production studio, Park Road Post. The studio explained that they had been following the campaign and wanted to know if they could be of any assistance in helping to preserve this important piece of Australia's film and animation history. Being very sympathetic to the team's dilemmas, Jackson's studio quickly agreed to restore the film and produce a Digital Cinema Package (DCP) for the same highly discounted rate that the previous company had promised (less than a tenth of their normal rate). Thus, within a short time, *Grendel Grendel Grendel* was digitally restored and subsequently released on DVD (and later made available for online streaming).[21] Because of the success of this grass-roots restoration effort, the film has now reached a much wider audience and effectively gained a much greater appreciation.

Notes

1. Newspaper clippings pertaining to *Grendel Grendel Grendel*, 1981, courtesy RMIT Design Archives.
2. The cover image of this book is derived from the artwork used in the production of this calendar.
3. Packaging material from commercial tie-in product for *Grendel Grendel Grendel*, 1981 (courtesy Bruce Smeaton).
4. Book cover text on Australian edition, John Gardner, *Grendel* (Melbourne: Penguin Australia, 1980).
5. Paddy Stitt correspondence 2019.
6. Paddy Stitt correspondence 2019.
7. Letter of invitation to the Australian premier of *Grendel Grendel Grendel*, 1981 (courtesy Bruce Smeaton).
8. David Atkinson, Interviewed by Dan Torre and Lienors Torre (2019).
9. Poster advertisement for *Grendel Grendel Grendel*, 1982 (courtesy RMIT Design Archives).
10. Frank Hellard, Interviewed by Dan Torre and Lienors Torre (3 September 2004).
11. Alexander Stitt quoted in 'Ustinov a natural Grendel' in *Screen International*, 22 May 1981, p. 50.
12. Jane Sullivan, 'A Spotty Ogre Comes to Life', *The Age*, 18 June 1981.
13. Keith Connolly, 'A Monstrous Achievement', *The Herald*, 18 June 1981. This quote is in reference to the American Ex-President Richard Nixon, who would begin many of his speeches by emphatically declaring, 'Let me make one thing perfectly clear'.
14. Geoff Mayer, 'Grendel, Grendel, Grendel', *Cinema Papers*, no. 33 (July–August 1981), p. 287.
15. David Bartholomew, 'Cartoon Separates the Myth from the Monster', *Cinefantastique*, June 1982.
16. 'Grendel' in *New Zealand Herald*, August 1982, p. 6.
17. Bill Plympton, quoted on *Grendel Grendel Grendel* DVD packaging (Sydney: Umbrella Entertainment, 1981).
18. Alexander Stitt, *A Film Study Guide – Grendel Grendel Grendel*, Melbourne: Al et al, 1981.
19. Alexander Stitt and Paddy Stitt, *Stitt Autobiographics – 50 Years of the Graphic Design Work of Alexander Stitt* (Melbourne: Hardie Grant Books, 2011), p. 184.
20. Correspondence regarding *Grendel Grendel Grendel*, 1981, courtesy RMIT Design Archives.
21. The print that was used for restoration, although untouched, had suffered from a degree of colour fading; thus, the resulting digital version does lack much of the original vibrancy of the cyan and yellow colour dye layers. The digital version also omits the film's original introduction sequence featuring Phillip Adams.

CONCLUDING GRENDEL

One of the things that Stitt found particularly appealing about Gardner's novel, *Grendel*, was that it expressed a 'simplicity of language, but a complexity of thought',[1] an approach that was mirrored in his animated feature. Stitt achieved a deceptively simple animated film. On one hand, it expresses highly reduced graphics, limited animation and cartoonish humour; yet on the other hand its visuals are extremely well planned, its ideas surprisingly nuanced and multifaceted.

This text has offered the foremost analysis of the animated feature, *Grendel Grendel Grendel*. By extension, it has provided a revised analysis of Gardner's novel, *Grendel*, and further contextualization of the original *Beowulf* poem. Chapter 1 of the text described how the character of Grendel, within the narrative of *Beowulf*, has changed and evolved over the centuries. Most significantly, Gardner's novel marked a pivotal turning point in Grendel's evolution – arguably, Stitt's film marked a further transitional milestone. Emanating from these seminal works (both the novel and the film), the character of Grendel and alternate retellings of the *Beowulf* story have flourished. The second chapter provided a scene-by-scene examination of the film, while offering comparisons to Gardner's novel and to the original Beowulf poem. Chapter 3 addressed a number of the film's pertinent themes, including the concept of monsters, the curse of Cain, the Dragon (and the Dragon God), literary allusions to Lewis Carroll's *Alice in Wonderland*, and the characters of the Shaper and the Sculptor. Importantly, several of these themes were originally devised by Stitt and are therefore unique to the animated film. Chapter 4 provided an in-depth look at the making of the animated film, while Chapter 5 looked at the film's innovative and original visual stylization. Finally, Chapter 6 considered the completed film's marketing and reception. From these discussions, it is hoped that this text contributes not only to providing a richer conception of Stitt's animated feature, but also serving to further *animate* the character of Grendel and the broader *Beowulf* narrative.

Gardner's novel, *Grendel*, marked a significant retelling of the *Beowulf* poem; in turn, Stitt's animated film, *Grendel Grendel Grendel*, features a significant retelling of Gardner's novel. The film simultaneously simplifies but also extends many of Gardner's ideas, supplementing a number of intriguing themes to the novel. Although the character of the Dragon plays an important role in both the novel and the film, Stitt uniquely clarifies its psychological origins. In the film, the humans worship a 'Dragon God' – and, as a result of their showy religious rituals, Grendel dreams up his own version of a Dragon. In this way, Stitt further amplifies the human's hypocrisy – absurdly, they hate Grendel *because* he is a monster, yet they themselves *worship* a monster. Following the conventions of cinematic narrative, on occasion Stitt's film also necessarily deviates from Grendel's perspective, situating the narrative within the human realm. Although this minimizes the intense psychological experience of the novel, it does advantageously allow for an overt depiction of the political upheavals and utter foolishness of the humans. As with the novel, the role of the Shaper is given great importance, but the film is able to amplify the prominence of this role through its musical genre. In this manner, the film is perhaps better positioned to demonstrate the significance and impact of the Shaper's vocal abilities. The film also introduces the character of the Sculptor as a medium specific analogue to the Shaper. Finally, while the novel describes Grendel as a readily identifiable character, the film further portrays him as an extremely affable character. This is expressed almost immediately, and most adroitly, through the film's opening theme song. There is perhaps no better means by which to transform a monster into a human than to make him the focus of a mother's love song.

The original *Beowulf* poem was written at a pivotal moment when society was transitioning between paganism and Christianity. Similarly, Gardner wrote his *Grendel* at a pivotal moment in which countercultures began to push back against general conservatism and the depravity of the Vietnam War, questioning, among other things, the validity of society's established ethics and its destruction of the natural environment. Stitt wrote and directed his film during the equally momentous era of Cold War tensions, when it had become clear that humans were not only capable of committing acts of monstrousness, but also had the capacity to obliterate the entire planet. Stitt's film also marked an important transitional period in which animated features were gradually transitioning from the realm of children's entertainment to an advocating of more mature and nuanced themes.

The film showcased a unique visual design, most notably, an aesthetic devoid of line work. In this way, the peripheries of the forms were not demarcated by black lines but by the natural edging of colour planes. Because of its meticulous design, universal absence of outlines and carefully planned colour schemes, the film's imagery appeared entirely unified. The production process was also unique – it was very much an auteur film that was realized by a small team of highly skilled and creative animators and artists. Some of these worked remotely, leaving director, Alexander Stitt and animation director Frank Hellard the challenge of maintaining a cohesive production.

Generally high praise was directed towards the film's striking visuals, its musical score and songs, its voice acting talent, as well as the humour and the intelligence of the narrative. However, a more in-depth analysis does point to a somewhat uneven animated feature. For example, the quality and timing of animation varies throughout the film, and some of the subtleties of the narrative are difficult to follow on first viewing. It was the first feature film to be produced by Al et al – a company that might be better described as a graphic design studio than strictly an animation studio – and its production was further hampered by an exceedingly low budget. It was also a very challenging film to make as it was based on a highly acclaimed, but exceptionally unconventional literary novel which was, in turn, based on a similarly unconventional Anglo-Saxon poem. Despite this, Stitt's film represents a unique vision that is executed through a blend of cohesive design and limited animation. As feature animated films have matured, and audiences have matured with them, many now regard *Grendel Grendel Grendel* as an outstanding example of animation and design. While it is by no means a perfect film, *Grendel Grendel Grendel* does contain many aspects that are perfectly brilliant.

Note

1 Paddy Stitt, correspondence with Dan Torre and Lienors Torre (2019).

A GUIDE TO FURTHER RESEARCH

Grendel Grendel Grendel is a unique animated feature with a rather unconventional lineage. It is an Australian animated feature that was written and directed by Alexander Stitt, which was based on John Gardner's novel, which in turn represented an unconventional retelling of the *Beowulf* poem. Consequently, this guide reflects this diverse heritage and includes a listing and brief expositions of additional texts and films covering the various topics of Australian animation, John Gardner's *Grendel* and the *Beowulf* poem. It is hoped that these will provide useful points of departure for researchers interested in gaining a deeper understanding of *Grendel Grendel Grendel*.

Australian animation and Grendel, Grendel, Grendel

Bendazzi, Giannalberto, *Animation: A World History. Volumes I, II, III* (Boca Raton: CRC Press, 2016).
This three-volume publication includes sections on Australian animation, including a brief discussion of *Grendel Grendel Grendel*.

Bradbury, Keith, 'Australian and New Zealand Animation', in *Animation in Asia and the Pacific,* ed. John A. Lent (Bloomington and Indianapolis: John Libbey Publishing/Indiana University Press, 2001).
This chapter provides a brief survey of Australian and New Zealand's animation history. A brief section of the chapter is devoted to the work of Alexander Stitt and his feature, *Grendel Grendel Grendel*.

Stitt, Alexander, *Grendel Grendel Grendel – The Book of the Animated Feature Film* (Melbourne: Penguin Australia, 1981).
This book recounts the narrative of the animated feature and is illustrated with over 200 colour images from the film.

Stitt, Alexander and Paddy Stitt, *Stitt: Autobiographics* (Melbourne and London: Hardie-Grant Books, 2011).
This lavishly illustrated text details the over fifty years of graphic design work by Alexander Stitt. Particularly relevant is chapter 12, which details the creative process involved in making *Grendel, Grendel, Grendel*.

Torre, Dan and Lienors Torre, *Australian Animation: An International History* (London: Palgrave, 2018).
This book represents the first comprehensive historical and critical study of Australian animation, commencing from the start of the twentieth century to the present day, and it represents the culmination of a decade long research project by the authors. Particularly

relevant is chapter 8, 'Alex Stitt – Animation by Design', which provides an overview of the significant contribution that Stitt made to Australian animation, including the feature, *Grendel, Grendel, Grendel*.

Grendel *(John Gardner's novel)*

Some texts that provide further insight into Gardner's novel:

Gardner, John, *Grendel* (New York: Alfred A. Knopf, 1971).
John Gardner's seminal retelling of the *Beowulf* narrative, which inspired Alexander Stitt's animated feature.

Gardner, John, *On Writers and Writing* (Berkeley: Counterpoint, 1996).
A collection of essays by John Gardner, some of which provide an author's perspective on *Grendel*.

Howell, John M., *Understanding John Gardner* (Columbia, SC: University of South Carolina Press, 1993).
This text provides a good general analysis of many of Gardner's works, including a substantial chapter devoted to the novel, *Grendel*.

Other useful readings include:
Fawcett, Barry and Elizabeth Jones, 'The Twelve Traps in John Gardner's Grendel', *American Literature* 62, no. 4 (1990), pp. 634–47.
Livingston, Michael and John William Sutton, 'Reinventing the Hero: Gardner's "Grendel" and the Shifting Face of "Beowulf" in Popular Culture', *Studies in Popular Culture* 29, no. 1 (October 2006), pp. 1–16.
Merrill, Robert, 'John Gardner's Grendel and the Interpretation of Modern Fables'. *American Literature* 56, no. 2 (1984), pp. 162–80.
Milosh, Joseph, 'John Gardner's Grendel: Sources and Analogues', *Contemporary Literature* 19, no. 1 (1978): 48–57.
Nelson, Marie, 'John Gardner's Grendel: A Story Retold and Transformed in the Process', *Journal of the Fantastic in the Arts* 18, no. 3 (2007), pp. 340–63.
Swinford, Dean, '"Some Beastlike Fungus": The Natural and Animal in John Gardner's Grendel', *Lit: Literature Interpretation Theory* 22, no. 4 (2011), pp. 323–35.

Beowulf

Some texts that provide more insight into the Beowulf legend and the original text – particularly ones that are useful in regards to Gardner's novel and Stitt's animated film:

Heaney, Seamus, *Beowulf* (London: Faber and Faber, 1999).
One of the most prominent of the recent English language translations is Seamus Heaney's *Beowulf* (1999). Heaney's translation has proven to be extremely popular and

is credited with spawning the production of the numerous Beowulf-themed films that appeared in the early 2000s.

Tolkien, J.R.R., *Beowulf: A Translation and Commentary* (Boston: Houghton Mifflin, 2014).
Another significant publication is J. R. R. Tolkien's long-awaited translation, *Beowulf: A Translation and Commentary*. This text was actually translated in 1926 but was not published until many decades later by his son, Christopher Tolkien, in 2014. The book also includes a previously unpublished Beowulf-themed fairy tale, 'Sellic Spell' (which Tolkien had originally written in the 1940s).

Tolkien, J.R.R., *The Monsters and the Critics and Other Essays* (London: HarperCollins, 2006).
This collection of Tolkien essays features his most famous writing about the poem, 'Beowulf: The Monsters and the Critics' originally presented as a lecture in 1936; it was subsequently published the following year. This essay was the first to champion not only the significance of the Beowulf poem, but also the importance of the monster characters, particularly Grendel, to the narrative. This collection of essays also includes Tolkien's brief essay 'On Translating Beowulf'.

Further useful readings include:
Forni, K., *Beowulf's Popular Afterlife in Literature, Comic Books, and Film* (London: Routledge, 2018).
Haydock, Nickolas and E.L. Risden, *Beowulf on Film Adaptations and Variations* (Jefferson, North Carolina and London: McFarland & Company, 2013).
Kim, Susan M. '"As I Once Did with Grendel": Boasting and Nostalgia in Beowulf', *Modern Philology* 103, no. 1 (August 2005), pp. 4–27.
Nelson, Brent. 'Cain-Leviathan Typology in Gollum and Grendel', *Extrapolation* 49, no. 3 (Winter 2008), pp. 466–85.

Published retellings of the Beowulf *narrative*

Canaway, W.H., *The Ring-Givers* (London: Michael Joseph, 1958).
This novel represents the first significantly altered retelling of the *Beowulf* poem. Like Crichton's later novel, Canaway retells the poem from a non-mythological perspective – describing the events of the Beowulf narrative without monsters or supernatural themes. This pioneering retelling of the poem was never acknowledged (and perhaps never read) by John Gardner, Michael Crichton or Alexander Stitt.

Michael Crichton, *Eaters of the Dead – The Manuscript of Ibn Fadlan, Relating His Experiences with the Northmen in A.D. 922* (New York: Random House, 1993).
This book represents a unique retelling of the *Beowulf* poem. It purports to be a translation of a newly discovered ancient manuscript written by Ahmad Ibn Fadlan, a tenth-century Arabic writer. In fact, the first two chapters of the book are direct translations from the actual ancient manuscript penned by the real-life Ibn Fadlan (an Arabic writer from the tenth century). The rest of the novel is fiction, although written

in a similar style, and describes Fadlan's imagined travels into Scandinavian territories where he encounters a Viking leader named Beowulf (here called 'Buliwyf'). In his telling of *Beowulf*, Crichton effectively declaws the monsters in the poem, indicating how their mythical status might have evolved from the mundane into the fantastic. For example, in his novel the monster 'Grendel' is revealed to be actually a tribe of surviving Neanderthal humans called the Wendol. Similarly, the purported sightings of a fire-breathing dragon are also debunked, these 'dragons' turning out to be simply groups of torch-wielding Wendol journeying through the fog. Crichton's novel suggests that monsters are simply manifestations of irrational fears and fanciful storytelling, while it is the very real barbaric acts committed by humans which are truly monstrous. The novel also details the supposed obsession and fear that these peoples had with injuring their noses. Crichton's novel was studied by the director Alexander Stitt and clearly had an influence on his treatment of the animated feature. This is most overtly (and humorously) referenced in his frequent mentioning of the King's obsession with his injured nose. Originally published in 1976, the revised 1993 edition includes the supplementary appendix which details the author's intentions for writing this fictional novel.

Sutcliff, Barbara, *Dragon Slayer – The Story of Beowulf* (London: The Bodely Head, 1966).
This retelling of the *Beowulf* poem was written for juvenile readers and introduced the poem, in a very accessible manner, to a very wide audience. It was originally published in 1961 under the title of *Beowulf – Retold by Rosemary Sutcliff*.

There have been a number of recent novels that have sought to recount the story of *Beowulf* from a variety of alternative perspectives, including:
Bourne, Ralph, *Grendel's Mother* (Tucson: Wheatmark, 2009).
Crownover, Ashley, *Wealtheow: Her Telling of Beowulf* (Nashville: Iroquois Press, 2008).
Headley, Maria Dahvana, *The Mere Wife* (Melbourne and London: Scribe, 2018).
Morrison, Susan Signe, *Grendel's Mother – The Saga of the Wyrd-Wife* (New Alresford: Top Hat Books, 2015).

Beowulf-*related media*

Grendel Grendel Grendel (Alexander Stitt, 1981). [Animated Film].
The animated version of Gardner's novel – also qualifies as the first feature film to deal with the *Beowulf* narrative.

Beowulf (Graham Baker, 1999). [Film].
The next major cinematic adaptation of *Beowulf*. It also marks a significant retelling of the narrative and is clearly influenced by Gardner's novel.

The 13th Warrior (John McTiernan, 1999). [Film].
A live-action adaptation of Michael Crichton's novel, *Eaters of the Dead* (1976). Stars Antonio Banderas as the main character, Ibn Fadlan.

Beowulf & Grendel (Sturla Gunnarsson, 2005). [Film].
A fairly liberal retelling of the poem, and also clearly inspired by Gardner's novel (and perhaps by Stitt's animated feature as well).

Grendel – The Legend of Beowulf (Nick Lyon 2007). [Film].
This relatively low-budget feature tellingly includes the monster Grendel in its title.

Beowulf (Robert Zemeckis, 2007). [Animated Film].
This film is significant for its use of technology and the manner in which it maintains the identity of its many celebrity voice and motion-captured actors. Co-written by Neil Gaiman, this film, as with Gunnarsson's and Baker's respective features, attempts to clarify the identity of Grendel's father.

Beowulf – The Game (Ubisoft 2007). [Video Game].
A video game based on Robert Zemeckis animated feature and features similar graphics to that of the film.

Beowulf – Return to the Shieldlands (2016). [TV Series].
This big-budget series, which was cancelled after the first season, picks up where the original *Beowulf* narrative ends.

BIBLIOGRAPHY

Adams, Phillip. 'Interview'. By Dan Torre and Lienors Torre (5 November 2019).
Ambrisco, Alan S. 'Trolling for Outcasts in Sturla Gunnarsson's Beowulf and Grendel'. *The Journal of Popular Culture* 46, no. 2 (2013): 243–56.
Atkinson, David. 'Interview'. By Dan Torre and Lienors Torre (1 August 2019).
Bartholomew, David. 'Cartoon Separates the Myth from the Monster'. *Cinefantastique* (June 1982).
Bellamy, Joe David, and Pat Ensworth. 'John Gardner'. In *The New Fiction: Interviews with Innovative American Writers*, edited by Joe David Bellamy. Urbana: University of Illinois Press, 1974.
Berzins, Andrew Rai. 'Screenplay of Beowulf & Grendel'. 2005. Available online: www.beowulfandgrendel.com (accessed 5 December 2019).
Bishop, Chris. 'Beowulf: The Monsters and the Comics'. *Journal of Australian Early Medieval Association* 7 (2011): 73–93.
Burton, Lee. 'Feature Films – Grendel Grendel Grendel'. *Metro Magazine*, no. 56 (1981): 64–5.
Canaway, W.H. *The Ring-Givers*. London: Michael Joseph, 1958.
Carroll, Lewis. *Through the Looking Glass and What Alice Found There*. London: Macmillan and Co., 1872.
Carroll, Lewis. *Symbolic Logic, Part 1, Elementary*. London: Macmillan and Co., 1896.
Carson, Rachel. *Silent Spring*. Boston, MA: Houghton Mifflin, 1962.
Connolly, Keith. 'A Monstrous Achievement'. *The Herald*, 18 June 1981.
Cooper, Mary Ann. '"Beowulf": Transforming an Ancient Epic into a High-Tech Blockbuster'. *Boxoffice* 143, no. 11 (November 2007).
Crichton, Michael. *Eaters of the Dead – The Manuscript of Ibn Fadlan, Relating His Experiences with the Northmen in A.D. 922*. New York: Random House, 1993.
Duncan, Jody. 'Beowulf All the Way'. *Cinefex*, no. 112 (2007).
Forni, Karen. *Beowulf's Popular Afterlife in Literature, Comic Books, and Film*. London: Routledge, 2018.
Gardner, John. *Grendel*. New York: Alfred A. Knopf, 1971.
Gardner, John. *Grendel*. Melbourne: Penguin Australia, 1980.
Gardner, John. *On Writers and Writing*. Berkeley: Counterpoint, 1994.
Geddes, Maggie. 'Interview'. By Dan Torre and Lienors Torre (13 August 2019).
'Grendel'. *New Zealand Herald* (19 August 1982).
Grigsby, John. *Beowulf & Grendel*. London: Watkins Publishing, 2005.
Heaney, Seamus. *Beowulf*. London: Faber and Faber, 1999.
Hellard, Frank. 'Interview'. By Dan Torre and Lienors Torre (3 September 2004).
Hill, John M. 'Beowulf and the Danish Succession: Gift Giving as an Occasion for Complex Gesture'. *Medievalia et Humanistica*, no. 11 (1982): 177–97.
Howell, John M. *Understanding John Gardner*. Columbia, SC: University of South Carolina Press, 1993.

Hutchinson, Ivan. 'Grendel Will Get You'. *The Sun*, 18 June 1981.
Jillett, Neil. 'Cheers, Cheers, Cheers for Grendel'. *The Age*, 19 June 1981.
Jolliffe, Anne. 'Interview'. By Dan Torre and Lienors Torre (15 January 2005).
Julius, Harry. *The Sydney Morning Herald*, 22 February 1938.
Lapidge, Michael. 'Beowulf and the Psychology of Terror'. Translated by E. Talbot Donaldson. In *Beowulf – A Prose Translation, Backgrounds and Contexts Criticism*, edited by Nicholas Howe. New York: W. W. Norton, 2002.
Livingston, Michael, and John William Sutton. 'Reinventing the Hero: Gardner's "Grendel" and the Shifting Face of "Beowulf" in Popular Culture'. *Studies in Popular Culture* 29, no. 1 (October 2006): 1–16.
Lonergan, David. 'Fooling Lc'. *Behavioral & Social Sciences Librarian* 16, no. 2 (1998): 63–72.
Lunden, Jeff. 'Grendel: An Operatic Monster's Tale', *National Public Radio*, 11 July 2006. Available online: www.npr.org (accessed 9 April 2021).
Mayer, Geoff. 'Grendel, Grendel, Grendel'. *Cinema Papers*, no. 33 (July–August 1981).
Mittman, Asa Simon. 'Introduction, the Impact of Monsters and Monster Studies'. In *The Ashgate Research Companion to Monsters and the Monstrous*, edited by Asa Simon Mittman and Peter J. Dendle. Farnham: Ashgate, 2012.
Nelson, Marie. 'John Gardner's Grendel: A Story Retold and Transformed in the Process'. *Journal of the Fantastic in the Arts* 18, no. 3 (2007).
Plympton, Bill. 'Review of Grendel Grendel Grendel'. Melbourne: Umbrella Entertainment, 2013.
Smeaton, Bruce. 'Interview'. By Dan Torre and Lienors Torre (15 November 2019).
Sporn, Michael. 'Grendel', *Michael Sporn Animation, Inc.*, 30 June 2006. Available online: www.michaelspornanimation.com (accessed 11 December 2018).
Stitt, Alexander. 'An Animated Progress Report on Grendel Grendel Grendel'. *Cinema Papers*, no. 21 (May–June 1979): 339–40.
Stitt, Alexander. 'Correspondence Regarding Grendel Grendel Grendel'. RMIT Design Archives, 1981.
Stitt, Alexander. 'A Film Study Guide: Grendel Grendel Grendel'. Melbourne: Al et al, 1981.
Stitt, Alexander. *Grendel Grendel Grendel – The Book of the Animated Feature Film*. Melbourne: Penguin Australia, 1981.
Stitt, Alexander. 'Interview'. By Dan Torre and Lienors Torre (17 April 2005).
Stitt, Alexander. 'Letter of Invitation to the Australian Premier of Grendel Grendel Grendel'. 1981.
Stitt, Alexander. 'Newspaper Advertisement Clippings of Grendel Grendel Grendel'. RMIT Design Archives, 1981.
Stitt, Alexander. 'Poster Advertisement for Grendel Grendel Grendel'. RMIT Design Archives, 1982.
Stitt, Alexander, and Paddy Stitt. *Stitt Autobiographics – 50 Years of the Graphic Design Work of Alexander Stitt*. Melbourne: Hardie Grant Books, 2011.
Stitt, Paddy. 'Interview'. By Dan Torre and Lienors Torre (10 October 2019).
Sullivan, Jane. 'A Spotty Ogre Comes to Life'. *The Age*, 20 October 1980.
Swinford, Dean. '"Some Beastlike Fungus": The Natural and Animal in John Gardner's Grendel'. *Lit: Literature Interpretation* 22, no. 4 (2011): 323–35.
Tolkien, J.R.R., *Beowulf: A Translation and Commentary*. Boston: Houghton Mifflin 2014.

Tolkien, J.R.R. *The Monsters and the Critics and Other Essays*. London: HarperCollins, 2006.
Torre, Dan. *Animation – Process, Cognition and Actuality*. New York: Bloomsbury, 2017.
Torre, Dan. *Cactus*. London: Reaktion Books, 2017.
Torre, Dan. *Carnivorous Plants*. London: Reaktion Books, 2019.
Torre, Dan, and Lienors Torre. *Australian Animation – An International History*. Cham: Palgrave, 2018.
Tulloch, Lee. 'Lee Tulloch Talks to Grendel and Friend, Grrumph!' *Vogue Australia*, January 1981.
Tupicoff, Dennis. 'Interview'. By Dan Torre and Lienors Torre (18 November 2019).
Uslan, Michael. 'Introduction'. In *Beowulf: Dragon Slayer*. New York: DC Comics, no. 1 (1975).
'Ustinov a Natural Grendel'. *Screen International* (22 May 1981).
Zeeman, Kenneth L. 'Grappling with Grendel or What We Did When the Censors Came'. *English Journal* 86, no. 2 (1997).
Zipes, Jack. *The Enchanted Screen – The Unknown History of Fairy-Tale Films*. New York: Routledge, 2011.

FILMOGRAPHY

The 13th Warrior (John McTiernan, 1999)
Abra Cadabra (Alexander Stitt, 1983)
Alice in Wonderland (Clyde Geronimi, Wilfred Jackson, Hamilton Luske, 1951)
Allegro Non Troppo (Bruno Bozzetto, 1976)
Around the World in 80 Days (API, 1974)
Around the World with Dot (Yoram Gross, 1981)
Arthur! And the Square Knights of the Round Table (Zoran Janjic, 1966)
The Beatles [TV series] (1965–7)
Beauty and the Beast (Gary Trousdale, Kirk Wise, 1991)
Beowulf (Yuri Kulakov, 1998)
Beowulf (Graham Baker, 1999)
Beowulf (Robert Zemeckis, 2007)
Beowulf – The Game, was released by (Ubisoft, 2007)
Beowulf & Grendel (Sturla Gunnarsson, 2005)
Beowulf – Return to the Shieldlands (2016)
The BFG (Brian Cosgrove, 1989)
The Cars That Ate Paris (Peter Weir, 1974)
Cartoons of the Moment (Harry Julius, 1915–16)
Casablanca (Michael Curtiz, 1942)
The Challenge of Flight & the Challenge of the Sea (API, 1962)
The Chant of Jimmy Blacksmith (Fred Schepisi, 1978)
A Christmas Carol (API, 1970)
The Curious Adventures of Mr. Wonderbird (Paul Grimault, 1952)
Diamonds Are Forever (Guy Hamilton, 1971)
Dot and the Kangaroo (Yoram Gross, 1977)
Eddie's Alphabet (Rowl Greenhalgh, 1967)
Fantastic Planet (Rene Laloux, 1973)
Freddo the Frog (Gus McLaren, 1962)
Fritz the Cat (Ralph Bakshi, 1972)
Gerald McBoing Boing (Robert Cannon, 1950)
Great (Bob Godfrey, 1976)
Grendel Grendel Grendel (Alexander Stitt, 1981)
Grendel – The Legend of Beowulf (Nick Lyon, 2007)
The Iron Giant (Brad Bird, 1999)
Journey to the Centre of the Earth (API, 1972)
Jungle Book, The (Wolfgang Reitherman, 1967)
The Little Convict (Yoram Gross, 1979)
The Lord of the Rings (Ralph Bakshi, 1978)
Marco Polo Jnr vs. the Red Dragon (Eric Porter, 1972)
Moby-Dick (API, 1973)

Monsters, Inc. (Pete Docter, David Silverman, 2001)
The Mouse and His Child (Charles Swenson, Fred Wolf, 1977)
One Designer, Two Designer (Alexander Stitt, 1978)
One Hundred and One Dalmations (Wolfgang Reitherman, Hamilton Luske, Clyde Geronomi, 1961)
Pete's Dragon (Don Chaffey, 1977)
Picnic at Hanging Rock (Peter Weir, 1975)
The Polar Express (Robert Zemeckis, 2004)
Popular Misconceptions (API, 1963)
The Prince and the Pauper (API, 1972)
Rip Van Winkle (API, 1971)
Robin Hood (Wolfgang Reitherman, 1973)
Shrek (Andrew Adamson, Vicky Jenson, 2001)
Shrek 2 (Andrew Adamson, Kelly Asbury, 2004)
Shrek the Third (Chris Miller, Raman Hui, 2007)
Sleeping Beauty (Clyde Geronimi, 1959)
Spartacus (Stanley Kubrick, 1960)
The Swiss Family Robinson (API, 1973)
The Thomas Crown Affair (Norman Jewison, 1968)
Those Magnificent Men in Their Flying Machines (Ken Annakin, 1965)
A Unicorn in the Garden (Bill Hurtz, 1953)
Yellow Submarine (George Dunning, 1968)
You Only Live Twice (Lewis Gilbert, 1967)
Wambidgee (Robert Knapp, 1962)
Watership Down (Martin Rosen, 1978)
Wizards (Ralph Bakshi, 1977)

INDEX

Note: Locators in bold indicate figures and locators followed by n denotes note number.

'2-I-C' 44
13th Warrior, The (1999) (film) 17, 189

A
A&M recording studio 141
Aanensen, Peter 139
Abel. *See* Cain
Abra Cadabra (1983) (film) 153 n. 1
accent (voice)
    Australian 3, 4
    as George Sanders 135
    London vs. Yorkshire 19, 29, 36, 42, 85
    mid-Atlantic 4
    as Terry-Thomas 54, 149
Adams, Phillip
    in introduction sequence 33–4, 99–101, 165, **166**
    as producer 2, 4, 20, 125, 126–7, 130, 131, 132, **133**, 174
Adams, Richard 176
Adelaide 135
Al et Al studio 121, 135, 141–3, **142**, **143**, 144, 185
    early history 124–5
Alice in Wonderland 6, 19, 32, 71, 99, 109, 110, 111, 112, **113**, 114, 124, 134, 143, 183
    Alice in Wonderland (1951) (film) 109, 112
    references in *Yellow Submarine* 113–4
Alice Springs 124, 143
Allegro Non Troppo (1976) (film) 176
Anglo-Saxon 1, 2, 9, 10, 12, 100, 111, 115, 118, 160
animals
    deer 46, 64, 65, 74
    fire snakes 19, 41, 69, 110, 141, 160, 171
    oysters 71, 72, 73, **73**, 112, **113**, 134
    pigs 38, 42, 47, 48, 72, 81, 111, 160

animal sacrifice **64**, 65, 74, 75, 105, 116
animation
    acting 123–4
    impact of character design 150–1
    impact of background design 159, **160**
    inconsistency of 152
    limited animation 1, 88, 124, 151, 167–8, 169, 183
    retreating walk 39, 53, 67, **153**, 167, 168
    walk cycle 168
API (Air Programs International) 4, 5, 124
apples
    as euphemism 78
    as humiliation 18, 22, 68, **68**, 70, 71, 78
    as non-violence 94, **94**
Around the World with Dot (1981) (film) 5
Arthur! And the Square Knights of the Round Table (1966) (TV series) 5, 124
Arup, Janet 125, 143, 150
Atkinson, David 125, 127, 129, 135, 142, 143, **143**, 144, 147, 150, 152, 174
Australian animation history 3–6

B
backgrounds 34, 114, 119, 122, 123, 124, 145, **146**, 157, 159, **160**, 164
Bakshi, Ralph 176, 177
Balty, Jean 122
Basil 34, **35**, 46, 139, 171
Bassey, Shirley 137
bear-trap 44, 56, 164, **164**
Beatles, The 113–15, 124
Beauty and the Beast (1991) (film) 102
Beowulf (character)
    in *Beowulf* (2007) (film) 24–7, **26**
    voice actor 24, 26
    Beowulf/Dragon connection 89, 93, 106, 131

in *Beowulf* poem 1, 10, 13, 35, 82, 93, 99, 101, 103, 104, 107
in Gardner's *Grendel* (unnamed) 15, 88–9, 93
in *Grendel Grendel Grendel* 2, 18, 19, 42, 49, 70, 82, 83, 84–9, **85**, **86**, 90, 91–2, **93**, 93–4, **94**, 100, 105–6, 138, **158**, **166**, 166
    design 106, 158
    voice actor 106, 131, 132, 135
in other sources 13–14, 17, 21–3, 28–9, 188–90
adaptations of 12–9, 188–90
original manuscript 9–10, **11**
translations of 12, 13
Beowulf (1998) (film) 21
Beowulf (1999) (film) 21–2
Beowulf (2007) (film) 23–7, **26**
Beowulf – The Game (video game) 27
Beowulf & Grendel (2005) (film) 22–3
Beowulf (original poem) 1, 2, 3, 9–13, 14, 15, 16, 20, 21, 22, 24, 25, 27, 28, 32, 35, 36, 39, 45, 49, 65, 76, 82, 84, 85, 93, 99, 101, 103, 104, 107, 137, 160, 178, 183, 184, 188–9
Beowulf – Retold (aka *Dragon Slayer – The Story of Beowulf*) 13
Beowulf – Return to the Shieldlands (2016) (TV Series) 190
Beowulfiana 33
Bird, Alison 139
BFG, The (film) (1989) 102
Bogart, Humphrey 82, **82**
Bond, James 36
Bourne, Ernie 139
Brecca 23
Bright, Bobby 139
brother-killer. *See* Cain
Brown, Jack 139
budgets
    of *Beowulf* (2007) 23, 26, 27
    of *Grendel Grendel Grendel* 126, 131, 141, 144, 145, 174, 185
    of *Grendel* opera 29

C

Cain
    in *Beowulf* poem 103

in *Beowulf* (1999) (film) 23
in Gardner's personal life 104
in *Grendel* (book) 15
in *Grendel Grendel Grendel* 56–8, 59, 87, 103–5, 137
camera
    animated camera move 80, 91, 152, 167
    camera operators 122, 143–4
Canaway, Hamilton. *See The Ring-Givers*
Cannes film festival 173–174
Carroll, Lewis. *See Alice in Wonderland*
Carson, Rachel 107
Cartoons of the Moment (film series) 4
Cartoon Filmads (studio) 4–5
Cars that Ate Paris, The (1974) (film) 130
Casablanca (1942) (film) 82
Castle Jackson Advertising 122
cave (Grendel's)
    in *Grendel Grendel Grendel* 39–41, **40**, 45, 67, 69, 89, 100, 110, 160, **161**
    in other sources 21, 24, 25
CD (soundtrack) 173
cels 121, 130, 144, 146, **146**, 147, **147**, 149, 150, 152, **153**, 159, 168
Cel-Vinyl 149. *See also* paint
Channel Nine (TV network) 122, 123, 124
Chant of Jimmy Blacksmith, The (1978) (film) 125
character designs 129, **140**, 150–1, 180
Cold War 100, 184
colour degradation 181 n. 21
colour design 1, 18, 34, 39, 44, 114, 145, 147, 148–9, 153, 157–8, 159, 160, 162–3, 166, 168, 169, 177
comic book 6, 9, 28
comic panel aesthetic 164
commercials (animated) 4–5, 19–20, 121, 122, 123, 124, 125, 126, 130, 139, 144, 178
concretized speech 118, **119**. *See also* typography
conservationists 107
Corman, Roger 127
credit/title sequence
    (closing) 96, **96**
    (opening) 36–9, **36**, 90, 118, **119**

Crichton, Michael 16–17, 66, 188–9
critical reviews of *Grendel Grendel Grendel* 1, 174, 176–80
CSIRO film department (123)
Curious Adventures of Mr. Wonderbird, The (1952) (film) 131

D

Dalgarno, David 125, 143, 150
Davies, Marilyn 143
Diamonds Are Forever (1971) (film) 137
Dickens, Charles 16
Dignam, Arthur 1, 24, 93, 131, 132, 134–5, **136**, 174
Disney 16, 54, 102, 109, 112, 114, 122, 131, 134, 135, 147, 176
Dot and the Kangaroo (1977) (film) 5
Dragon (character)
   (in *Beowulf* poem) 1, 10, 13
   (in Gardner's *Grendel*) 15, 71, 89, 93
   (in *Grendel Grendel Grendel*) 18, 19, 24, 60–3, **60**, 67, 74, 81–3, **82**, 89, 105–9, **109**, 110–11, 116, **116**, 118, **119**, 164–5, **165**, 183–4
   animating 147, 168–9, 108–9
   voice actor 131–2, 134–5
   (in other sources) 13, 17, 21, 25, 189
Dragon God 6, 58, 63, **64**, 74, 75, 76, 99, 105, 116, 119, 184
dragons 100, 102
Dragon's lair 60–1, **60**, 81, 168
dualism 106–7
Dung 18, 34, 35, **35**, 42, **43**, 44, 45, 46, 47, 49, 50, 51, 53, 54, 55, 65, 66, 74, 84, 115, 139, 160, 171

E

Eaters of the Dead (book) 16–17, 66, 188–9

F

Fadlan, Ahmad Ibn 17, 188–9
Fanfare Films 124–5
Fantastic Planet (1973) (film) 176
Ferro, Pablo 165
film rights (of *Grendel*) 20, 121, 126, 127, 129

Fitzgibbon, Smacka 138
flash-backs (time) 2, 41–2, 45
Ford, Cam (and Diana Ford) 120 n. 21
Foreign King 54–5, **55**, 139, 149
Freddo the Frog (1962) (TV series) 5, 124
Fritz the Cat (1972) (film) 176–7

G

Gaiman, Neil 24
Gardner, John
   on animation 7, 16
   personal life 14, 16, 104
Geddes, Maggie 114, 123, 125, 143, 145, 147, 150
Georges Borchardt Agency 126
Gerald McBoing Boing (1950) (film) 122
Gibbins, Helen 180
Glover, Crispin 24
Godfrey, Bob 124
Goldenthal, Elliot 29
Gollum 13
Gordon, John (Prime Minister) 4
Great (1976) (film) 124
Grendel (character)
   in *Beowulf* 2007 (film) 24–5
   in *Beowulf* poem 1, 9, 10, 12, **12**, 13, 101, 160, 183
   in Gardner's *Grendel* 1, 2, 9, 14–16, 39, 40, 42, 43, 53, 59, 66, 68–9, 70, 71, 81, 89, 93, 96, 102, 105, 106, 108, 115, 118, 160, 161, 183
   in *Grendel Grendel Grendel* 2, 4, 9, 18–20, **20**, 32–3, 34, **35**, 36–42, **38**, **40**, 43, **43**, 44, 45–53, 55–75, 76–83, 89, 91–2, 93–6, **92**, **93**, **94**, **95**, **96**, 99–101, 102–12, **109**, **113**, 113–19, 137, 138, 141, 142, **146**, **147**, 149, 152, **153**, **158**, 159–61, **161**, 163, 165, **165**, 167–9, 171, 172–3, **172**, **173**, 174, 183–4
   voice actor 41, 130–2, 134
   in other sources 12, 13, 14, 21–3, 27–9, 189
Grendel (Gardner's novel) 1, 2, 4, 9, 12, 14–16, 18, 19, 20, 22, 23, 24, 28, 29, 31, 32, 36, 39, 40, 42, 43, 45, 49, 53, 56, 58, 59, 60, 68, 70, 71,

80–1, 84, 87, 88–9, 91, 93, 96, 99, 102, 104, 106, 107, 115, 118, 121, 131, 134, 137, 138, 139, 160, 173, 177, 178, 183–4, 187
  controversy 59
  popularity of 15–16, 29, 126, 127, 130
Grendel – The Legend of Beowulf (2007) (film) 190
Grendel – Transcendence of the Great Big Bad (opera) 29
Grendel Grendel Grendel –The Book of the Animated Feature Film 2, 61, 186
'Grendel'll Get You' (promotional catchphrase) 7, 171–2, **172**, **175**, **179**
Grendel's mother
  in *Beowulf* (2007) (film) 24–7
  in *Beowulf* poem 1, 10, 99, 107
  in Gardner's *Grendel* 43, 70, 139
  in other sources 21, 22, 29
Grendel's Mum (in *Grendel Grendel Grendel*) 19, 36, 37, 38, 40–1, 43, **43**, 44, 45, 53, 59, 67, 89, 90, 95, 118, **119**, 137, 139, 163, 184
Gross, Yoram 5
Gunnarsson, Sturla 22–3, 190

H
Harris, Suzan 143
Hay, Phyllis 122
Heaney, Seamus 13, 187
Hellard, Frank 33, 78, 81, 108, 121, 122, 123, 124, 126, 127, 139, 142, 143, **143**, 149, 151–3, 167, 168, 176, 184
Heorot (see meadhall)
heroism
  in *Beowulf* 10, 13, 99, 104
  in *Grendel Grendel Grendel* 18, 19, 33, 48, 51, 53, 59, 65, 66, 67, 69, 70, 75, 84, 86, 100, 115, 178
Hill, Barry 54, 139, 149
honour 48, 52, 53, 66, 141
Hopkins, Anthony 24, 26, **26**
Hrothgar, King,
  in *Beowulf* (2007) (film) 24, 25, 26, 27
  in *Beowulf* poem 1, 10
  in Gardner's *Grendel* 15, 71

  in *Grendel Grendel Grendel* 18, 19, 32, 34, 35, **35**, 39, 41, 42, **43**, 44, **44**, 45, 46, 47, **47**, 48, 49, 50, 51, 52, 53, 54, 55, **55**, 56, **57**, 58, 63, 65, 66, 67, 69, 70, 73, 74, 75, 76, 77, 78, 79, 80, 83, **83**, 84, 85, 86, 87, 88, 89, 91, 92, 94, 100, 103, 105, 111, 112, 115, 116, 119, 137, 141, 152, 160, 162, 163, 164, **164**, 165, 166, 171
  voice actor 139
  in other sources 21, 22
Humphries, Barry 131

I
insanity 71, 73, 74, 75
Introduction. *See* Adams, Phillip)
Iron Giant, The (1999) (film) 102
irony. *See also* litotes 18, 36, 76, 77, 80, 105, 137

J
Janjic, Zoran 124
jazz 129, 138
Jigsaw Factory 124
Jolie, Angelina 24, 26
Jolliffe, Anne 114, 123, 124, 142, 143
Johnson, Sharon 143
Julius, Harry 3, 4
Jungle Book, The (1967) (film) 135

K
kangaroo 3–4
kenning 12
King. *See* Hrothgar

L
Laine, Cleo 138
layouts 18, 121, 143, **144**, 153
Lennon, John 113–14
Life. Be in It 19–20
line work (outlines)
  black 145, **146**, 157
  coloured 147
  line-free 1, 7, 34, 145–9, **147**, 159, 166, 169, 184
  loss of detail 149, **158**

litotes 76
Little Convict, The (1979) (film) 5
Lord of the Rings, The (1978) (film) 176
Lord of the Rings, The (book) 13

M
McClatchy, J.D. 29
McEwan, Colin 139
Mackay, Fiona 143
McKenna, Julia 1, 36, 137–8, 171, 174
McLaren, Gus 123, 124, 125, 142, 143, 151
Malkovich, John 24, 26
Marceau, Marcel 123–4
Marco Polo Jnr vs. the Red Dragon (1972) (film) 5
Matthews, Connie 122
Matthews, Pat 122–3
mead 10, 87
meadhall (Heorot)
  in *Beowulf* poem 10, 39, 101
  in Gardner's *Grendel* 15, 71, 93–4
  in *Grendel Grendel Grendel* 39, 41, 48, 49, 50, 51, 52, 55, 56, 58, 67, 68, 69, 70, 76, 80, 84, 85, **86**, 88, 91, 94, 112, 115, 117, 137, 152, 164, **164**, 166, **166**, 168
  in other sources 24
Melbourne 3, 114, 121, 122, 124, 134, 135, 139, 141, **142**, 174, 179
Melbourne International Animation Festival (MIAF) 180
metamorphosis (*also as* transform) 21, 25, **60**, 61, 62, 82, 108, 109, 114, 163, 168
Michell, Keith 1, 33, 135, 137, 174
Miller, Seton 102
mock-runes 63, 67, **117**, 118–19
Monahan Dayman Adams (MDA) 125, 139
monsters 9–29, 99–103, 105–9
Monsters, Inc. (2001) (film) 102
Moldoff, Sheldon 5
motion-capture 24, 26, 167, 190
Mouse and His Child, The (1977) (film) 131
music. *See* Smeaton, Bruce. *See also* recording sessions

musical (genre) 18, 19, 29, 114, 115, 116, 184
musical instruments
  guitar 141
  ocarina 141
  piano 129, 132, 134, 137, 138
  prepared piano 141
  shakuhachi 141
  waterphone 69, 141

N
Neely, Christine 143
New Zealand 20, 176, 177, 180
Norm (see *Life. Be in It*)
noses (obsession with) 17, 46, **47**, 49, 50, 51, 52, **52**, 53, 66, 68, 80, 94, 173, 189
nudity
  in *Beowulf* (2007) (film) 24, 25
  in *Grendel Grendel Grendel* 80, **80**, 177, 180

O
Old English 1, 10, **11**, 29
One Designer, Two Designer (1978) (film) 125
One-eyed Arthur 34, **35**, 46, 139, 171
One Hundred and One Dalmations (1961) (film) 147
opera (see *Grendel – Transcendence of the Great Big Bad*)
Owens, Eric 29

P
paint 114, 122, 123, 125, 141, 142, 143, 145, 146, 147, 148, 149, 150, 161, 162, 167, 168
paper cut-out aesthetic 166–7
Park Road Post 180
pattern 34, 36, 158, 159, 160, **161**
Penn, Robin Wright 24, **26**
Pepperland 113–14
personification. *See* plants
Pete's Dragon (1977) (film) 102
Pete's Dragon and the USA (Forever After) (book) 102
Peverill, Ralph 123, 124, 125, 142–3
Picnic at Hanging Rock (1975) (film) 130

pig-latin 141
plants
   carnivorous plants 160
   personified plants 39, 67, 159, 160, **161**
   trees 34, 39, 42, **43**, 47, 92, 114, 159, 160, 161, 163, 166
Plympton, Bill 177
poison 83–4, **83**, 93
Polar Express, The (2004) (film) 26
Pollard, John 143
Porter, Eric 5
premiere screening 174
priests 55, **64**, 65, 74, 75, **87**, 88, 139, 141
profanity 179–80
promotion (of *Grendel Grendel Grendel*) 171–80
Pryor, Denis 143

Q
Queen. *See* Wealtheow

R
radio actor 14, 130, 138, 139
rating (censorship) 45, 174, 176, 177
recording sessions
   music 34, 121, 141
   vocal 34, 121, 132–9, **133**, **136**, 141
restoration of film 180
riddles 82, 83, 89, 111
Ring-Givers, The (book) 13–14, 17, 188
RMIT University 122
Roald Barre's animation studio 4
Robin Hood (1973) (film) 54, 131
Rosser, Ed 139
Rozario, Sally Anne 143
runes *see* mock-runes

S
Satori (distributor) 174
Sawers, Dick 114, 123–4
Schepisi, Fred 125
Schepisi, Rho 139
school children 178–80
Sculptor 6, 49, 63–4, **72**, 99, 115–18, 183, 184
   stone carvings 49, 50, 63–4, **72**, **153**
Selma 22, 23

shading (on characters) 148, 159, 161–2
Shaper, the
   in comic book 28
   in Gardner's *Grendel* 15, 23, 53, 84, 118
   in *Grendel Grendel Grendel* 18, 49, 50, 51, 52, **52**, 53, 55, 56, 57, 58, 59, 63, 64, 65, 66, 67, 69, 74, 75, 76, 77, 78, 79f, 80, 81, 83, **83**, 86, 90, 99, 103, 104, 115, 116, 131, 134, 135, 137, 138, 141, 162, **162**, 171, 183, 184
   as blind 50–1, 74, 137, 138
Shaper's Boy 50–1, **52**, 76, 78, 79, **79**, 90, 91, 118, 137, 138, 171
   as mute 50, 51, 90, 138–9
Shrek (2001) (film) 102
Shrek 2 (2004) (film) 102
Shrek the Third (2007) (film) 102
silhouette
   in *Beowulf* (1998) (film) 21
   black 21, **43**, 44, 47, **153**, 159, 162–3, **162**, 165, 168, 169
   strong pose 149
Sinatra, Nancy 137
Sleeping Beauty 147
Smeaton, Bruce 1, 2, 31, 33, 121, 129–30, 132, 134, **136**, 137, 138, 141, 153
songs (in *Grendel Grendel Grendel*)
   'Creation Song' 56–7, 104, 137
   'Dragon's Song' 62–3, 106–07, 109, **109**
   'Grendel Grendel Grendel' 36–8, 118, **119**, 137
   'Grendel's Soliloquy' 71–4, **72**, **73**, 112, 117, 118, 134
   Grendel's theme song 42, 90–1, 118, **119**, 134
   'Moon is Rising, The' 90–1, 138
   'Revenge of Wiglaf, The' 51, 137
   'We Know a Lovely Monster' 77, 78, 79, **79**, 137
Spartacus (1960) (film) 131
speech disorder 54
Spencer, Norm 122
Sporn, Michael 126–7
Stitt, Alexander **3**

as Director of *Grendel Grendel Grendel* 5–6, 126–53, **133**
  narrative and creative approach 3–4, 18–20, 31–96, 99–119, 157–69
  early years in animation 122–5
  promoting *Grendel Grendel Grendel* 171–80
Stitt, Paddy 139, 173–4
Stone, Ric 139
storyboards (*Grendel Grendel Grendel*) 80, 121, 126, 127–9, **127**, **128**, 130, 131, 145, **148**, 149
storyboards (*Life. Be in It*) 125
Study Guide (for *Grendel Grendel Grendel*) 118–19, 177–8
Sutcliff, Rosemary 13, 189
Swinburne University 149
Sydney 4, 5, 124, 132, 133, 134, 135

T
Taymor, Julie 29
Terry-Thomas 54, 149
Thomas Crown Affair, The (1968) (film) 165
Thorkel 23
Those Magnificent Men in Their Flying Machines (1965) (film) 97 n. 16
Through the Looking Glass and What Alice Found There (see *Alice in Wonderland*)
Tolkien, J. R. R. 13, 33, 188
transitions (animated) 39, 165–6, **166**
translation of *Beowulf* 10, 12, 13, 17, 187, 188
Troll 85, **86**, 87, 88, 92, 103
Tupicoff, Dennis 143, 144, 149, 155 n. 50
Turner, Malcolm 180
typography (animated) 36–7, 118, **119**
  in *Yellow Submarine* 114

U
uncanny valley 26–7
Unferth
  in *Beowulf* (2007) 24, 26
  In *Beowulf* poem 104
  in *Grendel Grendel Grendel* 18, 19, 22, 44, **44**, 45, 46, **47**, 48, 52, 53, 54, **55**, 56, 58, 65, 66, 67, 68, **68**, 69, 70, **70**, 71, 75, 76, 78, 80, 81, 86, 87, 91, **92**, 94, 103, 105, 137, 162
  voice actor 139
Unicorn in the Garden, A (1953) (film) 122
UPA 122, 123, 124, 125, 151, 177
Uslan, Michael 28
Ustinov, Peter 1, 19, 32, 33, 40, 41, 42, 54, 131, 132, 133, **133**, 134, 135, **136**, 174

V
Victorian Film Corporation 126, 174
video game 23–4, 27, 190
Vietnam War 16, 33, 100, 110, 184
Vikings 17, 66, 157, 159, **160**, 189
violence 23, 27, 39, 45, 46, 47, 48, 66, 103, 176, 177

W
Wagner, Matt 28
Wambidgee (1962) (TV series) 5
Ward, Vincent 20
Watership Down (1978) (film) 176
Wealtheow, Queen
  in *Grendel Grendel Grendel* 19, 54–5, **55**, 56–7, 65, 67, 69, 75, 80, **80**, 81, 88–9
  voice actor 139
  in other sources 22, 24, **26**, 29
Weatherhead, Bruce 123, 124
Weatherhead & Stitt 124
Weir, Peter 130
Whitehead, Alfred North 15, 106
Wiglaf
  in *Beowulf* poem 10
  in *Grendel Grendel Grendel* 18, 19, 35, 42, **43**, 44, 45, 46, 50, 51, 52, 65, 66, 103, 137, 160, 171
  voice actor 139
  in other sources 21, 25
Wilson, John 122, 124
Winstone, Ray 24, **26**
Wizards (1977) (film) 176
Wizard of Oz, The 105

Wonderland (see *Alice in Wonderland*)

X
X-rated 176
xerography 147

Y
Yellow Submarine (1968) (film) 113–5, 124–5, 176

yobbos 34, **144**
You Only Live Twice (1967) (film) 137

Z
Zemeckis, Robert 23–7, 190
Zipes, Jack 110
zoophytes 160

www.ingramcontent.com/pod-product-compliance
Lightning Source LLC
Chambersburg PA
CBHW061826300426
44115CB00013B/2269